ADULT CHILDREN AND AGING PARENTS

Jane E. Myers

With contributions by Novella Perrin
Preface by Thomas J. Sweeney

KENDALL/HUNT PUBLISHING COMPANY
2460 Kerper Boulevard   P.O. Box 539   Dubuque, Iowa 52004-0539

Cover design by Sarah Jane Valdez

American Association for Counseling and Development
5999 Stevenson Avenue
Alexandria, VA 22304

Library of Congress Cataloging-in-Publication Data

Myers, Jane E.
    Adult children and aging parents.

    Bibliography: p.
    Includes index.
    1. Aged—Counseling of—United States.
    2. Adult children—Counseling of—United States.
    3. Aging—United States—Psychological aspects.
    4. Life change events—United States.

    I. Perrin, Novella.
    II. Title.
    HV1461.M94   1989   362.6'042   89-6485
    ISBN 0–8403–5448–7

Printed in the United States of America
10 9 8 7 6 5 4 3 2 1

To

John M. and Geraldine M. Myers

in memoriam

CONTENTS

PREFACE

Thomas J. Sweeney

This book could not be available at a better time. Those of us already aware of the need for resources to guide professional practice in working with older persons welcome this work. The author, Dr. Jane E. Myers, is widely known to have a scholarly background in the theory, methods, and research associated with older persons, aging, and the circumstances that challenge not only aging persons but their families as well. What is less well known are the many and varied experiences that Dr. Myers has had in coming to the point of writing this work.

A recipient of the American Association for Counseling and Development (AACD/APGA) Research Award for her work on older persons in our society, Dr. Myers has been a prolific contributor to the professional literature on this topic for over a dozen years. A leader in the field of counseling, she is Past-President and Executive Director of Sigma Phi Omega Gerontological Honor Society, Past-President of the Association for Evaluation and Measurement in Counseling and Development, Past-President of Chi Sigma Iota Counseling Academic and Professional Honor Society International, Founding President of the Association for Adult Development and Aging, and President-Elect of AACD. She also has been a recipient of numerous awards for her leadership in the counseling profession.

First, as a staff member of AACD and more recently as a university faculty member, Dr. Myers has directed four national projects on counseling older persons funded by the U.S. Administration on Aging. In the process, over 3,400 counselors and counselor educators have received inservice training in counseling older persons. In addition, curriculum materials, guides, and video resources have been developed and distributed nationally. Currently, competency statements and examination items on gerontological counseling are being developed for use by professional accreditation and credentialing bodies.

Finally, as is true of an ever-increasing number of us reading this work, Dr. Myers has had the experience as a youngest daughter of working out a new relationship with her own mother in her later years of life. Even while she was writing this book, her mother's physical decline and death brought with it many opportunities to review, relive, and reintegrate her life experiences with this person who was very special to her. Out of these experiences comes a rare combination of insights and knowledge about counseling adult children and their aging parents.

Chapter 1 provides the foundation for understanding the magnitude of the problem we face in both the near and long-term future. The demographics on our aging population leave no doubt that the needs of the aging are among the most pressing to be addressed by the helping professions. The "state of the art" in theory, methods, and research is reviewed throughout the work, but this chapter provides a context for what follows. As the author notes, there is room for more research, better theories, more tools, and greater evaluation of intervention methods.

Critical issues and helping responses to aging compose chapter 2. In a manner of speaking, this chapter addresses the "hot spots" of the aging population right from the very beginning. The reader will become aware that contrary to common myths, most older persons are not in nursing homes nor are they living with their children. Concerning the latter, it is often the last place that they would choose to live in their later years. For a variety of reasons, however, depression, suicide, and substance abuse are serious problems among our older population. Organic brain syndromes constitute a special class of problems for older persons, their loved ones, and those in a position to help them. The contents of this chapter are essential to any professional working with this population. Especially noteworthy are the sections on implications for counselors and strategies for assessment.

Chapter 3 helps to focus upon later life development and transitions for both older persons and their families. Although losses are often the source of issues with older persons, we should not overlook the real and potential gains that growing older brings to each of us. The tendency to focus exclusively on problems is a negative bias that can enter the counseling process if not confronted by the service providers themselves. The author's attention to the gains and potentials in aging offers just such an opportunity to the reader.

The circumstances that evoke stress responses in older persons and their families are many. In chapter 4, Dr. Myers addresses the predominant themes around which stress responses evolve. Two of these, caregiving and elder abuse, have been receiving increasing attention in recent years within the popular press. Unfortunately, even greater attention is needed through more and better facilities, substantive programs, and trained service providers in order to ameliorate the problems being identified. Although death and dying issues have been addressed in a variety of forms over the last 10 to 15 years, the death of a parent always has a special effect on the children. Institutionalization, on the other hand, is a growing concern about which most people know little until there is a crisis. Information important to counselors is presented in this chapter in a concise, useful format that should prove practical to the reader.

The concluding chapter provides the foundation for responsible practice with adult children and their aging parents. Building healthy, positive relationships is the goal. Assessment and intervention techniques for helping move toward that goal are presented. Drawing upon the community resources available to help achieve that goal is introduced. This chapter helps place the topic in proper perspective. Our goal as counselors with these family members is not only to remediate but to enrich their relationships with one another. The purpose is not only to relieve guilt, reduce stress, or redirect anger, but to induce joy, highlight satisfaction, and promote love and appreciation for the courage upon which all family members draw daily to meet the challenges and opportunities of life together. Dr. Myers helps us maintain the proper focus while providing tools and references needed to achieve our goal.

In summary, I have found this work to be timely, relevant, and altogether scholarly in its presentation. As a text or reference, it will be useful to a variety of professionals. The genuine concern the author feels for older persons and their families comes through in the positive, caring way that each topic is covered. The readers can expect to place this book among their special collection of desk references for continuing use.

ACKNOWLEDGMENTS

When I told my feisty 75-year old mother I was writing a book about mental health issues for adult children and aging parents, her reply was an enthusiastic, "Well, you should be an expert at that!" Well, I'm not. Her unexpected death during the early stages of writing taught me that and much more. In fact, at times this book was more of a grieving project than a writing project. In reflecting on the nature of relationships between adult children and aging parents, it is clear that I must acknowledge both of my parents for their input into this book. My father's love of both reading and writing, my mother's intellectualism, and the encouragement of both to reflect on my thoughts and experiences were major contributors to my development as well as to the ideas in this book.

My friend and colleague, Novella Perrin, made numerous contributions to the content of this text, particularly for the sections on demography, theories of aging, attitudes toward older persons, and grandparenthood. Were it not for an untimely illness, her participation would have been even more extensive and significant.

Tom Sweeney, another dear friend and colleague, and his mother, Cissie, have been a stimulus for this writing as well as healthy role models for relationships between adult children and aging parents. I am especially appreciative of Tom's suggestions and encouragement both personally and professionally during the difficult months of writing this book.

Richard Blake and Richard Johnson provided thorough reviews and insightful suggestions for the final development of this book. Linda Lewis assisted in developing the annotated list of tests as well as in obtaining numerous references for preparing the literature reviews. W. Mark Hamilton, Director of Professional Publications at AACD, provided suggestions and encouragement as my "friendly publisher."

Many other friends have lent their support, shoulders, listening ears, companionship, and love. My thanks are expressed also to them: Linda Fowler, Lois Wedl, Jana Raup, Cindy Cugno, Sandy Watt, Louise Forsyth, Sr. Immaculata Paisant, and my own sister, Jill Williams. Special thanks are due to Brooke Collison for his continual encouragement and support, and the gentle manner in which he *always* asked, "How's the book coming . . .?"

INTRODUCTION

At the turn of this century, the average life span in America was 47 years. Few persons reached midlife with their parents still alive. As the life span has increased to the late 80s, the potential for three-, four-, and even five-generation families has increased significantly. Today, most persons reach adulthood with their parents alive, independent, and active. During the midlife period, most adults experience both the pleasures and the problems of relating to their aging parents.

The potential exists for positive and satisfying relationships between adult children and their aging parents. While parents are "young-old," meaning that they are relatively healthy physically and mentally and are basically independent in their daily functioning, these relationships occur quite naturally. (Young-old persons are generally considered to be those between 60 and 75 years of age. Old-old persons are those aged 75 and above.) When parents grow older and experience physical or mental decline that *may* accompany the aging process, these relationships may be disrupted. New patterns of relating may be required—and these can be painful. For some families, coping with the consequences of aging represents a continuation of a lifetime of healthy relationship patterns. For others, it is necessary to renegotiate relationships as adults. Dysfunctional family patterns, perhaps softened by time and distance, may, under the stress of caregiving needs, result in a reactivation of disruptive and disturbed ways of relating. Dysfunctional patterns can lead to a plethora of negative feelings and reactions when attempting to cope with role reversals, caregiving needs, or other stressful situations that adult children of aging parents may encounter.

Clearly, aging parents represent an increasingly common concern for their adult children. The issues include personal as well as interpersonal concerns. A comprehensive approach to meeting the information needs of counselors must include attention to *both* adult children and their aging parents. Some general theory and research data on the normative concerns of each will be useful. In addition, specific, commonly encountered issues must be addressed. The entire repertoire of counseling skills will be needed to meet the broad, complex, interacting, and multifaceted needs of families with older members.

With these issues in mind, this book is divided into five parts. The first chapter addresses normative developmental issues in later life. This includes the demography of aging, theories of aging, and attitudes toward older persons. As is true in each of the first four chapters, some suggestions for identifying at-risk populations and implications for counselors are included. Criteria for choosing assessment instruments for older persons are discussed, and specific instruments for assessing attitudes and counseling needs are identified.

The second chapter addresses several issues of aging, including depression, suicide, drug and alcohol abuse, and organic brain diseases, that are critical for counselors. Implications for counseling and strategies for assessment are included with each of these issues.

The third chapter addresses the needs of caregivers as well as the needs of older persons. Psychosocial concerns of caregivers and adult children as well as family relationships and patterns in later life are examined. Several common late life transitions and the effect of each transition on family relationships are reviewed. These include aging and loss, the retirement transition, and the transition to grandparenthood. Again, implications for counselors and strategies for assessment are included.

The fourth chapter deals with four family stress situations and possible responses. These are caregiving, institutionalization, elder abuse, and death and dying. For each issue, the needs of both older persons and adult children are considered. Implications for counseling and strategies for assessment for each issue are also discussed.

The final chapter provides general information useful to counselors working with adult children and aging parents. The focus is on building and maintaining healthy, positive relationships. Family counseling is discussed in terms of applying family therapy literature in working with adult children and aging parents. Several counseling methods are described that can be useful in this context. These include the use of bibliotherapy, life review, genograms, and early recollections.

An annotated list of assessment instruments referenced in the text is provided in the appendix. Publishers' addresses are included.

This book was developed to assist counselors in working with adult children and their aging parents. It will be useful to counselors and human development specialists at all levels— students, faculty, private practitioners, community agency counselors—in helping adult children and aging parents. It can also be helpful, on a personal level, to both adult children and their aging parents.

It is important to recognize that, at times, the counselor will be the client. Each of us, at some time, must confront the aging and eventual death of our parents. Therefore, this book is for all of us.

At the same time, this book focuses on the issue that the counselor must deal with helping others. The concern is with the basic knowledge necessary for counselors to be helpful to adult children and their aging parents who need assistance with mental health concerns. It is impossible to provide *all* the answers to *all* the questions in only one source. The areas selected represent those considered to be most commonly encountered and most important for counselors to understand. References and suggested resources for additional information and assistance are included to help counselors obtain information beyond the scope of this book. Counselors and other helpers are encouraged to view this book as a beginning resource, and to understand that meeting the needs of adult children and aging parents is something for all of us to work at, work for, and work toward as we, our parents, and our society grow older.

—Jane E. Myers

CHAPTER I

AGING: AN OVERVIEW

Understanding the mental health needs of adult children and their aging parents requires, first of all, an understanding of normal development in adulthood and later life. Developmental issues for older persons are the focus of this chapter. Normative aspects of development for adult children are discussed in chapter 3.

The context for viewing the needs and concerns of older persons is both global and individual. That is to say, we must view older persons as a whole and discuss their social roles and status as a population subgroup before we can fully comprehend their needs. Therefore, the focus of this chapter is on the older population in general. The demography of aging is described in detail in terms of the current situation as well as population projections. The major theories of aging—biological, sociological, and psychological—are reviewed to provide a summary of the state of the art in understanding the aging process.

Attitudes toward older persons exert a pervasive effect on their lives. Hence, common myths and stereotypes about older persons are discussed in this chapter. The normative aspects of aging suggest a number of risk factors that place certain older persons in potentially vulnerable positions. These risk factors are identified in terms of demography, theories, and social stereotypes. Implications for counselors are discussed, including considerations in the assessment of older persons.

1

Demography of Aging

In 1900, there were 3.1 million persons or 4.1% of the U.S. population aged 65 and over. By 1986, the number of individuals aged 65+ had reached 29.2 million, which represented 12.1% of the total population (American Association of Retired Persons [AARP], 1986a). By the year 2030, it is projected that 64.3 million persons or 21% of the population will be in this age group (Special Committee on Aging [SCOA], 1983). Stated another way, the proportion of older persons in the population was 1:25 in 1900, 1:9 in 1986, and is projected to be 1:5 in 2030.

The number of older persons has grown tremendously. In fact, in the last 20 years the over 65 population increased by 24% compared to a 6% increase in those under age 65. Among persons aged 65 and over, those aged 85 or older deserve special attention. This group is now and is expected to remain the fastest growing age segment in the total population. The number of persons aged 85 or older has increased 22 times since 1900; the number of persons aged 75 to 84 has increased 11 times; and the number of persons aged 65 to 74 has increased 8 times. By the year 2010, there will be 6.8 million persons over age 85, or 2.4% of the total population (SCOA, 1983).

Although many assume that the current growth of the older population is due to increased longevity, the primary reason has been the growth in numbers of older persons, reflecting the high birth rates in the years prior to 1920 and during the post-World War II "baby boom" of 1945–1959 (SCOA, 1983). Demographic data describing subgroups of the rapidly growing older population are included in the following sections.

Race, Sex, and Marital Status

There is significant variation within the older population with regard to race, sex, and marital status. In 1982, approximately 90% of persons aged 65+ were White, 8% were Black, and 2% were members of other races. This is in contrast to the total population, in which 80% of persons are White and 20% non-White, of whom 8% are Hispanics. The non-White older populations are growing faster than the White older population because of higher birth rates and more rapid gains in life expectancy (SCOA, 1983). It is estimated that 21% of the older population will be non-White in 2020, and 30% by 2050 (AARP, undated). The major subgroups of minority elderly, in decreasing order by number, are Blacks, Hispanics, Native Americans, and Asian Americans, including Pacific Islanders.

Life expectancy for both men and women has increased steadily since the turn of this century. A person born in 1900 could expect to live an average of only 49 years, whereas a person born in 1986 can expect to live 74.9 years (AARP, 1986a). The longer one lives, the longer one may expect to live. This "survivorship" phenomenon results in differential life expectancies for persons at birth and at age 65. In 1900, persons who had reached the age of 65 could expect to live an additional 11 years (Decker, 1980). Currently there are 5,900 persons reaching age 65 each day, and these persons can expect to live an additional 16.9 years (AARP, 1986a). Thus, the life expectancy *at age 65* today is 81.9, in contrast to 74.9 for those *born* today.

Because the life expectancy for women is greater than that for men, it should not be surprising to find that older women outnumber older men by three to two (SCOA, 1983). In 1986, there were 17.4 million women and 11.8 million men aged 65 and over (AARP, 1986a). The statistics change with increasing age within the older population, so that the ratio of women to men increases from 122:100 for those aged 65 to 70 to 251:100 for those over age 85 (Butler & Lewis, 1982).

It is not surprising to find that over 50% of all older women are widows and most of them live alone. In fact, because women tend to marry older men, and also to outlive men by several years, the average American woman can expect to be a widow for 25 years (SCOA, 1983)! In contrast, older men generally are married and living with their spouse. Because older men tend to remarry if they lose a spouse, currently 83% of older men live in family environments compared to only 57% of older women. These figures decrease with advancing age, especially for women.

Geographic Location

The states with the largest numbers of older persons are also the states with the largest total population. The largest numbers of older people reside in California (2.4 million), New York (2.2 million), Florida (1.7 million), Pennsylvania (1.6 million), Texas (1.4 million), Illinois (1.3 million), and Ohio (1.2 million) (SCOA, 1983).

However, the states with the largest numbers of older persons are not the same as those with the highest proportion of older persons in their total population. Florida and Pennsylvania are the only exceptions because they have both high numbers and high percentages of older persons. The states with the highest proportions of older persons and the percentages of older people in their populations are: Florida (17.7%), Pennsylvania (14.6%), Rhode Island (14.6%), Iowa (14.5%), Arkansas (14.5%), South Dakota (13.9%), Missouri (13.7%), West Virginia (13.6%), Nebraska (13.6%), and Massachusetts (13.6%) (AARP, 1986a). For most of these states, the large proportion of older persons is the result of heavy outmigration of younger persons rather than an influx of older individuals.

Regardless of the state of residence, most older persons now live in metropolitan areas. However, there has been a steady increase of approximately 2.5% per year in the older population in small towns and rural areas (SCOA, 1983).

Contrary to popular myths, most older adults live in the same place where they lived in midlife. Of those aged 60+ who have made interstate moves, approximately 50% moved to five states: Florida, California, Arizona, Texas, and New Jersey. Of those who moved intrastate, 50% moved within the same metropolitan area. Those who do move, either inter- or intrastate, are more likely to be married, not working, well educated, and relatively affluent compared to those who do not move (SCOA, 1983).

Income and Poverty Rates

Almost half of the income older persons receive comes from retirement benefits, including Social Security and public and private pensions, one third comes from employment earnings, and the remainder from savings, investments, and gifts (Cook & Stewart, 1985). In 1940, fewer than 100,000 persons received retirement benefits under the Social Security system. Today more than 21 million Americans receive such benefits (Cunningham & Brookbank, 1983). Fixed incomes are common, with increases in Social Security payments not keeping pace with rising inflation. Most people experience a one-half to two-thirds drop in income at retirement, therefore the financial status of older persons in general is not as good as that of the rest of the population.

Because the majority of older adults are not in the labor force, it is not surprising to find lower median incomes for those aged 65 and over. In 1980, the median income for all persons aged 65+ was $6,593, compared with $12,387 for individuals aged 25 to 64. Older persons who live alone are further economically disadvantaged, as their median incomes are only $5,096 compared to $12,882 for families with a head of household over age 65.

Among older adults living alone, 60% receive $6,000 or less per year, with 32% having incomes under $4,000. About one in five older persons are "poor," with 21% of families with a head of household over age 65 having incomes of $7,500 per year or less. Eighteen percent of families with a head of household over age 65 had incomes of $25,000 or more, compared to only 18% of older adults living alone having incomes of $10,000 or more (SCOA, 1983).

The poverty rate for the general population stands at 13%, compared to the following rates for persons aged 65 and over:

- total population   16%
- White men   8%
- White women   17%
- Black men   33%
- Black women   40%

About one in every seven older persons is poor, and an additional 10% of the older population is classified as "near-poor," with incomes between the poverty level and 125% of the poverty level. Poverty rates are higher for older individuals living in rural rather than urban areas. The highest poverty rates for persons aged 65+ are found in Mississippi (34.3%), Alabama (28.4%), and Arkansas (28.2%) (SCOA, 1983).

Employment and Retirement

Although retirement was once viewed as a luxury, today it is considered the norm. In 1900, 66% of older men were employed in the labor force. By 1950, this figure had dropped to 50%, and by 1970 to 25%. Today, fewer than 18% of men aged 65+ participate in the labor market. Labor force participation rates for older women, however, have remained fairly stable.

In 1900, 10% of older women were in the work force, compared with 8% today (SCOA, 1983). Projections for 2010 indicate that these percentages will further decline to 11% for men and 7% for women (Cunningham & Brookbank, 1983).

The occupations in which most older persons remain employed include professional and crafts positions. Many of these occupations permit self-employment, thus there is no mandatory retirement age. Older people also tend to be overrepresented in lower paying jobs such as building maintenance and retail sales.

Even though the mandatory retirement age has been raised to almost 70 for most occupations, retirement at age 65 or earlier is still the trend. Changes in the mandatory retirement age combined with the results of inflation have increased the desire of many older persons to remain working or to return to work (Kieffer, 1980). A recent study showed that 41% of retired women and 32% of retired men were forced to retire, either because of poor health or employer policies (Harris & Associates, 1974). A follow-up study in 1979 revealed that 46% of older retirees would prefer to be working, whereas 50% preferred not to return to paid employment (Harris & Associates, 1981). More than half of the older persons currently working want to continue to work. More than two thirds of older persons would prefer at least part-time employment to full retirement after the age of 65 (National Alliance for Business, 1985).

Health Status

The self-reported health status of older persons is generally either "excellent" (42%) or "good" (38%). A minority report their health as "only fair" (15%) or "poor" (5%) (Harris & Associates, 1981). Although chronic illness increases with age, the majority (80%) of older persons are able to carry out their activities of daily living without assistance. For most persons, health status and independent daily functioning are not significantly reduced until at least age 75, but most likely are reduced by age 85 or older.

Most older persons visit doctors for treatment of chronic physical conditions. The conditions most often reported as limiting activity for older persons, and the percent of older persons who report having these conditions are (Brotman, 1982):

- arthritis   44%
- hypertension   39%
- hearing impairment   28%
- heart disease   27%
- arteriosclerosis   21%
- visual impairment   12%
- diabetes   8%

These chronic conditions create increasing disability over time; however, most older persons cope with physical limitations without disruption of their activities. The three leading causes of death in older persons, heart disease, stroke, and cancer, account for more than three fourths of all deaths. All three are due to conditions creating increasing physical disability over time.

Older persons compose only 12% of the population yet use 40% of all prescription drugs. They purchase an average of 15.5 prescriptions per year, with 37% using five or more concurrent prescriptions and 19% using seven or more (Wolfe, Fugate, Hulstrand, & Kamimoto, 1988). Older persons account for over 31% of total health care expenditures nationally.

A common misconception is that the majority of older persons live in long-term care facilities such as nursing homes. In reality, only 5% of all older persons are institutionalized at any given time. This represents 1.3 million older persons. By the year 2000, this figure is expected to rise to 2.2 million, and by 2030 to 5.4 million. About one in five older persons may expect to be institutionalized at some time in their lives.

Mental Health

It is commonly recognized that the incidence of mental health concerns increases with advancing age (Butler & Lewis, 1982). Both preventive (preretirement counseling, life coping skills enhancement) and remedial assistance are important. Older persons experience multiple losses, changing life circumstances, and needs for significant adjustments at a time when their resource base may be declining significantly.

An estimated 25% of all older persons experience treatable mental health problems (Kramer, Taube, & Redick, 1975). Depression in older persons, discussed in chapter 2, is perhaps the most common mental health concern. About one fourth of reported suicides (also discussed in chapter 2) occur among older persons, with the highest rates occurring among older White men.

Older persons are overrepresented in public mental hospitals, where they occupy some 60% of available beds, and underrepresented in outpatient service delivery programs. Community mental health clinics serve only 2% to 4% of older persons among their case loads (Patterson, 1978). Despite federal mandates, the rate of underservice to older persons in community mental health settings contributes to the high incidence of problems with this population (Myers, 1983).

Education

Most of today's older persons did not have access to the types and extent of educational experiences available to young persons today. Thus older persons lag behind the younger population in educational attainment. However, the discrepancy between the younger and older populations in median years of school completed is decreasing. By 1980, older adults had completed an average of 10.2 years of education, with 41% finishing high school and 9% completing 4 or more years of college (Siegel, 1976). By 1985, the median years of education completed was 12 for older Whites, 8 for older Blacks, and 7 for older Hispanics.

The number of older persons enrolled in educational programs has increased steadily in recent years. Between 1974 and 1981, the number of older persons enrolled in community education programs through schools, industry, and community and senior centers increased from 13% to 29%. Educational enrollments occur most frequently among college graduates (Harris & Associates, 1981).

Older persons frequently take adult education courses to advance job skills, but do so primarily for personal growth and development. In 1986, 2,500,000 students nationwide, or 10% of adult education participants, were aged 65 and over. More than 800,000 participants were over age 75 (U.S. Department of Education, 1988). Survey data from the National Council on Educational Statistics indicated that 16% of all persons enrolled in continuing education programs are over age 65. Older persons compose only 1% of those enrolled in academic programs and 3% of those enrolled in vocational education courses (U.S. Department of Education).

Older Persons and Their Families

Approximately 80% of persons over age 65 have living children, most of whom are middle-aged (i.e., 35–64). Some older adults, however, have adolescent and preschool children. About 10% of older persons have children who also are over age 65 (Cicirelli, 1983a).

Of the older persons who have children, half have one or two children and half have three or more. Most older persons (94%) have grandchildren and approximately 50% have great-grandchildren (Brubaker, 1985). Because of the increased life expectancy, there are more four- and five-generation families than in the past. Reduced fertility rates, however, result in increasingly fewer children, grandchildren, and great-grandchildren among the kinship networks of persons as they grow older.

More couples are electing to remain childless than ever before. It is estimated that 5% of older persons are married (or widowed) and voluntarily childless and another 5% single and childless. Combined with the possibility of parents outliving their children, which increases with fewer offspring, it seems that at least 10% of the future older population will have no children to whom to look for needed care and support.

Theories of Aging

Gerontology, or the study of aging, is a relatively new field, with fewer than 40 years to its record, and its theory is still evolving. In fact, some scholars would argue that the so-called theories of aging that do exist are nothing more than descriptions of what happens to individuals as they age, rather than explanations of *why* they age. Without these explanations, prediction is difficult if not impossible (Kart, 1981). Theory, such as it is in gerontology, has been guided by the traditional discipline of the theorist (e.g., biology, sociology, psychology), rather than the more comprehensive field of aging itself. Thus, gerontology has three distinct theoretical units: biological, sociological, and psychological. Theories of aging are discussed in this section from all three perspectives. Because the orientation of this book is psychological in nature, the biological theories are discussed in less detail than are sociological and psychological theories.

Biological Theories of Aging

The biological theories of aging can be divided into two broad categories—those with genetic and those with non-genetic themes. There are several major theories in each category. Empirical evidence supports each of the theories, all of which offer some explanation of the aging process. However, at this time none of these theories offer much in the way of predictive value. We still do not understand how or why people age biologically.

The *wear and tear* theory of aging is perhaps the oldest biological theory. It explains aging as a normal process wherein body parts, like machine parts, simply wear out. Similarly, the *genetic clock theory* asserts that a definite time limit is programmed into each of our cells. After reproducing 50 times, cells will die. Thus, the maximum possible human life span is between 110 and 120 years (Hayflick, 1977).

The *error catastrophe theory* postulates that mistakes are made in the RNA and DNA of cells as they reproduce. Faulty cells accumulate with age and become incapable of normal functioning. In contrast, the *somatic mutation theory* was developed to explain how cells mutate, and thus how aging occurs as damaged cells accumulate in the body.

Among the non-genetic theories, the *fixed amount of time* theory suggests that each person is born with a predetermined amount of time to live. Related to this is the *declining energy theory*, which suggests that each person has a fixed amount of energy and will die when it is used up. The *autoimmune* theory of aging was proposed to explain how the body's immune system turns against itself and tries to destroy itself. Related to this is the *immune* theory of aging, which suggests that immunity to disease decreases with advancing age after midlife. Older persons are thus more susceptible to numerous diseases that limit their life span. Additional information on both genetic and non-genetic theories of aging is available in many gerontology textbooks (e.g., Cox, 1988; Harris & Cole, 1980).

Though little is known about the causes of biological changes associated with aging, the fact remains that all body systems change and decline. These changes are progressive and universal, and result in a decreased ability to handle both physical and psychological stress. Recent research on physiology and aging suggests that at least two factors can slow or even reverse the normal processes of aging: first, exercise (about 20 minutes of aerobic exercise three times a week), and, second, proper nutrition. Clearly, wellness life styles can improve the health of individuals at all ages. Because the link between physical and mental health has been identified, it is also significant that wellness life styles can contribute to positive aspects of mental as well as physical health as persons age.

Sociological Theories of Aging

Sociological theories of aging share the common view that aging occurs within a societal context. These theories attempt to explain the aging process in the context of the interaction of older individuals with other persons and social institutions. The major theories included in this section are: disengagement, activity, subculture, exchange, social breakdown, and age stratification. Each theory can contribute to our understanding of older persons.

Disengagement Theory

Cumming and Henry (1961) developed the disengagement theory and explained it in their book, *Growing Old*. The theory was based on cross-sectional research with 275 people aged 50 to 90 living in Kansas City. All 275 were physically and financially self-sufficient.

The basic premise of disengagement theory is that, as aging occurs, there is:

> . . . an inevitable mutual withdrawal or disengagement resulting in decreased interaction between the aging person and others in the social system he (sic) belongs to . . . . When the aging process is complete the natural equilibrium which existed in middle life between the individual and his (sic) society has given way to a new equilibrium characterized by a greater distance and altered type of relationship. (Cumming & Henry, 1961, pp. 14–15)

The process of withdrawal or disengagement is desired by older persons as well as society. It ensures optimal personal gratification as well as continuation of the existing social system. When the process of mutual withdrawal occurs, there is a shrinkage of social interaction opportunities that becomes self-perpetuating. The pool of contacts, and hence activity, decreases until the older person eventually dies. This process is believed to be both inevitable and universal.

Activity Theory

The activity theory is consistent with the American work ethic (Maddox, 1970). According to activity theory:

> . . . the older person who ages optimally is the person who stays active and who manages to resist the shrinkage of his (sic) social world. He (sic) maintains the activities of middle age as long as possible and then finds substitutes for those activities he (sic) is forced to relinquish. (Havighurst, Neugarten, & Tobin, 1968, p. 161)

The activity theorists suggest that a person's sense of personal worth or self-concept is based on different roles. As a person ages, and their roles are changed or lost, the potential for diminished self-worth arises. In order to maintain high levels of self-worth, the older person must replace lost roles with compensatory activities (Lemon, Bengtson, & Peterson, 1972). Thus, to remain emotionally and psychologically well, older persons must remain active.

Subculture Theory

Rose (1965) suggested that the aged cohort is in fact an aged subculture or a culture within a culture. He theorized that older adults interact more among themselves than with persons in other age categories and that new norms emerge to guide their behavior. Good physical and mental health and high levels of social activity have a special value in conferring status within this subculture.

Although some stigma may be attached to belonging to the older subculture, certain demographic and social trends contribute to its perpetuation. One such factor is the sheer number of older persons who are both healthy and mobile enough to interact with one another. This interaction may be by design, such as older people electing to move into a retirement community, or it may simply be the result of an unplanned occurrence such as the outmigration of younger persons from rural or inner-city areas. Other factors that aid the establishment of a subculture are mandatory retirement policies and social services that include all older persons in one category. Yet other factors might include biological changes, different socialization experiences early in life, and different normative expectations for older persons.

Conversely, a number of factors prohibit the development of subcultures. These include sustained contact with family members, continued employment, and an attitude of active resistance toward aging. In other words, factors that act to integrate older persons into society effectively act against the formation of subgroups.

Exchange Theory

The tenets of exchange theory were developed by Homans (1961), empirically tested by Blau (1961), and applied to older adults by Dowd (1981). The basic premise of exchange theory is that people act to optimize their rewards and minimize their costs. Unfortunately, Dowd saw older persons as having nothing to exchange, leaving them no options except to be compliant in accepting their life circumstances and lack of social status. The exchange theory may be better understood by the following example:

> A resident in a long-term care facility pushed the call button for assistance to the bathroom. Unfortunately the nurse's aide did not respond rapidly enough and "an accident" resulted. Rather than confronting the nurse's aide regarding the slow response, the resident apologized in an attempt to avoid retaliation from the employee or added delays the next time a request for help would be made. Thus, the resident *exchanged* compliance for future assistance.

Exchange can be positive as well as negative. Businesses and political candidates are beginning to recognize this phenomenon and are trying to offer products and promises in exchange for the older consumers' market and vote.

Social Breakdown Theory

The social breakdown theory has its roots in labeling theory (Coser & Rosenberg, 1976), which infers that older persons become what other persons believe them to be. In effect, the negative aspects of aging become self-fulfilling prophecies. According to Kuypers and Bengston (1973), society holds negative stereotypes of older persons and views them as less capable. When older persons experience role losses, they perceive that others expect them to be less able, and they internalize the view that others communicate. This internalization results in increasingly dependent behavior that is first seen by members of society and then reinforced in the minds of others as "normal" for older people. Denied access to roles and independent functioning, older persons increasingly withdraw and their functional level declines, causing observers to view them as even less capable. Thus, the cycle is established and is self-perpetuating, beginning with the perceptions of others that a person is "old."

The social reconstruction syndrome, also developed by Kuypers and Bengston (1973), offers a model for interrupting the negative breakdown cycle by providing opportunities for older persons to enhance their sense of competence. These opportunities must be free from negative societal values, and in some instances, the environment of the older person must be carefully reconstructed. When others begin to communicate confidence in the older person's abilities, self-fulfilling prophecies can occur in a positive direction. Thus, social breakdown theory is a systematic explanation of the dynamic interchange between society and older persons, whereas social reconstruction theory offers a model for developing helping interventions.

Age Stratification Theory

The age-stratification theory postulates that there is a hierarchy of age strata (Riley, 1971). Each age stratum is associated with certain social roles and expectations. When one is fulfilling these roles and expectations, little attention is given to one's behavior. However, when an individual behaves differently from the norm, that person is viewed as atypical or perhaps even abnormal. Thus, wearing miniskirts is appropriate for a 16-year-old girl but inappropriate for a 72-year-old woman.

When all age strata are combined, a type of social clock is developed. It is expected that persons will marry in their early 20s, have children in their late 20s, experience a career peak in their mid-40s, and retire at about age 65. Because everyone is expected to follow the same social clock, the entire society becomes synchronized. If persons do not marry until age 35, for example, they are said to be out of synchronization, or asynchronized with society.

Psychological Theories of Aging

Most people are familiar with the behavioral/personality typologies associated with early childhood ages and stages. These include the "terrible twos," "trusting threes," "fascinating fours," and "frustrating fives." Based on the logic that there is one unique personality characteristic associated with a specific age, many researchers have tried to identify *the one* characteristic that best describes the behavior of older persons. Disengagement and activity theories are examples of these attempts. The older population, some 25 million persons, is extremely diverse. Based on this heterogeneity, typologies of multiple personality styles in later life rather than a single type of personality have proven to be more useful in explaining the psychology of aging.

In reviewing the psychological theories of aging, an understanding of the concept of life satisfaction is helpful. Life satisfaction refers to a feeling of happiness, contentment, or high morale. Empirical research in gerontology includes numerous studies of life satisfaction. Most such studies focus on correlates of life satisfaction such as employment, social support and health (Krause, 1987), religion (Markides, Levin, & Ray, 1987), race and socioeconomic status (McKenzie & Campbell, 1987), and leisure (Sneegas, 1986). Each of the psychological theories of aging attempts to explain why some older persons are satisfied and content with their lives (i.e., have high life satisfaction) whereas others have low levels of life satisfaction.

Personality Theories

Perhaps the best-known personality typology of aging was developed by Neugarten, Havighurst, and Tobin (1968) following an analysis of data from the Kansas City studies gathered by Cumming and Henry (1961). According to Neugarten et al. (1968), there are four major personality types among older persons: integrated, armored-defended, passive dependent, and unintegrated. Each type includes several subtypes.

The *integrated* personality is well adjusted and mature. This personality type includes three subtypes, all of which are high in life satisfaction. These are the reorganized, focused, and disengaged types. The person can be well adjusted (integrated) by being extremely active, or what is termed *reorganized*. Persons who display this personality have replaced one activity with another, (i.e., they volunteer 8 hours a day at a social agency rather than being employed for pay). At the other end of the continuum are those with a *disengaged* personality type. They are not active but are content to lead a quieter life. In between these poles is the *focused personality*. The focused person is active but specializes in selected activities.

The *armored-defended* person has relatively high levels of life satisfaction but generally is not happy about aging. Within this category are two subtypes, the *holding-on* personality type and the *constricted* personality type. The holding-on person tries to "hold on" to middle age. Such persons may continue to wear "younger" clothing styles and adopt the behaviors of younger people. Constricted personality types limit their activities much as focused-integrated persons do. However, constricted individuals are not happy about their restricted activities and perceive them to be caused by old age.

Passive-dependent persons are much less independent than either of the first two types. Within this general type are the subtypes termed *succorance seeker* and *apathetic*, both of which have medium to low levels of life satisfaction. Succorance seekers are heavily dependent on others for their happiness and need others for emotional support. Apathetic persons are passive and uninvolved in social activities. However, their apathy has been a lifelong pattern rather than a characteristic newly developed in old age.

Unintegrated, or *disorganized* individuals have gross defects in their psychological functioning. They may be recognized by lack of attention to dress, housekeeping, and other aspects of personal care. There were no subtypes identified in this category. All disorganized persons experience low levels of life satisfaction.

Reichard, Livson, and Peterson (1962) also developed a typology of personalities among older persons. They proposed the following personality types: (1) *mature* (a person who is well adjusted to aging); (2) *rocking chair* (a person who is also well adjusted to aging but is more dependent than the mature type); (3) *armored* (a person who has high levels of self-control and self-reliance, a person who exemplifies rugged individualism); (4) *angry* (a person who is hostile and not well adjusted, a person who blames others for all of their problems); and (5) *self-hater* (a person who is also poorly adjusted but who blames him- or herself for any problems).

Obviously there are parallels between these theories. They share the recognition that no one personality type accurately describes all older persons, and that different behaviors characterize individuals who are well adjusted and experience high levels of life satisfaction.

Continuity Theory

Many of the early personality theories focused on changes that occurred within persons as they grew older. However, most of these changes were identified as a result of cross-sectional research, meaning that cohort differences rather than change in persons over time were identified. Longitudinal studies were needed to determine age-related changes in personality. In the second phase of the Kansas City Studies of Adult Life, a brief 6-year longitudinal study of 70 noninstitutionalized older adults aged 40 to 90 was conducted. Using objective tests and interviews, the researchers were able to show that a person's basic personality remains stable over the life span. This stability, or *continuity*, as it is termed, is believed to be the most representative aging pattern. Basically, the theory that Havighurst, Neugarten, and Tobin (1968) postulated states that as persons grow older, they become more like themselves and less like other individuals.

Again reverting to cross-sectional interpretation, Neugarten et al. (1968) did find two changes that seem to accompany the aging process. Both changes were discovered using Thematic Apperception Test (TAT) data. In the Kansas City studies, TAT stories were compared between persons in different age groups. Respondents in the older age categories tended to provide stories concerning greater introspection and self-reflection or interiority. Older respondents told stories with less conflict and less activity than their younger counterparts. Older respondents also were more likely to tell stories in which the hero relied on magic, luck, or the help of others to succeed. This is contrary to the active mastery stories of younger persons who based their hero's success on their (the younger persons') own competencies.

The second change Neugarten et al. (1968) identified was a blending of sex roles. Women tended to become more assertive and aggressive, whereas men tended to become more nurturing and affiliative. These studies support earlier theories by Jung explaining increased interiority with age as well as "reversal into the opposite," wherein masculine and feminine roles become less divergent (Jacobi, 1962).

Life-Span Development Theories

The concept of continuity is consistent with theories of life-span development. Among the many that have been proposed, those of Erikson (1963), Peck (1968) and Havighurst (1972) are reviewed here because they contribute most to an understanding of the needs of older persons in relation to their adult children.

Erikson's Eight Stages of Humanity. Erikson (1963) suggested that personality develops as a result of a person's meeting a series of psychosocial crises or challenges, each of which occurs around a certain age or age range. Each stage (crisis) must be addressed during the life course. A positive resolution of the crisis of each stage is necessary for successful resolution of the crisis of each succeeding stage. The first four crises are those of trust versus mistrust, autonomy versus doubt, initiative versus guilt, and (childhood) industry versus inferiority. The crisis of identity versus identity confusion is most salient during adolescence, but is one that appears and reappears throughout the life span. Intimacy versus isolation, the central challenge of young adulthood, also resurfaces throughout life, particularly when partners are lost as a result of separation, divorce, or death.

In the seventh stage, generativity versus stagnation, which occurs during midlife, generativity refers to "concern in establishing and guiding the next generation" (Erikson, 1963, p. 267). Stagnation, in contrast, is characterized by a preoccupation with oneself. The central concern of midlife adults is to raise their children to be independent persons in society. The final stage in Erikson's typology is the crisis of ego integrity versus despair. This is the culmination of all the crisis resolutions. Older persons who achieve integrity are able to look back on their lives and appreciate what has occurred. They believe the life they have lived is the best that could have been lived. In despair, however, the older person looks back in anguish and disgust, wishing that his or her life could have been different. A pervasive depression ensues with the knowledge that it is too late to make significant changes.

Peck's Conflicts of Old Age. In contrast to Erikson's two final stages, which are broad both in scope and years covered, Peck (1968) proposed three essential psychological conflicts specific to old age. These are: ego differentiation versus work-role preoccupation; body transcendence versus body preoccupation; and ego transcendence versus ego preoccupation. In successfully resolving the conflict of ego differentiation versus work-role preoccupation, the older person must learn a variety of social roles other than a single work role. These varied roles will allow for continued self-esteem after the major work role is lost via retirement or children leaving home.

Chronic illness affects many older persons. How a person copes with the increased likelihood of illness and pain is the conflict of body transcendence versus body preoccupation. Those who become overly dependent on medication or doctors in effect give in to body preoccupation. Those who learn to cope with their illnesses and lead productive, happy lives are successful at body transcendence.

Ego transcendence versus ego preoccupation refers to the view one takes of the world after one's own eventual death. If persons have a desire to leave a legacy and share their knowledge, and believe that life will continue after their death, then they have attained ego transcendence. If, on the other hand, persons make no plan beyond their own demise, then they have achieved only ego preoccupation.

Havighurst's Tasks of Old Age. Havighurst (1972) also followed a developmental perspective in identifying six primary tasks of old age. These are: (1) adjusting to decreasing physical strength and health; (2) adjusting to retirement and reduced income; (3) adjusting to the death of a spouse; (4) establishing an explicit affiliation with one's age group; (5) adopting and adapting social roles in a flexible way; and (6) establishing satisfactory physical living arrangements.

The primary tasks of old age are associated with lost social roles and physical decline. Successful adjustment to these tasks requires learning new roles and behaviors to cope with changes. These issues have been addressed in other theories. Interestingly, Havighurst does not address the issue of facing one's own death, a task that seems to take on added significance as one grows older.

Other Psychological Contributions to Theory

The needs of older persons and persons of other ages are known to be of the same type, but they differ in degree. Thus, older people may experience a greater array of needs at a time when their resources to meet those needs are declining. Because they are based on the commonalities of development and life circumstances, many psychological theories can contribute to an understanding of older persons.

Maslow's (1954) needs hierarchy, for example, is equally valid for older as well as younger persons. It is necessary to satisfy one's basic needs—food, clothing, shelter, medical care—before the higher order needs—love, belonging, self-esteem—can be met.

The results of recent research on locus of control suggest age-related differences. Though independent and internally oriented throughout their lives, many persons react to the losses of aging, over which they have no control, with an interpretation that increasingly emphasizes an external locus of control. They also may be increasingly willing to accept external control. For many older people, this is a realistic adaptation (Troll, 1982a).

A related concept, that of learned helplessness, also contributes to an understanding of personality in later life. When attempts to control one's environment consistently fail, older persons may *learn* that they are "helpless" and thus fail to try to remain independent. Self-efficacy may be both frustrating and unrealistic under certain circumstances, especially those related to losses over which the older person has no control. In contrast to self-efficacy, passive mastery, which can result from a reframing of life events, can lead to greater life satisfaction (Simons & West, 1984–85). These concepts are closely aligned with the social breakdown theory, and have implications similar to those of the social reconstruction model.

Each theory—biological, sociological, and psychological—contributes to an understanding of the needs of older persons. Such an understanding is necessary for counselors and other helping professionals who work with older persons and their families. An understanding of "normal" development and change provides a framework for viewing individual older persons and at least a starting point for the process of assessment, as discussed further in chapter 3. Certainly, knowing what is "normal" for many older persons can help families better understand individual older persons, though theories provide only guidelines and not rules when counseling with older persons. Theories alone, however, provide insufficient data and may be supplemented with an explanation of how attitudes toward older persons affect their lives and, in particular, their psychosocial development in the later years.

Attitudes Toward Older Persons

The term *ageism* was first coined by Butler (1975) in his Pulitzer Prize winning book, *Why Survive? Growing Old in America.* Ageism describes the negative stereotypes and discrimination toward older persons prevalent in our society. Similar to the stereotyping that racism and sexism describe, ageism is viewing all older persons in a similar and negative fashion, for example, that they are all unattractive, senile, and in poor health. The practice of ageism feeds negative stereotypes regarding older people.

A number of prevalent and commonly accepted myths about older people have been identified. These overgeneralizations are absolutist in nature, yet each contains a kernel of truth. More important, perhaps, is the cognitive distortion that occurs when an older person internalizes one or more of these myths and acts accordingly. According to the National Council on the Aging, the most persistent negative and untrue stereotypes regarding older persons in America are (Kermis, 1984):

- Old people are all alike.
- Old people are all poor.
- Old people are all sick.
- Old people are all depressed.
- Old people are all a drag on everyone else.
- Old people can't function in society.
- Old people all live alone.
- Old people all die in institutions.
- If we live long enough we will all become senile.

Yet another myth is that all old people want to live with their adult children. An examination of the facts simply does not support any of these myths. As was discussed earlier, old people are a very heterogeneous group; hence, the development of theories of multiple personality types in older persons has been necessary.

Although poverty rates are higher for older persons than for adults under the age of 65, not all older persons are poor. In fact, 25% of all older persons have incomes of over $25,000 per year (SCOA, 1983).

Approximately 86% of older persons have chronic health conditions such as arthritis, heart disease, and diabetes; however, these conditions do not result in total disability. As noted earlier, most noninstitutionalized older individuals report no limitation in their activities of daily living (Brotman, 1982). Because most older peole are able to live independently, the myths that they cannot function and are a drag on society are completely unfounded.

Research on the incidence of depression provides discrepant figures, but most studies reveal that between 10% and 25% of older persons are depressed. Although these rates are higher than for some other age groups, they certainly do not represent "all" older people.

As reported earlier, the majority of older men and almost half of older women live in a couple relationship. Almost all older persons—95%—live outside an institution. These figures help dispel the myths related to older people's living arrangements.

Although the facts do not support commonly repeated myths, they tend to be pervasive and universal. We learn these myths at a very young age, and from a variety of sources. Negative stereotypes are particularly damaging if persons internalize them as they age. Because these views are commonly believed, many older persons *do* internalize them, resulting in negative self-images that become personally self-defeating. In fact, there is some evidence that the healthiest, most satisfied older persons are the ones who refuse to refer to themselves as old (Barbado & Feezel, 1987)! Apparently, this denial serves to enhance the self-concept of older persons, inhibit internalization of a devalued status, and increase their sense of self-esteem and self-efficacy.

Harris and Associates (1974) conducted a national poll regarding the perceptions of younger and older adults about persons aged 65 +. Responses indicated that young people viewed older people as senile, inactive, unfriendly, and uncooperative. Persons in the 65 + category were also asked how they perceived other older people and how they perceived themselves. Though they perceived themselves as intelligent, active, and friendly, they had negative perceptions of their age peers—"those old people."

Negative societal views also affect those who work with older persons. Many nurses, social workers, counselors, and other professionals who work with geriatric populations are forced to defend their choice of occupation against the prevailing negative attitudes. These attitudes have become an economic issue as well, because long-term care workers are paid lower wages than similar workers in hospital or orphanage settings.

Fighting negative societal attitudes toward older persons is even more difficult when professionals ascribe to the same beliefs. Unfortunately, research indicates that as many as 80% of all nurses, and 50% of all long-term care workers do not like the older clients whom they serve (Chandler, Rachal, & Kazelskis, 1986). It is widely believed among those who specialize in counseling older persons that counselors in general hold negative attitudes toward aging and older people.

In the mental health as well as the medical fields, negative myths and misconceptions influence the services provided to older persons. For example, many depressed older individuals are not treated because depression is viewed as a "normal" aspect of aging. Clients are denied access to counselors' time because of an industrial mentality that states that older persons cannot return as much to society as younger persons, so time is better spent on younger persons (Bearden & Head, 1985). In other words, there is a higher rate of return when limited resources are focused on younger clients. Time, of course, is not the only resource withheld from older persons based on the supposed lack of return. Vital organs, experimental drugs, and life-saving technologies all may be denied to older persons where age is a selection criterion.

Helping Responses and Aging

Identifying At-Risk Older Persons

Counselors working with older persons and their families need to be able to assess factors that contribute to making persons at risk in terms of need for mental health intervention.

Knowing that older persons possessing certain characteristics may be more vulnerable to the circumstances of aging can be important information for counselors in at least three ways. First, by identifying at-risk populations, counselors can target their limited resources toward helping persons most in need of interventions. Second, counselors can use this information to develop and implement preventive services to assist vulnerable persons in coping successfully with the circumstances and changes of later life. Third, when working with families, counselors can provide information to assist family members in helping older persons meet the challenges they will experience as they grow older.

Using the data provided in this chapter, a number of potential risk factors may be identified. These are discussed below in terms of demography, theories of aging, and attitudes toward older persons.

Demographic Risk Factors

The increasing numbers and proportions of old persons in the population make it increasingly likely that most counselors will have occasion to work with older persons or their families. Hence, some basic knowledge in the following areas is necessary: needs of older people, normative aspects of late life development, physical, social, and psychological changes in later life, and mental health concerns of older persons. Increasing numbers of older minority individuals in the population also mean that counselors must know about the unique concerns of subcultures within the older population. Of course, when counselors lack specific knowledge, they need to know where and how to refer persons for needed assistance.

Because the old-old group is the fastest growing in the population, and because this group tends to be the most frail, most vulnerable, and most in need of both physical and mental health care, counselors and other helping professionals will need to target services to this group. Their health care and independent living needs will be a high priority; however, quality of life may best be ensured through mental health interventions. The decision to change a primary residence, from independent living to assisted living or long-term care, will arise more commonly with old-old persons and their families than with young-old persons.

Decisions regarding institutionalization are discussed in more detail in chapter 3. What is important here is to identify those older persons most in need of assistance. In addition to age, other criteria or special groups that should alert counselors to potential needs for multiple social service and counseling interventions are these:

- physical disabilities that are multiple or severe and that restrict activities of independent daily living;
- low income and poverty, especially when combined with large medical expenses;
- old persons living in rural areas or isolated in retirement or housing complexes;
- single old persons living alone;
- old persons living without family members in close proximity and seemingly without multiple sources of support or well-developed support networks; and
- older women, especially those who are childless.

Statistics on employment and retirement suggest potential concerns for older persons who are forced to retire. Counselors may find it useful to ascertain the reasons for retirement as well as satisfaction with retirement when working with older persons, especially older men. Many older people may request or need assistance in obtaining gainful employment.

Among older persons who are members of ethnic minority groups, the problems and changes of aging may be compounded by a lifetime of discrimination, with all the associated social, economic, physical, and psychological effects. Older women who are members of minorities are described as being in "double jeopardy." In actuality, these women experience at least "triple jeopardy," being at once old, female, and minorities. Almost by definition, to be old, female, and a minority is to be very poor. So, the circumstances of many older persons are best described as a situation of "multiple jeopardy," with numerous risk factors contributing to their vulnerability.

Risk Factors Linked to Theories of Aging

Knowledge of how persons are expected to age, based on available theories, is important for counselors in order to assist older persons with normative developmental issues. Furthermore, an understanding of normative aspects of development is important in identifying those aspects of an individual older person's life that may be pathological and thus require intervention.

Many older persons expect to experience physical limitations and decline as they age; hence they fail to seek medical care when it could be useful to them. Moreover, families may maintain similar expectations and fail to encourage aging parents to seek needed medical—or psychological—evaluation and treatment. Armed with the knowledge of normative biological changes, as well as theories of aging, counselors can refer older persons for medical care when changes seem pathological. Furthermore, counselors can assist family members in understanding and accepting normal aspects of aging. A general rule of thumb is to seek medical evaluation whenever changes are sudden, because most age-related changes occur gradually. At the same time, it is important to remember that not all "slow" changes are necessarily normal either—many are correctable and treatable.

Comprehensive assessments by trained geriatric specialists are available in many communities, particularly through hospitals, and are preferable to multiple consultations with specialists in the community. Such consultations can result in numerous referrals that may be both physically exhausting and emotionally difficult for older persons. In the absence of a clear leader of the medical team, resulting data may be confusing or contradictory, and a clear diagnosis and treatment plan may emerge slowly or not at all. Comprehensive assessments, on the other hand, include medical as well as psychological evaluations. These are discussed in more detail later in this chapter.

Although physical decline and limited activity tend to accompany the aging process, those older persons who experience rapid decline or significant limitation of activities are those potentially most in need of intervention. On the positive side, counselor interventions with young-old persons and their families can be targeted toward achieving wellness life styles. From this perspective, virtually all older persons may be seen as at risk! Certainly, older persons with unhealthy life styles, including poor nutrition and lack of exercise, may be most vulnerable to illness, both physical and emotional.

Sociological theories of aging emphasize the importance of social roles, and the difficulties of older persons who experience role losses and changes. Older persons expected to be most at risk are those who experience, or are expected to experience, role changes. For example, persons approaching retirement or those who have recently retired, those who have lost a spouse or other loved one, those who have lost a job, volunteer position, or physical health, or those who experience a significant drop in useful income due to retirement, job loss, or increased expenses may be expected to be more at risk and potentially in need of helping interventions.

Psychological theories of aging posit various personality types as more or less adaptive to the aging process. If counselors use the various typologies as a basis, then older persons who are succorance seekers, apathetic, and unintegrated may be expected to have the lowest life satisfaction and be less able to cope with the changes of aging. Older persons with low self-esteem may be identified by examining their locus of control to determine if it is internally or externally oriented, with the latter being most at risk. Older persons whose basic needs are not met may require community services before counseling interventions can be effective.

Older persons who have learned to be helpless in response to their changing life circumstances also will be vulnerable to emotional as well as physical crises. Older persons who are under stress, depressed, or those who experience significant life changes may be expected to be at risk, in a psychological sense, and potentially in need of helping interventions.

Implications for Counselors

In planning counseling services, some attention to the needs of subgroups of the older population who are most at risk in terms of services is important. Counselors may need to learn about these various subgroups, and should be prepared to refer older persons for a variety of services they may need. Some subgroups are defined by ethnicity, requiring counselors to be sensitive to ethnic and cultural values, traditions, and language. Other subgroups may be defined by geographic location, including rural and urban older persons, urban "ghetto" dwellers, "Appalachian" persons, and so forth. Older women, older men, older workers, single older persons, older gays and lesbians—all are subgroups that counselors may encounter. Some knowledge of the special needs and circumstances of each subgroup, and its attitudes toward the care of older persons and relatives, is necessary for effective interventions.

Literature in the field of gerontological counseling within the past 10 years yields the firm conclusion that the needs of older persons are multiple and interactive. The response of counselors must be holistic, with a team approach and a willingness to work cooperatively with other service providers and family members whose assistance is essential to the success of helping interventions. Some suggestions for working with family members are provided in chapters 2 and 5. Service providers may include physicians and other health care providers, staff of housing units and senior centers, beauticians, and any other individuals from whom older persons receive or purchase services. Counselors must be prepared to work closely with these providers while maintaining respect for the confidential nature of communications with older clients and their families.

The types of services provided to older persons may vary according to their age. For example, old-old persons may be most in need of remedial services, with the counselor functioning as a member of a medical team of care providers. Young-old persons may require more preventive approaches, with counselors assisting in life planning endeavors. Helping older persons manage their time and resources, learn new skills, develop satisfying leisure pursuits, and plan where and how to live for the remainder of their lives can be both challenging and rewarding. By emphasizing a desire to help all persons live until they die, counselors can assist older persons and their families, of any age and circumstances, in developing and maintaining healthy, satisfying life styles.

Counselors need to be aware of and sensitive to cultural issues for older minority persons. Though discussion of these issues is beyond the scope of this book, the interested reader will find useful information in a number of sources provided in the reference list (e.g., Lawrence, 1981; Markides, 1986; Solomon, 1984). Meeting the needs of other subgroups of the older population will require the application of generic counseling skills (e.g., reflective and facilitative listening and responding) combined with sensitivity to the specific circumstances of each group. For example, the problems of aging have been defined as the problems of women, because there are many more older women than older men, and they experience multiple jeopardy situations—being female, living in poverty, being isolated, and so forth. Helping older widows and other single older persons develop new and satisfying life styles and expanding their networks of support will be important roles for counselors and other helping professionals.

Counselors play a major role in the area of retirement planning and counseling. It is known that persons who plan their retirement experience greater life satistfaction than those who fail to plan. Counselors may conduct retirement planning seminars and provide retirement counseling to older persons and their families in order to facilitate the retirement transition. Because some older persons choose or need to work, counselors may find themselves conducting career and vocational counseling and planning activities. Assessment resources such as those discussed in chapter 3 may be helpful. In addition, some older persons may choose to pursue educational experiences, now that they have more free time. Counselors can assist and encourage older individuals in choosing satisfying, fulfilling avocational activities.

Because many older persons experience physical changes and decline, it is important for counselors to be aware of normal changes and to help older persons and their families understand and accept these changes. Adjusting to physical decline may be expedited when those changes are understood and strategies for coping are explored. Furthermore, through sharing their understanding of biological aging processes, counselors can assist older persons in planning their lives to ensure remaining as independent as possible regardless of their physical condition. We know that wellness life styles retard or even reverse the aging process, therefore helping older persons achieve and maintain positive wellness attitudes can assist them in remaining healthier and happier longer.

The various social and psychological theories of aging provide numerous clues to assist counselors in helping older persons adjust to role changes and losses. Simply being able to predict that changes will occur is important in helping persons prepare for change and improving their ability to adapt to change. In particular, the social breakdown syndrome offers a useful model to help counselors understand how vital, active persons can become vulnerable and dependent as a result of societal labels that accompany the definition of "old person." By listening to the self-talk of older persons, identifying a change in locus of control from internal to external, and identifying the symptoms of learned helplessness, counselors can plan interventions, with the assistance of family members, to help older persons maintain, or regain, a sense of independence in their lives.

By identifying persons who are most likely to age unsuccessfully (i.e., those with low levels of life satisfaction), counselors can target them for services. Moreover, counselors can assist family members in understanding the personality types and coping styles of older individuals. The psychological theories of aging can be useful guidelines for understanding personality types; however, each older person still must be approached as a unique individual.

Some of the most compelling research on the need for counseling in the lives of older persons is that of Butler (1975) on the role of the life review. The process of reviewing one's life, useful in counseling with persons of any age, is virtually universal in older persons. The outcome of the life review process can be either ego integrity, as defined by Erikson (1963), or despair and depression. Counselors can both facilitate the life review process and, more important, encourage reframing of experiences to achieve a positive outcome. The use of techniques such as Early Recollections (Sweeney & Myers, 1986) can help older persons identify their successful coping strategies and use these to deal with current life circumstances. (Both life review and early recollections are discussed in detail in chapter 5.) Hence, the potential exists for counselors to assist all older persons in achieving ego integrity and life satisfaction.

A final note may be made concerning the effect of negative attitudes and ageism on older persons and the counseling process. The pervasive effect of negative stereotypes has been mentioned. Again, a major consideration is that older persons are all members of a society that denigrates persons because of their age. Older persons themselves tend to believe the negative misconceptions about "old people." It is the internalization of the myths that contributes to a decline in their self-esteem and thus to decreased coping abilities through a self-definition as being less capable.

Family members of older persons also tend to believe the stereotypes. Adult children may both label older persons as incapable *and* communicate to older parents a need to act in certain ways because of the parents' age. Even when an older person asserts, "I am not old!", family members may unknowingly encourage dependence through negative attitudes. Paradoxically, family members may be most disturbed and frightened by signs of increasing dependence in older parents—while being primary contributors to the development of that dependence.

Assessment and Older Persons

Counselors working with older persons and their families will find it helpful as well as necessary to conduct a variety of both informal and formal assessments. Informal techniques include clinical judgments made through interviews and behavioral observations, as well as data gathering techniques to obtain historical data from older persons, family members, and friends. Structured or unstructured diagnostic interviews may be conducted as part of informal assessment approaches.

Formal assessment methods include all of the paper-and-pencil, performance, and other measures used to evaluate intelligence, aptitude, achievement, interest, personality, and career development of individuals. A number of special considerations have been identified when using these assessment methods with older persons. These are discussed below, followed by a review of currently available instruments to assess counseling needs of older persons, life satisfaction, and attitudes toward aging. Assessment of health and wellness, including multidimensional functional assessments, also is discussed.

Considerations in Assessing Older Persons

Special considerations in the assessment of older persons have been reviewed in several sources (e.g., Aiken, 1980; Gallagher, Thompson, & Levy, 1980; Myers & Rimmer, 1982). These considerations include difficulties in assessing older clients, factors affecting test selection for older persons, and alternative assessment strategies.

Difficulties in Assessing Older Clients

As a group, older persons lack a test-taking set. Today's older persons were raised in a time when most available tests were used to assess classroom achievement or work potential. Many view testing as a negative means of evaluation and are uncomfortable in testing situations. Also, the high proportion of illiteracy among older persons makes the use of many pencil-and-paper tests inappropriate.

Because they do not have a strong history of test taking, many older persons will fail to see the purpose of tests and may not understand the goals of testing. Rapport can be compromised by pursuing a testing program in the absence of client motivation and cooperation. On the other hand, older persons may fail to ask questions when they do not understand, and provide responses they think the tester desires. Acquiescent response sets are common when testing older persons, as is easy distractibility and failure to complete sections of the tests.

As persons grow older their reaction time decreases. Tests requiring speeded (timed) responses may yield erroneous information about older clients simply because of physiological response capability and not innate ability or potential. For example, multiple aptitude batteries that include performance items, such as the General Aptitude Test Battery, have been used in longitudinal testing to determine the effect increasing age has on various aptitudes. Manual and finger dexterity both decline with age. They are related to reaction time, tactile decrements that naturally accompany aging, and tactile decrements that result from conditions such as arthritis. Hence, the test scores of older persons on timed (speeded) tests and some performance tests (those requiring manual or finger dexterity) cannot be compared to younger persons' scores if accurate conclusions are to be reached.

Older persons who are frail or ill will fatigue more easily, thus requiring shorter testing sessions. Sometimes it will be necessary to schedule several brief sessions rather than attempting to obtain all the information desired in one session. Communication or sensory impairments further may slow testing efforts and can contribute to erroneous results in the absence of compensatory testing procedures.

Selecting Tests for Older Persons

The most important factor in test selection for older persons is the same as that in any test administration, namely, determining the purpose of the assessment. Ethical concerns dictate that consideration also be given to the use and distribution of test scores, particularly with older persons who are frail or dependent. Because adjudication of competence and decisions regarding institutional care may be made on the basis of test results, test users must exercise care in selecting and using appropriate instruments with this population. This need is emphasized further when tests are used to determine the differential diagnosis of organic or functional disorders.

Differential diagnosis is a process of using multiple diagnostic procedures to help determine a diagnosis. The possibility of certain conditions or disease processes are eliminated or ruled out, whereas others are considered as possibilities. The purpose is to differentiate the source or cause of symptoms in order to evaluate the prognosis and develop a treatment plan. Implications for treatment (or nontreatment) may differ considerably based on the outcomes of assessment or testing sessions in the diagnostic process. For example, given identical or similar symptoms, the differential diagnosis of a physiological (organic) disease would lead to a different treatment plan than the diagnosis of a psychosomatic (functional) condition.

Most available psychometric instruments were developed for use with younger persons; they may or may not be appropriate for use with older clients. Test users should examine information about potential tests carefully, paying special attention to validity, reliability and normative data, and standardization samples. If older persons were not included in norm groups, test users should establish the validity and reliability of the test with an older population. In so doing, local norms may be created to guide users in interpreting test results. Item and test discrimination power among older and younger persons and subsets of the older population should be explored.

Test users should examine test instructions and items carefully when choosing tests to use with older people. Attention should be given to the reading level and format of items and responses, including size of type and contrast of colors. Dot matrix answer sheets requiring filling in squares or circles or marking between lines that are close together may be difficult for older persons with visual impairments. Instruments developed with ipsative, or self-norming, scoring systems may seem repetitive and useless to older persons. Rather than using a sample of persons to develop norms for the interpretation of scores, ipsative scoring is a system for comparing a person with him- or herself. To determine the relative strength of an individual's values, it is necessary to repeat various items in juxtaposition to two or more other items. Those items consistently marked high in relation to others provide evidence of stronger values. Because explaining this fact could invalidate the results, and because older persons may react negatively to being asked "the same question" repeatedly, their motivation to complete these assessments seriously or accurately may be impaired.

Alternative Assessment Strategies

Given the limitations described above, alternative assessment strategies may be more appropriate with older persons. These might include structured interviews or behavioral observations, either with self-ratings or ratings by others. Clinical interviews and careful history taking may provide as much data as do some available tests, although these methods may take more time to complete.

It is possible to overcome many of the limitations inherent in testing older persons. One strategy is to involve older clients in the test selection process by explaining the value and nature of a variety of tests and then having them select those that would have most value for their purposes. Counselors can make an effort to overcome fears and anxieties about testing through carefully establishing rapport. Older clients can be made more comfortable with psychological tests and helped to feel less threatened over the outcomes and potential uses of test data. In addition to helping older clients overcome fears of the assessment process, counselors can assist them in overcoming the effects of disabling conditions that may limit test performance. Ensuring adequate lighting, providing large, readily readable type, and engaging in oral administration may be necessary in some instances.

Assessing Counseling Needs of Older Persons

Blake (1982) stressed the importance of assessing counseling needs because counselors are especially prone to misunderstanding the counseling needs of older persons. Such assessments can assist in screening and referral of clients as well as program planning and evaluation. Two assessment instruments for assessing counseling needs have been developed specifically for older persons.

Ganikos (1977) developed a survey form to examine expressed counseling needs and perceptions of counseling of older community college students. Myers (1978) developed a scale to assess the counseling needs of a broad spectrum of older persons. The Older Persons Counseling Needs Survey (OPCNS) has been published (Myers & Loesch, 1981) and may be useful as a screening instrument to determine older persons' needs for assistance in personal or interpersonal areas, activities, or responding to environmental demands.

Assessing Life Satisfaction in Older Persons

As mentioned earlier, life satisfaction or well-being has been studied as a primary factor in successful aging. Several instruments have been developed and validated specifically to determine life satisfaction of older persons. The most widely used scale is the Life Satisfaction Index (LSIA) (Neugarten, Havighurst, & Tobin, 1961) and its major modification, the LSIZ (Adams, 1969). The items, scoring, and norms for the LSIA and LSIZ are available in professional journals and hence easy to obtain and use.

The Lawton Philadelphia Geriatric Center Morale Scale (PGC) is similar to the LSIA and also readily available (Lawton, 1975). The Affect Balance Scale (Bradburn & Caplovitz, 1965) was designed for use with a general adult population and has been found useful with older persons to measure life satisfaction.

Salamon and Conte (1981) published the Salamon-Conte Life Satisfaction in the Elderly Scale, a multifactor scale for measuring life satisfaction. This commercially available instrument assesses eight categories of influence, including pleasure in daily activities, meaningfulness of life, mood tone, self-concept, perceived health, financial security, social contact, and the fit between desired and achieved goals.

Assessing Attitudes Toward Older Persons

Finnerty-Fried (1982) reviewed instruments for assessing attitudes toward older persons and concluded that they can be useful tools for research and clinical practice in counseling. Palmore's (1977) Facts on Aging Quiz has been used extensively to assess attitudes toward aging and older people. This is a knowledge-based true-false inventory that assesses what respondents know—or think they know—about older people. It is a useful tool for exploring myths and stereotypes about older people and offers an opportunity for correcting misconceptions. Finnerty-Fried reviewed several other inventories; however, the Palmore Quiz remains the most widely used instrument for assessing attitudes toward older persons.

Assessing Health and Wellness

Assessing the overall health and wellness of older persons is an important part of a holistic approach to working with people in the later years. Assessments can provide baseline data to assist in proactive planning for healthy life styles as well as in diagnosis of existing problems. Because the interrelationship of physical and mental concerns is known to increase significantly with advancing age, any change in functioning needs to be carefully evaluated.

The La Crosse Wellness Project recently developed the La Crosse Wellness Inventory (LWI) and the Wellness Development Process (WDP) to promote wellness through educational interventions and a holistic perspective. Though not yet normed with older persons, the LWI and WDP provide a potentially viable means of assisting older persons to plan and implement healthy life styles.

Multidimensional measures, or multidimensional functional assessments, have been developed to assess in a holistic sense the needs of impaired older persons. They provide a mechanism for assembling a vast amount of diverse data, and also analyzing and summarizing the findings through a type of scoring formula. Multidisciplinary teamwork is essential to the success of these assessment methods. Kane and Kane (1983) noted that reliability and validity measures are not readily available for most of these types of assessments; however, they provide a wealth of useful data depending on the skill level of the team members.

Among the more widely used multidimensional assessment methodologies are the Older Americans Resources and Services (OARS) methodology, the Sickness Impact Profile (SIP), the Comprehensive Assessment and Referral Evaluation (CARE), and the Patient Appraisal and Care Evaluation (PACE). These methods were reviewed by Kane and Kane (1983).

Whanger and Myers (1984) provided a detailed analysis of the OARS methodology, one of the more widely used multidimensional functional assessment techniques. It includes two parts, the first being a functional assessment and the second a services assessment. It requires a team approach and enlists the joint services of physicians, nurses, social workers, occupational therapists, counselors, and others who may be required to evaluate comprehensively the needs of older persons and develop a plan of action to meet those needs. An extensive questionnaire is used to gather information from members of the team working with the older person, family members, neighbors, friends, and other service providers working with the older person. A team leader is required to complete the analysis and arrange a meeting of the team to develop a treatment plan. Clinical evaluation and judgments form an important part of the assessment process, which in general is time-consuming but often necessary in the case of older persons with severe mental or physical impairments.

Summary

This chapter provided an overview of the demography of aging; biological, psychological, and sociological theories of aging; and attitudes toward older persons. Implications for counselors stressed the importance of identifying older persons who are most at risk in terms of need for counseling interventions. These include persons who are older (those who are "old-old"); members of minority groups; women; those who are widowed, divorced, or single; those with low incomes; those who are unemployed involuntarily or retired involuntarily; those in poor health; those with low educational levels; and those with poor support systems.

Theories of aging were discussed to provide an overview of normative aspects of development in old age. Implications for counselors include the need to distinguish normative from pathological development and functioning when working with older clients and their families.

When conducting assessments with older persons, counselors must be sensitive to considerations relating to the nature of the clients as well as the tests themselves if valid results are to be achieved. Available tests to measure counseling needs of older persons, life satisfaction, attitudes toward older persons, and health and wellness were reviewed.

CHAPTER II

AGING: CRITICAL ISSUES AND HELPING RESPONSES

A number of critical issues will be of concern to counselors in working with adult children and their aging parents. Issues involving relationships between adult children and their aging parents are discussed in chapter 3. In this chapter, critical issues *some* older persons face are discussed. These include depression, suicide, drug and alcohol abuse, and organic brain disorders.

To enhance the usefulness for counselors, a similar format is used for each topic in this chapter. This includes an overview of the incidence and prevalence of the concern in the older population, a review of some of the known causes and contributing factors, an overview of risk factors that may predispose some older persons to experience the problem, and a discussion of the diagnosis and prognosis for the condition. The effect on the interaction between older persons and their adult children is also included for each issue, in addition to implications for counselors and strategies for assessment.

Depression

Depression, the "common cold" of mental disorders, is known to increase in incidence as persons grow older. Although it is only one of a number of mental health problems that increase with advancing age, the tremendous incidence of depression in older persons, the overwhelming problems that can result when it is not diagnosed and treated, and the difficulty in obtaining accurate diagnosis and treatment are the main reasons it is singled out for discussion here. The need for attention to depression in older persons is supported by the following statistics (Special Committee on Aging, 1980):

- Older persons compose 12% of the total population and over 60% of the occupants of public mental hospital beds.
- More than 50% of older persons in public mental hospitals received *no* psychiatric care prior to admission.
- More than 25% of reported suicides occur among older persons.
- Over 50% of older persons in nursing homes have a diagnosis of "senility," which could be a result of a treatable problem such as depression.
- Only 2% to 4% of persons seen in outpatient mental health clinics are older.

Incidence and Prevalence of Depression in Older Persons

Persons over the age of 65 are known to be among the most vulnerable to experience episodic or chronic depression. Many researchers link this phenomenon to the increasing numbers and variety of losses as persons grow older. Because of the reluctance of older persons to seek mental health care, combined with the failure of mental health professionals to provide outreach and treatment to older individuals, it is difficult to assess accurately the extent of depression in the older population. Depression is underdiagnosed, and physicians are more likely to conclude that an older person has an organic brain syndrome than symptoms of depression. Moreover, older depressed persons are referred for treatment less frequently than younger individuals because of the bias among mental health providers that older persons cannot be helped (Zarit & Zarit, 1984).

Diagnosis of depression is further complicated by differences in symptomatology between older and younger persons, as discussed below, and frequency of reported symptoms. Although significant numbers of older persons report dysphoric mood states, the proportion of the older population who qualify for diagnosis of major depressive disorder is much smaller. Some estimates of depression allow for differences based on severity whereas others do not.

Estimates suggest that as few as 8% to as many as 65% of older persons evidence symptoms of treatable depression. Fry (1986) estimated that 15% to 20% of older persons living in the community have significant depressive symptomatology. The prevalence of major depression in such older persons has been variously determined to be less than 5%, or more specifically 1.8%, with 1.9% having a secondary depressive disorder (Blazer, 1982). The difference in reports of significant depressive symptoms and the prevalence of major depressive disorders in older persons complicate the estimates of incidence. Apparently, though older persons experience more bereavement and consequently lowered life satisfaction, " . . . there is little evidence that community-dwelling older adults suffer appreciable and continuing dysphoria secondary to bereavement" (Blazer, Hughes, & George, 1987, p. 281).

The implications from the literature are that older persons do, in fact, experience more losses than younger persons. However, because many of these losses are expected as concomitants of aging, they are perceived as "on-time" events and thus are better tolerated. Therefore, although the incidence of depressive episodes is greater in older persons because of a greater incidence of precipitating life events (e.g., losses), at the same time the potential for depression to be treatable is excellent. A very small percentage of severely depressed older persons may not respond to treatment.

Depression tends to occur more frequently in women than men for most ages, with the exception that men over 80 experience a considerably higher rate of prevalence (Zarit & Zarit, 1984). Over half of all older persons with physical health problems have depressive symptomatology. Because 86% of older persons have one or more chronic physical health impairments that limit their daily living activities (Brotman, 1982), the actual incidence of depression, considering underreporting of symptoms as well as diagnoses, may be greater than 50% of the older population.

Causes and Contributing Factors

Life stresses are known to increase the risk of depression— and older persons have many. Satisfaction with life across the life span differs somewhat for men and women. Flanagan (1982) reported that the determinants of life satisfaction in older men were the presence of a spouse followed by having children, and the reverse order was true for older women. By implication, the loss of a spouse or children, and disrupted family relationships, are major sources of stress in older persons. In general, all types of losses—people, things, hopes, roles—are highly correlated with depressive symptoms in older persons.

The self-rated causes of depression among older women include the following (Essex, Klein, & Benjamin, 1985):

- health problems   20%
- worry about children   17%
- marital problems   10%
- job-related problems   10%

Though little specific research is available, it seems that the loss of a job and the loss of work-related roles are contributing causes of depression for older men. The retirement transition seems to be particularly stressful. This transition requires adapting to the loss of a job, which had served as the primary source of identity, assuming a new and less valued social role (retiree), and creating a new self-definition based on a devalued social status.

Life changes are the primary antecedents of depression. Among depressed older persons, the severity of symptoms may preclude the reporting of life changes or distressing life events. They simply may not have the energy to recall or to report precipitating events, or, lacking a psychological vocabulary or sophistication, they may assume events to be unimportant or unrelated to their current condition, and thus not report them. However, a diagnosis of reactive depression, based on the absence of precipitating events, typically will be changed as depression is treated and lethargy gives way to a fuller reporting of life circumstances (Zarit & Zarit, 1984).

In many cases, depression results when an older person makes an objective analysis of his or her situation and fails to perceive that the future will or can be better than the past has been. A shortened future time perspective can lead to a sense of negative expectation or hopelessness about the future (Fry, 1984). Loneliness and isolation contribute to the development of negative self-talk and negative expectations.

Another factor that contributes to depression in older persons is learned helplessness. Faced with an increasing array of life changes and especially losses over which they have no control, the reaction of many older persons is to learn to be helpless. Previously successful coping strategies may no longer be effective. What seems to be most effective instead is a sense of passive mastery, wherein withdrawal and depression are functional means of coping with significant negative life changes and undesired processes and events.

The reality is that older persons have diverse needs and face a series of diverse challenges. They experience losses, often multiple in nature, and endure bereavement overload—the failure to fully grieve one loss before the onset of the next. They age biologically, psychologically, and socially at varying rates with varying results. They experience the cumulative effects of ageism and often internalize negative stereotypes with resultant lowering of their self-esteem. For many reasons, old age often is viewed as the most difficult of all life stages. A feeling of vulnerability can be a realistic reaction to the realities of later life.

Persons who feel old, regardless of their age, tend to be significantly more depressed than their counterparts (Baum & Boxley, 1983). In later life, depression as a reaction to loss is more common than in younger persons (Whanger & Myers, 1984). Depression in older persons is best predicted by their general state of health and purpose in life, both of which seem to be related to feeling younger (Baum, 1983–84).

An additional cause of depression is medication, either prescribed or over-the-counter, either taken as directed or misused. Recent estimates are that 43% of older persons abuse prescription and over-the-counter drugs (Raffoul, Cooper, & Love, 1981). Commonly taken drugs and their reactions and interactions can cause or contribute to depression in older persons (Wolfe et al., 1988).

Disruptions in family relationships are common causes of depression in older persons. Unfortunately, role changes and reversals occur when older persons cease to be independent and family members are placed in the role of caretakers. Caring for older relatives often occurs at the expense of other family relationships, increasing the potential for depression in younger as well as older persons.

Risk Factors

Certain characteristics of older persons may increase the risk of depressive episodes. Many of these are linked to demographics. For example, increases in the life span, differential life expectancies, and age of marriage combine to place older women at risk for loss of a spouse with ensuing depressive reaction. Older persons who are unmarried are more likely to be institutionalized (itself a precipitator of severe depression) and less able to cope independently with the demands of daily living. This is true for both men and women.

Older persons who are uneducated, or in low socioeconomic groups are more prone to depression, presumably linked to their having fewer resources for coping with the losses and changes of the later years. Because many older minority persons live at or below the poverty level, minority status may be included as a risk factor for depression. Any of these factors in combination can increase the likelihood of depression, such as being female, poor, and a member of a racial minority. An additional major risk factor is the presence of physical illnesses or disabilities.

It is known that life changes, even positive ones, can be stressful. Those older persons who experience life changes thus are more at risk for depression. Common changes include role losses, physical changes, loss of significant others (including pets), and loss of status. Acceptance of the aging process, a normative developmental task, may itself predispose an older person to depression. Geographic moves, whether desired and anticipated or sudden and not wanted can contribute to depression. When a move is made to an assisted living environment, the recognition of decreased ability to live independently can be a significant source of distress for an older individual, as well as his or her family members. In fact, recognition of the loss of their own physical capacities and the aging of their parents are major sources of stress, discomfort, and depressed feelings for midlife adults.

Diagnosis and Prognosis

Accurate diagnosis of depression in older persons is essential for treatment planning, and is in turn dependent on accurate assessment of contributing factors as well as symptoms. The differential diagnosis of depression and dementia is especially critical and complex. Dementia can contribute to depression, and the symptoms of both conditions may be similar. Depression resulting from organic brain syndromes may be resistant to treatment, whereas depression linked to psychosocial stressors tends to be treatment-responsive.

The differential diagnosis of depression and dementia is discussed in several sources (e.g., Fry, 1986; Zung, 1980). Primary diagnostic criteria include differences in affect, memory, intellect, orientation, judgment, somatic complaints, psychotic behavior, and neurological symptoms. Some of the major diagnostic indicators are as follows:

- Persons with dementia experience labile, or unstable, affect and impairment of normal emotional control, whereas depressed persons exhibit pervasive feelings of despair and anxiety. The affect of depressed persons is not affected by suggestion.
- Dementia is accompanied by a decreased attention span, decreased short-term memory, perseveration (continuing or repeating an activity after the causal stimulus has stopped), and confabulation (making up ready answers and reciting experiences without regard for truth). Depressed persons report difficulty concentrating, impaired ability to learn new information, decreased attention, and secondary decrease in recent memory functions.
- Intellect is impaired with dementia (serial 7s—the ability to repeat a sequence of seven numbers—are impaired, along with similarities and recent events) and also with depression (serial 7s may be performed, memory for recent events is intact).
- Both demented and depressed persons may be disoriented; however, confusion is more continual and severe with dementia.
- Judgment may be poor for both conditions, with deterioration of personal care and possibly loss of bowel and bladder control in dementia.
- Demented persons complain of failing health and fatigue; depressed persons complain of loss of sleep, appetite, and decreases in other physical functions.
- Neurological symptoms (dysphasia—impairment of speech, and apraxia—inability to carry out purposeful movements) are present in dementia but not in depression.

Depression in older persons may be reactive (endogenous), can be the result of medications or medication interactions, or may be the result of preexisting personality predispositions. Depressive reactions may be associated with unknown biological or psychosocial stressors. The causes are complex, hence diagnosis can be difficult. Diagnosis is compounded by problems such as accompanying physical illness or disability, fatigue, psychomotor retardation, organic brain disease, or the client's inability to describe symptoms or a history of precipitating factors.

The diagnosis of severe depression is easier, and is based on the presence of a dysphoric mood, loss of interest in activities, and even suicide attempts. Less severe depression is more difficult to diagnose because the older person may deny depression, fail to complain of sadness or dysphoria, and may complain of memory disturbances that could indicate other disorders. Furthermore, somatic problems present in other diseases may complicate diagnosis, a significant concern because hypochondriasis is present in about two thirds of older depressed individuals. Over two thirds of depressed older persons report physical symptoms as precipitating factors.

A number of typologies are available to assist in the diagnosis of depression. Davidson (1976) suggested the following four commonly used categories of symptoms: dysphoria, behavioral deficits and behavioral excesses, somatic symptoms, and cognitive manifestations.

- *Dysphoria* refers to overwhelming sadness, loss of interest and gratification, boredom, and apathy.
- *Behavioral deficits* refer to the older person's inability to participate socially, decreased verbal or physical activity, and psychomotor retardation evidenced by slowed or slurred speech, decreased speech volume, and so forth. Lack of attention to grooming and loss of the ability to laugh are additional deficits.
- *Behavioral excesses* include excessive complaints about one's life situation, feelings of guilt, and feelings of self-doubt and uncertainty.
- *Somatic symptoms* include headaches, fatigue, sleep disturbances, increased or decreased appetite, and physical complaints such as urinary tract disturbances, chest pains, loss of libido, and dizzy spells.
- *Cognitive manifestations* include recurrent and persistent feelings of poor self-esteem, negative expectancies, feelings of inadequacy, dependency, and self-criticism.

Diagnosis is complicated by lack of a "mental health" vocabulary in older persons. In contrast to younger persons, older persons tend not to identify themselves as sad or depressed. Younger depressed persons more commonly report feelings of guilt and self-blame, low self-esteem, and loss of appetite. Younger depressed persons also commonly report suicidal thoughts and use suicidal gestures and the threat of suicide for manipulation. In contrast, older depressed persons may complain primarily of physical problems that, in as many as one third of these persons, may lead to unnecessary surgery (Davidson, 1976).

Fry (1986) suggested several clusters of symptoms that may distinguish later life from earlier life depression. These include verbal, cognitive, and overt motor symptoms such as verbalizations of dependency and helplessness, pessimism, hopelessness, guilt, and withdrawal. Another cluster includes somatic symptoms such as insomnia; loss of appetite; headaches; difficulty in breathing; excessive fatigue; weight, hearing, or vision loss; and memory complaints unrelated to cognitive impairment. Of course, an actual physical problem could exist, making diagnosis much more difficult. Vegetative symptoms, such as constipation, are more common in older persons.

The prognosis for treatment is good when:

- onset occurs for the first time in old age;
- organic impairments are not present;
- there is a supportive environment; and
- the causes of the depression are pyschosocial or linked to medication mismanagement.

The prognosis, given early intervention, is good, especially in young-old persons. Unfortunately, the prognosis is less favorable with increasing age. This may be explained by the variable nature of depression and by the effect of prolonged depression on physical and social functioning (Epstein, 1976). The prognosis depends on the physical health of the older person, mobility limitations, availability of social supports, personality characteristics before the onset of symptoms, personal resourcefulness, and a sense of confidence and optimism (Whanger & Myers, 1984).

Effect on Family Members

Depression in older persons leads to a number of interpersonal problems with their family members as well as friends and acquaintances. Withdrawal is a common response to depression, and one that some family members experience as rejection. Older depressed persons can evidence extreme dependency and be excessively demanding, complaining, and manipulative. They simply are not fun to be around. Any of these reactions can serve to alienate others from the depressed older individual.

Not understanding the nature of depression, family members can lose patience and react with hurt and their own withdrawal from the older person. Rather than encouraging the older person to seek treatment, and participating in the treatment plan, hurt feelings may prevent family members from interacting with older relatives. Of course, this only intensifies the aging parent's depression and continues a spiral of negative symptomatology. Arguments and negative interactions with older family members also can contribute to depression in adult children. Again, the cyclical nature of the problem is apparent.

Faced with the depression of an aging parent, adult children may feel overwhelmed and helpless. Feelings of guilt are common, first, over being a possible contributor to the depression and, second, over being unable to alleviate the older person's trauma. Adult children may view their parent's depression as a normal response to the circumstances of their life. Sharing the older person's feelings of hopelessness for a better future, the adult child may become further immobilized. Often it seems that the only way to assist the older parent is through extensive personal sacrifice. The needs of the depressed parent can include extreme dependency on an adult child as the main source of emotional gratification. The tendency of many older persons to become increasingly isolated, to lose friends and peers through geographic moves and deaths, leaves them increasingly dependent on their adult children for emotional support and social interaction. Unfortunately, the needs of their adult children may be in direct contrast, because adult children are apt to have their own network of nuclear family, work, and friendship relationships in which they have invested their emotions as well as their time.

Thus, adult children may feel trapped between the excessive demands of their parent and their own needs for independence. Eventually each must confront the following question: To what extent am I responsible for the emotional reactions and life circumstances of my parent? This seems to be a question that seldom has an easy answer.

Eyde and Rich (1983) noted that " . . . the family system is the primary articulator of mental health needs across the lifespan of the individual . . . " (p. 1). It is imperative that older persons maintain linkages with family members if depression is to be accurately diagnosed and assessed and successfully treated. Clearly, the needs of adult children must be addressed in the process, sometimes raising the important and difficult question of who is the client: the adult child, the aging parent, or the family system?

Implications for Counselors

Depression in older persons is treatable, and the best prognosis occurs when family members are involved in planning and implementing treatment. Accurate assessment is essential, and requires differential diagnosis between depression and dementia and depression and physical illness.

Whanger and Myers (1984) provided several guidelines to assist in differential diagnosis of depression. First, they stressed the importance of differentiating normal from pathological symptomatology, which of course is difficult. Depression is a normal reaction to loss in old age, and it may take some time after a loss before pathology can be delineated. In contrast to persons with hypochondria, depressed older persons do not have a variety of bodily complaints and do not enjoy talking about their bodily functions. In contrast to persons with paranoia, older depressed persons do not have loose associations and thought disorders. Persons who experience adjustment disorders in reaction to later life circumstances also tend to have a reduction of depressive symptoms when the adjustment is made, and tend to focus on the adjustment problem and not depressive symptoms.

Early identification of depression is critical, because early treatment may prevent intensification of symptoms. It is important to consider the history of symptoms and how the depression affects the person's daily life, as well as to perform a differential diagnosis. Goals developed for treatment should be modest and include consideration of directive, supportive approaches. Cognitive, behavioral, and cognitive-behavioral approaches have proven to be the most successful with older depressed persons. It is important to set reasonable goals for treatment and measure behavioral changes in small, easily achieved increments. Treatment programs typically last only a few months, with weekly sessions. Helping the older person identify pleasant life events and encouraging the older person to engage more frequently in such events both alleviates the depression and develops a renewed sense of control over his or her life and emotional reactions.

It is important in working with older depressed persons to obtain a medical evaluation to rule out physical pathology. Often medications are prescribed for older depressed persons, requiring counselors to consider the effects of medications when planning their own interventions.

In addition to the cognitive and behavioral therapies, psychoeducational and client-centered approaches have been used to treat depression in older persons. Psychoeducational approaches may use paraprofessionals and involve caregivers. The focus is on developing strategies for early self-identification of depressed mood states and implementing self-interventions. Client-centered approaches provide opportunities for catharsis and open expression of grief, and place the counselor in a supportive role where growth and self-fulfillment may be encouraged.

Barriers to the treatment of depression exist in both older clients and counselors. Clients may have given up hope of improvement and may lack faith in the potential of successful therapy. Feeling both unloved and unlovable, they may lack an expectation of getting better. Counselors may believe that older persons are rigid and cannot change, that they are more likely to have organic than functional pathologies, and that feelings of joylessness are quite normal in later life (Wolberg, 1977). Counselors who want to be successful in helping older depressed persons and their families must first confront their own negative stereotypes about older persons and develop a positive view of the capabilities of older people to solve their own problems and to grow and change in response to the challenges of later life.

Strategies for Assessment

Assessment of depression in older persons is at once extremely important and often difficult. The symptoms of depression are similar to the symptoms of many conditions common in older persons, including some organic brain syndromes. In the absence of accurate differential diagnosis, potentially treatable depressions may be misdiagnosed and thus assumed to be untreatable syndromes. In the absence of needed treatment, older persons may experience a severe and irreversible decline in functioning.

Both clinical interview methods and more formal methods for assessing depression have been used successfully. Blazer (1982) reviewed several of the most widely used assessment instruments and compared them on the extent to which each measured symptoms of depression. The symptom clusters included emotional, cognitive, worry, delusional, physical, and volitional concerns. The most comprehensive instruments according to Blazer's analysis include the Beck Depression Inventory, Hamilton Rating Scale for Depression, and the Zung Self-Rating Depression Scale. Each of these scales is brief and has been used successfully to assess depression in older persons. Additional information on these scales is found in the appendix.

One of the newer scales, which is also easy to score and interpret, is the Geriatric Depression Scale (Yesavage, Brink, Rose, Lum, Huang, Aday, & Leirer, 1983). Fry (1984) developed the Geriatric Scale of Hopelessness, based on the high correlation of depressed affect with feelings of hopelessness and pessimism about the future. Numerous other instruments for assessing depression in older persons are reviewed in currently available sources (e.g., Blazer, 1982; Fry, 1984).

One of the more recent strategies for assessing depression is examining recent life events older persons have experienced. These strategies are based on earlier research by Holmes and Rahe (1967) with the Social Readjustment Scale. An underlying assumption of these instruments is that life events can have a positive or negative valence in terms of the effect on people's lives. The Psychiatric Epidemiology Research Interview (PERI) Life Events Scale (Dohrenwend, Krasnoff, Askenasy, & Dohrenwend, 1978) and the Geriatric Scale of Recent Life Events (Patrick & Moore, 1985) are examples of life events scales. These instruments also may be useful in assessing suicide potential; this is an important assessment because depressed persons are more at risk for suicide.

Suicide

Suicide is one of the 10 leading causes of death in the United States. It is the 7th leading cause of death for men of all ages and the 10th leading cause of death for women (Osgood, 1985). As is true of depression, the incidence of suicide among older persons is greater than that among the general population. Moreover, suicide among older persons has a greater lethality. In contrast to younger persons, older persons tend not to give warnings prior to effecting suicides (Jarvis & Boldt, 1980). Thus, it is even more important that counselors help family members to be alert to risk factors and intervene before problems become extreme.

Incidence and Prevalence of Suicide in Older Persons

Fry (1986) noted that older persons account for 12% of the population and about 25% of reported suicides. The exact suicide rate among older persons is difficult to determine, as discussed below, but seems to be almost triple that of the general population, a ratio that has remained stable over several decades. Each year up to 10,000 older persons kill themselves. In contrast to these data, the Harvard Medical School reported that 40% of suicides occur among persons aged 60 and over. The suicide rate after age 65 is three times the national average, and three times as many older men as older women take their lives (Suicide, Part I, 1986; Suicide, Part II, 1986).

The highest suicide rate in the older population is among White men in their 80s. Suicide rates for non-Whites are lower and peak in the late 20s, whereas rates for White women peak in middle age (Butler & Lewis, 1982). Among non-Whites, suicide rates are highest for Asian Americans and lowest among Blacks and Native Americans (McIntosh & Santos, 1981).

The incidence of suicide among older persons probably is vastly underreported. Older persons tend to be serious in their suicide attempts and quite successful. They are able to disguise suicidal behaviors through drug overdoses or underdoses that seem to be accidental and the result of organic brain impairments or depression. The ratio of attempted to completed suicides among older persons is 2:1, whereas the ratio among younger persons is 7:1 (Fry, 1986). Older persons seldom fail in their suicide attempts.

Causes and Contributing Factors

The many psychosocial and physical losses and stresses that accompany the aging process may contribute to suicidal ideation in older persons. These factors will vary for different individuals. In general, prolonged depressed moods precede suicide attempts, making the early intervention and treatment of depression in older persons even more critical.

Serious physical illnesses, especially those that are progressive, painful, and debilitating have been linked with increased suicide potential. Virtually any terminal illness, especially cancers and carcinomas, can stimulate suicidal ideation. Furthermore, progressive organic brain impairments may be a precursor of suicide in an older person. Affective disorders such as depression and loneliness, and substance abuse are additional predisposing factors (Fry, 1986).

A variety of losses, as well as prolonged grief and bereavement, have been linked to suicide. Of course, the depth of the reaction to loss depends on the salience of the lost object to the person and the availability of replacements. Loss of social roles, occupational roles, and family roles can contribute to depression and the possibility of suicide. For example, an older person who experiences increasing physical losses and decreasing independence may find his or her status within the family structure diminished. This in itself can contribute to significant depression, especially when the future seems to offer no hope for improvement. Older persons who experience environmental deprivation through abusive situations in the home or institutional settings are also at risk.

Osgood (1985) discussed several clues that may alert caregivers and mental health professionals to the possibility of suicide in older persons. The first of these are verbal clues, which may be direct (e.g., "I'm going to kill myself") or indirect (e.g., "Everyone would be better off without me"). Both direct and indirect statements may be mistaken for attempts to manipulate or control adult children. In fact, sometimes such statements *are* attempts at manipulation; however, they also are signs of depression or generalized unhappiness. The rule of thumb for persons of other ages should be followed with older persons as well. That is, *all* suicidal statements must be considered seriously. Medical and psychosocial evaluations are essential, particularly when direct or indirect statements are repeated.

Behavioral clues also may be direct (e.g., a suicide attempt) or indirect. Indirect clues may include putting one's affairs in order, making funeral plans, and sudden changes in behavior. Situational changes also are important clues. These may include recent moves, deaths of family members or friends, arguments with family members, or other crisis situations. Other clues include constellations of symptoms most often associated with suicide. For older persons, these include depression combined with anxiety, isolation and loneliness, and threatened dependency needs.

Risk Factors

Osgood (1985) identified a number of risk factors for suicide in older persons. It is clear that older White, protestant men are most likely to take their lives, especially those over the age of 80. Widowed or divorced older persons have a higher risk than those who are married. Persons who have held blue-collar jobs, especially those that were low paying and resulted in disorderly careers, are at risk. White-collar professionals have a lower suicide risk, as do older persons who are employed. Those who are retired take their lives more frequently.

Risk factors related to living environments in older persons include living in urban areas, living alone, having moved recently, and being isolated. Those in poor health, who suffer chronic pain, and who have a terminal illness are more likely to take their lives. Mental health concerns that correlate with high suicide potential include depression, alcoholism, loneliness, rejection, and low self-esteem.

Osgood further noted factors in the older person's background that are correlated with higher suicide potential. These include a history of a broken home, critical or rejecting parents, a dependent personality, shyness, poor interpersonal relationships, and a history of being a "loner." In addition, a history of familial mental illness, poor marital history, poor work record, tunnel vision, and circular reasoning seem to be predisposing factors.

Effect on Family Members

The effect of suicide on survivors is similar regardless of age. Those left behind usually suffer feelings of extreme shock, denial, guilt, and depression. If the older person suffered from a terminal illness or chronically painful condition, or loneliness over the loss of a spouse, the feelings of guilt may be combined with feelings of relief that the older person no longer has to suffer. Family members may experience conflicting feelings.

They may feel confused and overwhelmed, all of which may interfere with the successful completion of the grieving process.

These effects can be pervasive and long-lasting. Also, in defense against an overwhelming array of negative emotions, family members may deny a suicide or fail to report it as such. Adult children even may keep the suspected suicide hidden from their own offspring and extended family members. Though research on persons who fail to report the suicide of older family members is not available, it may be conjectured that they would experience significant emotional disturbance as a result of keeping the suicide a secret. Additional stress occurs when explanations to friends and relatives must be made.

At the same time, survivors of suicide must confront guilt and fear over their own part in the reactions of an aging parent. There are always the questions of what more could have been done to assist the older person or to prevent or alleviate their emotional distress. A common notion is that the suicide could have been prevented "if only" the adult child had not been so "selfish" in living his or her own life, rather than responding to the needs of aging parents.

How an adult child views aging and the aging process can be profoundly affected by the suicide of an aging parent. Fears of the aging process can be stimulated and shared with other family members in direct or indirect ways. Gerontophobia, or fear of growing old, can interfere with successful passage through many transitions in life, particularly those in midlife and beyond.

Implications for Counselors

Clearly, when older persons commit suicide, there is a need for counseling interventions for their survivors. This is particularly true when the suicide is not reported as such because fear, shame, and guilt may be intensified through the stress of hiding the family stigma. As is true with suicides of any age, counselors may expect to find themselves in highly stressful situations, needing to help family members respond to unanswerable questions. Both individual and family systems approaches may be helpful, and will be complicated when survivors choose to hide the actual suicide from certain members of the family.

Adult children and their families should be encouraged to seek counseling assistance and also to join support groups to help them cope with the suicide of an aging parent. Educational programs that help them prepare for the emotions they may experience, anniversary reactions, and so forth are important. When the parent is survived by a spouse, the spouse should be included in the sessions. The idea that older persons are emotionally fragile and could not tolerate the family counseling needs to discarded. Older persons are survivors, and the survivors of suicide can use all the help available to cope with their feelings and emotions. Becoming widowed as a result of a natural death can be difficult, at best. When suicide is involved, the grieving process can be exceedingly more difficult.

It is important for adult children dealing with the suicide of a parent to confront their own feelings of guilt, shame, and remorse over "not having done more" while the parent was alive. Furthermore, it is essential that adult children be encouraged to express and resolve their own feelings about the aging process and fears of growing older. It is only through open expression of these feelings that adult children can be helped to plan more constructive ways to approach their own aging, and help their children to do the same.

Strategies for Assessment

Osgood (1985) completed an extensive review of assessment strategies designed to determine the lethality potential of older persons who may attempt suicide. She pointed out that over 75% of older persons who commit suicide visit a physician shortly before doing so. Few visit counselors or therapists. Accurate assessment of suicide risk requires knowledge of the relevant demographic variables identified above, personal background and history of the individual, history of past and present crises and methods of coping with crisis situations, history of mental disorders, availability of social and interpersonal supports, health status, and relationships with significant others. Osgood noted that careful listening, attention to behavioral changes, knowledge of a suicide plan, and assessment of lethality are essential steps in evaluating suicide potential.

Although questions about suicide are asked in some depression scales, no specific instrument has been developed to measure only suicide potential in older persons. Assessment requires clinical judgment combined with the ability to ask questions to elicit the presence of a plan and evaluate the lethality, availability, and accessibility of the methods proposed.

Alcohol and Drug Abuse

According to the American Psychiatric Association's *Diagnostic and Statistical Manual of Mental Disorders, Third Edition* (DSM-III, 1980), there are five classes of substances involved in abuse and dependence. These include alcohol, barbiturates, opiods, amphetamines, and cannabis. Apparently the incidence of use of illegal drugs, amphetamines, hallucinogens, and inhalants by older persons is rare (Peppers & Stover, 1977). Rather, the greatest substance abuse among older persons falls into two categories: (1) the intentional use or abuse of alcohol and (2) the misuse of legal drugs.

Whanger and Myers (1984) noted that the change in DSM-III-R (the revised edition) terminology from "substance abuse" to "substance use disorders" has been important in understanding the nature and extent of these problems in older persons. Substance use disorders in older persons tend not to involve illegal but rather legal substances. The stereotype of the streetwise adult who uses mind-altering drugs to achieve a temporary state of euphoria simply does not apply to older persons. Nor does the image of the binge drinker who sacrifices job and family and frequents detoxification units describe the majority of older alcohol abusers.

A more accurate picture of some older problem drinkers may incorporate a view of an older, isolated, depressed person drinking in response to a series of unreplaced, not fully grieved losses. The typical picture of drug misuse could be in one of three commonly occurring categories among the older population: the misuse of legally prescribed medications, the misuse of over-the-counter drugs, and iatrogenic, or physician-induced, disorders (Whanger & Myers, 1984).

In this section, alcohol and drug misuse in older persons are discussed separately in terms of incidence, causes and contributing factors, and risk factors. Diagnosis and prognosis, the effect on family members, and implications for counselors of both types of substance abuse are discussed in the final sections.

Incidence of Alcohol Abuse in Older Persons

The incidence of alcohol abuse among older persons is comparable to that of younger persons. Stern and Kastenbaum (1984) estimated that between 2% and 10% of older men experience severe alcohol problems and 2% of older women do so. Barnes (1982) suggested that heavy drinkers, or those who consume more than one ounce of alcohol per day, include 14% of older men and 7% of older women. These figures are in contrast to estimates of overall drinking rates, which include persons for whom alcohol consumption is not a problem. Barnes noted that the drinking rate for older persons is lower than for those in younger age groups, and that the drinking rate is 75% for older men and 62% for older women. The comparable figures for persons in their fifties is 90% for men and 83% for women. Thus, a number of authors have concluded that drinking behaviors decrease with advancing age.

It is difficult to determine the exact incidence of problem drinking among older persons for several reasons. First, many older persons are "closet drinkers" who are mainly isolated, not employed, and thus do not come to the attention of persons who might recognize or report their problem. Second, many older persons are reluctant to admit drinking problems, and their families assist in hiding their condition out of shame and embarrassment. Third, physicians may fail to diagnose alcohol problems because many of the symptoms of abuse are similar to symptoms associated with the aging process. These include organic brain dysfunctions, gastrointestinal disorders, and cardiovascular diseases, among others. Fourth, due to metabolic changes that are normal age-related processes, the amount of ethanol required for intoxification decreases with advancing age. Thus, the quantity of alcohol ingested is not an accurate criterion, though a commonly used one, for assessment of older alcohol abusers (Mishara & Kastenbaum, 1980; Stern & Kastenbaum, 1984).

Yet another factor that complicates estimates of the incidence of "problem drinking" among older persons is the fact that there seem to be basically two types of older drinkers. First, there are those who experienced episodic drinking problems in their younger years, and, second, those whose abuse problems began—or were recognized—for the first time in later life. The former are more likely to have had contact with alcohol treatment programs and therefore are more likely to be counted when statistics are compiled.

Whanger and Myers (1984) summarized the results of several epidemiological studies and concluded that among the older population, 20% of medical inpatients and 15% of medical outpatients have serious alcohol-related problems. The rates are probably higher for persons in psychiatric facilities. When alcohol-drug interactions are added to these figures, considering that older persons are heavy consumers of prescription drugs, the rate of serious problems could be even higher. Because the proportion of older drinkers in the population is expected to remain stable while the proportion of older persons in the general population is expected to increase, an increase in the numbers of older problem drinkers may be anticipated over the next few decades (Brody, 1981).

Causes and Contributing Factors to Alcohol Abuse in Older Persons

Gomberg (1982), in an extensive review of alcohol problems in older persons, concluded that little is known about the psychological and social characteristics of persons who become problem drinkers in later life. They tend to report greater feelings of depression, alienation, and isolation than their age peers, but it is not known whether these feelings are antecedents or consequents of their drinking behaviors. Older persons tend to drink to alleviate depression and escape life problems, particularly with family, health, and the police.

Factors that may promote increased alcohol abuse in older persons include: retirement with its associated role losses and changes, as well as reduction in income; death of significant others and confronting their own mortality; declining health and physical disabilities; and loneliness, a particularly severe problem among older women (Brody, 1981). Early-onset drinkers seem to have personality disturbances, particularly neurosis and deviant personalities. Late-onset drinkers, in contrast, may drink in reaction to the external stressors of aging (Stern & Kastenbaum, 1984). In fact, Gomberg (1982) suggested that the stresses of aging, most of which fall in the general category of losses, are antecedent factors for drinking in *all* older persons.

The drinking patterns of older persons include daily consumption, but of less quantity than among younger drinkers.

Social drinking, in moderate proportions, even has a beneficial effect on older individuals. As Stern and Kastenbaum (1984) noted, wine for centuries has been termed the "milk of old age" (p. 165). The social drinking patterns that may be quite acceptable to many older persons may be seen as excessive to some observers. Furthermore, because the biological effect of alcohol is greater for older than younger persons, social drinking patterns that seem innocuous may contribute to physical decline. The key seems to be in moderate use of ethanol. Mishara and Kastenbaum (1980) noted that moderate alcohol consumption among older persons can contribute to increased self-esteem and morale, improved social interaction, and decreased difficulties with sleep.

Risk Factors for Alcohol Abuse in Older Persons

Older persons with drinking problems tend to be those who are single, separated, divorced, widowed, or living alone (Brown & Chiang, 1984; Stern & Kastenbaum, 1984). Other circumstances that place older persons at risk for alcohol problems include the following: retirement, financial troubles, loss of significant others, and loneliness (Berger, 1983). Lowered physical tolerance for ethanol and the potential for drug interactions in older persons who take multiple prescriptions are additional risk factors.

The universal experience of loss among older persons contributes to increased risk for alcohol abuse. The failure to fully grieve losses with subsequent bereavement overload can impair the older person's ability to function and contribute to a vulnerability to abuse (Kastenbaum, 1969). Depression seems to be a strong antecedent of alcohol abuse in older persons (Dupree & Schonfeld, 1985), as does the absence of well-developed support networks.

An additional set of risk factors may be stated. Motto (1980) identified several factors as estimators of suicide risk among older alcoholics. These include impaired health, job instability, living in an apartment complex, and low income.

Diagnosis and Prognosis for Alcohol Abuse in Older Persons

Older alcohol abusers are less likely to be identified in the work place or through the legal system, and are less likely to seek out treatment programs than are younger abusers. Because many of the processes of aging present symptoms similar to those of alcohol abuse, the likelihood of diagnosis by physicians and care providers is small (Crook & Cohen, 1984). Even when health care providers recognize that a problem exists, they may be reluctant to encourage the older person to seek treatment that would remove one of his or her few remaining sources of pleasure (Stern & Kastenbaum, 1984). Moreover, families and friends avoid dealing with the problem from their own sense of embarrassment or to protect the older individual.

As is true of severe depression, severe cases of alcohol abuse are easier to diagnose. Older persons may have Korsakoff's disease, a nonreversible alcohol-induced organic brain disorder. Symptoms include confusion, amnesia, gait disturbances, memory loss, and neurologic involvement. Butler and Lewis (1972) suggested the following diagnostic clues for the clinical presentation of alcoholism in old age: insomnia, impotence, problems with control of gout, rapid onset of a confused state, uncontrollable hypertension, and unexplained falls. Prolonged alcohol abuse may contribute to varying degrees of organic brain disorders (Whanger & Myers, 1984).

Obviously, early identification is essential to successful treatment of alcohol problems in older persons. Typical symptoms of alcohol abuse, such as blackouts and morning shakes, are diagnostic indications, as is a high tolerance for ethanol consumption. Older persons who drink in contradiction to medical, psychosocial, or other warnings should be suspect (Whanger & Myers, 1984). Older persons who are isolated and have experienced significant losses may be evaluated using one of the available alcohol assessment scales, which are discussed later in this chapter.

The prognosis for treatment of older alcoholics is good. When family members and other social supports are involved, the prognosis increases significantly (Blai, 1987). The prognosis may not be as good for older persons who abuse alcohol along with other drugs. Using a sample of older alcohol abusers, Edwards (1985) found that 29% used other drugs in connection with alcohol. Thus, a small proportion of the 10% of older persons who abuse alcohol may be singularly resistant to treatment.

Incidence of Drug Abuse in Older Persons

Rather than abusing drugs, older persons tend to *misuse* them, and they are assisted in doing so by physicians untrained in geriatric medicine. (In fact, few trained geriatric physicians are available nationwide. This situation is slowly changing.) Although only one in six adults is over the age of 60, older persons use almost 40% of all prescription drugs. Older persons filled 613 million prescriptions in 1986 at retail drugstores, an average of 15.5 prescriptions per year per older person (Wolfe et al., 1988).

Older persons use one third of the minor tranquilizers, one third of the antipsychotic medications, one half of the sleeping pills, and one third of the antidepressants sold annually. The risk of adverse drug reactions is high. An estimated 9 million adverse reactions occur among older persons annually. More than one third of these are not reported to physicians, possibly because older persons are not aware of the possible side effects or medication interactions (Wolfe et al., 1988). Because they are not reported, many medication interactions remain untreated or unresolved. Hip fractures due to falls are common, as is misdiagnosis of organic brain syndromes or psychosis when confusion or hallucinations result from accidental medication overdoses or interactions. About two thirds of persons in long-term care facilities (nursing homes) receive psychotropic drugs, yet only 20% have a psychiatric diagnosis (Butler & Lewis, 1982).

As people age, the decreased ability of the kidneys to filter toxic substances, decreased liver functioning, decreased plasma volume, and other physiological changes drastically reduce the ability to metabolize drugs. Thus, older persons are particularly susceptible to adverse reactions as a result of accidental overdoses because their changed physiology prolongs the effects of medication. Because most drug dosages are set using young persons, physicians who fail to compensate by lowering doses for older persons may contribute to iatrogenic (e.g., physician-induced) disorders. Because such disorders are frequently misdiagnosed, the actual incidence of this type of drug misuse is unknown.

However, it is known that the incidence of reported adverse drug reactions is 21% among persons aged 70 to 79, yet only 3% for persons aged 20 to 29 (Wolfe et al., 1988). Drug-induced illness accounts for between 5% and 30% of hospital admissions for older persons, compared to only 2% for the general population. Butler and Lewis (1982) noted that half of all older persons who take drugs do not take them as prescribed, and at least 25% make serious errors resulting in drug-induced illnesses. Furthermore, older persons compose half of all persons admitted to hospitals for drug intoxication.

More than two thirds (75%) of all older persons use some medication on a regular basis. One third of these medications are purchased over the counter. Of these drugs, 26% are self-prescribed, 11% are physician prescribed, and 3% are prescribed by a friend (Wolfe et al., 1988).

Causes and Contributing Factors to Drug Abuse in Older Persons

As mentioned above, older persons consume a large quantity of medications and many use multiple medications. If physicians and pharmacists fail to explain possible side effects, older persons may not recognize adverse drug reactions as such and fail to compensate for them. Misdiagnosing symptoms of confusion or organic brain syndromes that result from drug interactions are common.

Wolfe et al. (1988) estimated that two thirds of prescriptions filled by older persons annually fall into one of three categories: " . . . the drug is: (1) not needed at all because the problem of the older patient is not one for which a drug is the proper solution, (2) unnecessarily dangerous because a less dangerous drug would give the same benefit with lower risk, and (3) the right drug but the dose is unnecessarily high, again causing extra risks with out extra benefits" (p. 3). Older persons also receive prescriptions from multiple medical providers, leading some researchers to conclude that up to 43% of older persons misuse drugs (Raffoul, Cooper, & Love, 1981).

Whanger and Myers (1984) noted that drug use among older women was significantly correlated with insecurity, sick role (behaviors one is socially allowed as a result of being sick), and fear of medications. They also noted that substance abuse is related to learned helplessness. Perceptions of control over one's environment affect levels of substance abuse or misuse.

Older persons may misuse drugs accidentally as a result of short-term memory disturbances, not taking drugs they think they have taken or taking drugs they already have taken. They may take too much or too little of a drug, or alter their medication schedule on the advice of a friend who was helped by some other procedure. They may have hearing or other im-

pairments that make it difficult to understand physicians' recommendations. Visual decrements may contribute to difficulty
in reading medication labels and instructions (Butler & Lewis,
1982). Medication management schedules, written records, and
other techniques can reduce self-management problems.

Another area of concern is the tendency of older persons
to quit taking a substance if they feel better, or to take more of
a substance that seems to be helping. Tolerance to certain drugs
develops over time, and some older persons may take more of
a drug to obtain a previously achieved effect. This is particularly
true of pain medications.

Risk Factors for Drug Misuse in Older Persons

Older persons who live alone, are depressed, or have low
incomes, those who take multiple medications, particularly from
different physicians, those who use different pharmacies, and
those with a history of poor medication self-management are
most prone to misuse drugs. Other high-risk groups include
older persons with visual impairments, who may have difficulty
reading prescription labels, those with tactile impairments, who
may have difficulty recognizing drugs by touch, and those who
have memory impairments or organic brain syndromes. Older
persons who abuse alcohol are likely to experience drug-alcohol
interactions. Finally, older persons who share their prescription
and nonprescription medications, and those who fail to ask
physicians for a list of possible side effects are most at risk for
drug misuse.

Diagnosis and Prognosis for Drug Misuse in Older Persons

Diagnosis of alcohol and drug misuse among older persons
is complicated by a number of factors, including bias among
medical and other health care professionals (which of course
reflects a general societal bias against older persons). Unfortunately, the symptoms of alcohol or drug misuse may mimic
those of numerous other conditions common to older people.
Differential diagnosis, though necessary, is time-consuming and
not always completed successfully. Diagnosis is complicated when
older persons are unable to provide accurate behavioral and
medication histories, sometimes because of organic or memory
impairments or because of selective reporting of information
they consider important. A common complaint is that physi-

cians are very busy, and therefore older persons do not take the time to provide a thorough history unless specifically questioned. This process can be time-consuming. There are some available instruments to assist in the assessment of alcohol abuse, discussed in this chapter, but drug misuse needs to be documented primarily through taking a client's history.

The diagnosis of drug misuse among older persons is essential if misdiagnosis, especially of organic brain syndromes, is to be avoided. Changes in physical condition, emotional or mental state, or social interactions need to be evaluated in terms of the older person's history, the medical history in particular. Many older persons report feeling differently after beginning a new drug regimen. They need to be encouraged to discuss this with physicians, rather than discontinuing the drug on their own. Sometimes a dosage needs to be changed and sometimes a new prescription medication is needed. Diagnosis is made easier if older persons remember to take all of their prescriptions along when they visit physicians and also pharmacists, who can be excellent sources of information concerning drug interactions and side effects.

A thorough history of medications taken, both prescription and over-the-counter, along with notations on when and under what circumstances each is taken, is important in determining a diagnosis. Simply talking to older persons about their medication habits can reveal instances of poor self-management or drug misuse. The prognosis for improvement is better in older persons who are capable of self-management and who are willing to learn strategies for taking medications as prescribed. Older persons who have organic impairments or who are poor self-medicators may be taught some useful strategies to avoid misuse of medications; however, some follow-up may be needed to ensure adherence to treatment regimens.

Gomberg (1982) noted that the prognosis for improvement is good for older persons with drinking problems. The prognosis is better for late-onset drinkers. In fact, older persons are more likely to complete therapy programs than are younger persons.

Effect of Alcohol Abuse and Drug Misuse on Family Members

Alcohol and drug misuse are primary contributors to accidents for older persons. These accidents include falls, hip fractures, and other conditions that can lead to incapacitation, inactivity, and a negative spiral of declining health. The secondary effects of substance abuse and misuse among the older population can necessitate hospital and long-term care, or other daily living care. Family members are among the first called upon to provide assistance. At the same time, family members may be enablers, or partners (codependents) in the abuse situation.

Where alcohol abuse is involved, families experience shame and guilt and frequently deny that a problem exists, or deny the seriousness of the problem. The older person may withdraw and become isolated or alienated. Family members may mistakenly attribute these behaviors to something other than alcohol abuse, thus delaying identification and treatment. On the other hand, they, like members of the medical profession, may hesitate to take away one of the few pleasures left to an older parent.

Family members may fail to understand medication problems and be intolerant of the symptoms. They may or may not understand the necessity of talking with physicians to develop an understanding of the medication needs of an older relative. Furthermore, they may not understand how it is that the older person is unable to obtain the information needed from his or her physician concerning the effects of medications. It would be helpful for family members to accompany an older person to physicians' offices, particularly if questions are discussed and written out in advance of the appointment.

The misdiagnosis of senility when adverse drug reactions or alcohol-drug interactions are involved has a major effect on family members of older persons. A diagnosis of senility removes hope for a better future. Accurate diagnosis of medication intoxication or misuse allows for rehabilitation and restoration of functioning. Family members may feel guilty or frustrated over their own lack of knowledge of prescriptions and their effects. Family members who are caregivers certainly could benefit from adequate information about the drugs older persons take and their potential side effects. Accurate information enables caregivers to help older persons remain independent for as long as possible.

Implications for Counselors

Alcohol treatment programs (ATPs) increasingly are including older persons in their patient populations. Schonfeld and Dupree (1984) conducted the Gerontology Alcohol Project (GAP) under the auspices of the National Institute for Alcoholism and Alcohol Abuse as a pilot program for older drinkers. The results of earlier research studies had indicated that relapse is predictable when the antecedents to drinking are not considered. The GAP thus developed four major approaches to treating older problem drinkers:

1. teaching older persons to break down their drinking behaviors in terms of antecedent conditions and to monitor their behaviors;
2. using behavior rehearsals, practice, and lectures in group sessions to help them deal with the identified antecedents;
3. teaching general problem-solving skills to deal with both present and future antecedents of drinking; and
4. teaching the consequences of alcohol abuse through group education.

A fifth strategy is to teach skills for expanding the social network of the older individual.

All treatment programs for alcohol or medication abuse in older persons should include a medical evaluation and monitoring by a physician. Whanger and Myers (1984) encouraged the use of a multidimensional functional assessment that would allow a holistic approach to evaluation and treatment of substance abuse disorders. It is important to consider medical, psychiatric, social, and family history, as well as current mental status, in determining treatment plans.

Eyde and Rich (1983) stressed the importance of a family systems approach to the treatment of substance abuse disorders in older persons. Families may have long histories of denial and avoidance of the problems or may be codependents, and thus may benefit from intergenerational involvement in treatment. Because the availability of support networks is one of the critical factors in recovery, and because families are among the primary supports of older persons, family involvement in treatment is essential. Dysfunctional patterns of relating may complicate treatment; however, both older and younger family members can develop insights about their behaviors and new patterns of relating.

Both broad-spectrum and single-treatment modality approaches are recommended for older substance abusers (Stern & Kastenbaum, 1984). The former include a multiplicity of strategies such as medication, socialization, group and individual counseling, and so forth. Single-treatment modalities might be antabuse, or some type of insight or group therapy. If the individual does not "fit" the treatment, the potential for relapse is greater. Therefore, multiple treatment strategies offer greater potential for success.

Fry (1986) suggested that helping older persons cope with changes in their life styles would be the primary strategy for situational or late-onset drinkers. Early-onset drinkers would require more conventional treatments, such as hospitalization, drugs, aversion therapies, and family interventions. Fry also cautioned that therapeutic regimens be entrusted to families only when family support is reliable and family members are responsible. Family therapy is indicated when family dynamics seem to have played a role in the onset of abuse.

Though physicians are the primary persons to consult regarding any medication issues, counselors and other helping professionals can assist in diagnoses by helping older persons to (1) prepare complete lists of medications taken and (2) develop a history of physical and behavioral changes that may be linked to drug use. In addition, counselors can help older persons evaluate their medication habits, apprise physicians of these habits, and work with family members for follow-through on treatment plans.

In the treatment of alcohol problems (and related substance abuse problems), group approaches are recommended. Reminiscence has been recommended as a useful strategy with older persons but may be contraindicated in the treatment of substance abuse. By placing emphasis on past events that may be painful, counselors can unknowingly stimulate the antecedents of problem behaviors (Kelly & Remley, 1987). Additional challenges in treating older abusers include the need, both for older persons and for their families, to consider all the concomitants of aging and accept the aging process as an integral part of treatment (Gross & Capuzzi, 1981; Kelly & Remley, 1987).

Strategies for Assessment

Strategies for recognizing older alcohol abusers were discussed above. Through careful attention to identified risk factors, counselors can assist family members and other helping professionals in early identification of older persons who may become abusers. The same factors can be useful in identifying active abusers. Physical examinations are important diagnostic tools for both alcohol and drug abuse in older persons.

The National Council on Alcoholism (1972) developed an extensive set of criteria for assessing alcoholism that is useful with older alcoholics. Fry (1986) suggested that these are the *only* available criteria for accurate assessment of problem drinking in older persons. These include attention to physiological and clinical factors, and behavioral, psychological, and attitudinal factors as both major and minor diagnostic criteria. It is important to remember that both frequency and amount of alcohol consumed may be over- or underrepresented and misreported in older persons because smaller amounts of alcohol will register higher blood alcohol levels.

Graham (1986) reviewed existing instruments for identifying and measuring alcohol abuse among older persons and noted several serious problems with these instruments. The instruments reviewed included the Quantitative Inventory of Alcohol Disorders (QIAD) (Stinnett & Schechter, 1983), the Structured Addictions Assessment Interview for Selecting Treatment (ASIST) (Beck, 1984), the Alcohol Dependence Scale (Horn, Skinner, Wanberg, & Foster, 1984), and the Severity of Alcohol Dependence Questionnaire (Stockwell, Hodgson, Edwards, Taylor, & Rankin, 1979), among others.

The first problem Graham (1986) identified is that self-reports of alcohol consumption may yield inaccurate results because these reports require accurate recent memory. Older persons may experience memory difficulties induced by medications, alcohol consumption, lack of time structure due to retirement, and other reasons. Second, social and legal problems related to alcohol consumption may be less conspicuous for older drinkers, who tend to drink alone and often live alone. Measures that indicate problems with family members, employment problems, problems with drinking and driving, neglecting responsibilities, and so forth may not be applicable to older drinkers. In the absence of these problems, older drinkers may not be identified with such measures. Third, it is difficult to distinguish alcohol-related health problems from many other health problems of aging. Fourth, symptoms of drunkenness and dependence may be confused in many existing measures. Alcohol dependence may be confounded with effects of prescription drugs or age-related changes in functioning. Fifth, many older persons do not recognize the existence of alcohol problems and thus fail to note them on self-report measures.

As is true with assessment of alcohol abuse, assessing misuse of prescribed and over-the-counter medications requires a carefully documented history. It is necessary to consider all medication use with attention to instances of misuse. These may include taking medications in other dosages or frequencies than prescribed, stockpiling medications beyond the date of usefulness or beyond the date when they are needed, taking medications prescribed for other persons or providing prescription medication to other persons, purchasing and using "quack" remedies, forgetting to take medications on schedule, or accidental overdoses. Direct observation and interviews with family members and friends may be necessary to obtain this information. Asking older persons to bring all available prescription bottles to counseling sessions provides a basis for reviewing medications taken and discussing medication management. Of course, medication always should be taken when visiting physicians for examinations.

Counselors also may benefit from knowing the side effects of medications used to treat common illnesses of older persons. Furthermore, a review of medications that are not recommended for use by older persons could be useful information for counselors and family members (see Wolfe et. al, 1988). Any attempts to change patterns of drug misuse in older persons will require active cooperation between counselors and family members and the older person's family physician.

Organic Brain Disorders

It has been estimated that as many as 15% of the older population have some form of mental disorder (Butler & Lewis, 1982). These disorders can be described in terms of two general classifications: functional disorders, which have no known physical cause, and organic disorders, or organic brain syndromes, which do have a physical antecedent. Functional disorders seem to be related to personality and life experience, and include conditions such as psychosis and affective and personality disorders. Organic brain syndromes have a physiological basis and are characterized by five major signs: disturbance or impairment of memory, impairment of intellectual functioning, impairment of judgment, impairment of orientation, and labile affect.

Organic brain syndromes include what formerly were termed acute or reversible, and chronic or irreversible disorders. Although Alzheimer's disease is the most well known, several other organic brain dysfunctions common among older persons are discussed in this section.

Incidence and Prevalence of Organic Brain Disorders

Butler (1982) noted that "most people never become senile no matter how long they live" (p. 75). Three fourths of all older persons maintain good mental functioning, between 10% and 15% experience mild to moderate memory impairment, and only 4% to 6% experience progressive, severe mental impairment known to laypersons as "senility" (Busse & Blazer, 1980). Though the prevalence of senile dementia increases with age, the incidence among persons in their 60s and 70s averages only 2% to 4%. By their ninth decade, some 20% of persons experience serious organic disorders and mental impairments.

Within the population of older persons having complaints of memory dysfunctions, the following breakdown of illnesses may be expected (Terry, 1982). Almost one third (10–30 per 100 persons) will have a condition that is treatable and reversible. About 20% will have a vascular disorder known as multi-infarct dementia (formerly and erroneously referred to as hardening of the arteries). A few will have one of the rare neurological diseases affecting primarily older persons, including Huntington's disease, Pick's disease, Korsakoff's psychosis, and Parkinson's disease. About 10% experience two or more of these conditions, usually multi-infarct dementia and a neurological condition. Most organically impaired older persons (55% to 65%) have senile dementia of the Alzheimer's type (SDAT). The latter group numbers between one and three million older persons. As the population ages, the incidence of SDAT is expected to increase proportionately.

Causes and Contributing Factors

The causes of most organic mental disorders in older persons are as yet undetermined. What is clear is that more than 100 temporary or acute conditions create symptoms that mimic those of chronic impairments. If these temporary conditions such as dehydration, malnutrition, heart diseases, anemia, head trauma, alcoholism, medication overdoses and interactions, and psychological stress are treated, the symptoms of "senility" may vanish and the older person can return to normal functioning. These conditions have been frequently misdiagnosed and hence left untreated. The results have been continued deterioration and eventual irreversible impairment for many older persons. Consequently, the National Institute on Aging has published for physicians a list of 100 disorders that commonly mimic symptoms of senility. Not all physicians have or use this list.

Probably the most commonly misdiagnosed condition that mimics dementia among older persons is depression, potentially a treatable condition. The differential diagnosis of depression and dementia, discussed below, is perhaps the greatest challenge in treating older persons with symptoms of mental impairment.

Multi-infarct dementia, a chronic disorder with an erratic progression (compared to senile dementia, which progresses in a somewhat steady manner), is associated with damage to cerebral blood vessels as a result of arteriosclerosis (Butler & Lewis, 1982). It is more common in men than in women, usually between the ages of 50 and 70, though the average age of onset is in the mid-60s. It frequently occurs in combination with hypertension or diabetes mellitus.

Huntington's disease is hereditary but there is no diagnostic test at present for its occurrence. Pick's disease and other neurological conditions seem to be genetically linked, but as yet they share the same place as SDAT in our medical knowledge: they are progressive and eventually fatal, have no known cause, no known effective treatment, and no known cure.

SDAT occurs more frequently in women, possibly because they live longer, though sex-linkage may be a factor (Butler & Lewis, 1982). A number of theories have been proposed to explain the causes of SDAT. One is that predisposed individuals have an excess of aluminum in their brain tissue. A slow-acting virus may be the cause, or age-related changes in the immune system.

Risk Factors

In the absence of known causes, known treatments, and known cures, the search for risk factors in relation to organic mental impairments is, at best, elusive. Certain risk factors may be identified with reversible impairments or acute conditions. For example, these include psychosocial stressors such as recent moves, losses, or family disruption. Older persons who are poor self-managers in terms of medication are more apt to experience interactions from over- or underdoses of medication. Lack of trained and interested geriatric physicians can contribute to iatrogenic disorders. Lack of attention to personal care and hygiene (possibly associated with low income, poor housing, and lack of access to transportation and medical care) can lead to malnutrition, dehydration, or anemia.

Several organic impairments seem to be sex-linked or otherwise genetically transmitted. For example, there is some evidence that SDAT tends to occur in families. Pick's disease seems to have a genetic link, as does Huntington's disease. For the latter, each child in an affected family has a 50% chance of developing this condition (Butler & Lewis, 1982).

Diagnosis and Prognosis

Organic brain syndromes include a constellation of five major features, not all of which are present in impaired persons to the same extent (Butler & Lewis, 1982). The signs of each of these may range from mild impairment to profound loss of functioning, with gradual or precipitous onset and progression.

- *Impairment of memory* is first evidenced in short-term recall, though in the later stages of organic brain impairments long-term memory is affected as well.
- *Impairment of intellect* refers to a decline in the ability to comprehend, calculate, learn, and retrieve one's fund of stored information.
- *Impairment of judgment* refers to a deterioration in the ability to make decisions based on circumstances, both for daily living needs and vocational/career demands.
- *Impairment of orientation* occurs with respect to time, place, and person, in that order, with the identities of others and oneself the last functions affected.
- *Lability and shallowness of affect* are common, including emotional excesses as well as numb or inappropriate expression of emotions.

Because the onset and course of organic brain disorders is so variable, a careful history-taking is important for accurate diagnosis. Often the older person cannot provide a clear and accurate history; therefore interviews in person or by telephone with relatives, neighbors, and friends are important (Busse & Blazer, 1980). Current mental and physical status must be assessed, as well as current medication and alcohol use and their history. In all cases, a physical examination is essential for accurate diagnosis.

As mentioned earlier, a differential diagnosis of depression and dementia is extremely important and exceedingly difficult. Physicians may be more likely to diagnose organic symptoms as reflecting senile dementia when a patient is older, and more apt to diagnose similar symptoms as indicating depression in middle-aged persons (Perlick & Atkins, 1984). The prognosis for depression is more positive than that for dementia, and therefore carries an implicit possibility of successful treatment.

Zung (1980) reviewed the essential components of the differential diagnosis between depression and dementia.

- In cases of dementia, affect is labile, inconsistent, suggestible, and may include depression, and normal control may be impaired. In contrast, the affect of depressed persons is not influenced by suggestion, and feelings of despair are consistent and pervasive.
- Dementia is accompanied by memory deficits, confabulation, and perseveration; depressed persons experience difficulty concentrating and learning new information.
- Intellectual decrements occur with dementia; some may occur but are not sustained for depressed persons.
- Persons with dementia experience fluctuating levels of awareness and disorientation to time, place, or person; those with depression may have some confusion but it is less profound.
- Poor judgment occurs with both conditions, as do somatic complaints.
- Psychotic behaviors, including delusions and hallucinations, may occur with both conditions.
- Neurological symptoms (dysphasia, apraxia) are common with dementias but not depression.

In many cases, differential diagnosis is not possible until a course of treatment has been attempted and the response of the older person, especially to drug therapies, has been determined (Barnes & Raskind, 1984).

The absence of clear diagnostic criteria, combined with the unknown etiology of organic mental impairments, necessitates team approaches to assessment and often results in tentative diagnoses and trial treatments. The only accurate, conclusive diagnostic test for most such impairments, particularly SDAT, is achieved through autopsy. The brains of SDAT individuals have clusters of neurofibrillary tangles or neuritic plaque that is characteristic of this disease. To date, even CAT scans (computerized-axial-tomography) cannot provide accurate diagnoses.

The prognosis for organic mental impairments is generally not good. In most cases, treatments are not able to reverse the conditions and in only a few instances is remission enabled. Most organic mental impairments result in progressive mental deterioration and eventual death. SDAT is fatal within 10 years of diagnosis (Whanger & Myers, 1984), though as many as 80% of hospitalized persons with this diagnosis will die within 2 years (Busse & Blazer, 1980). Persons may live with multi-infarct dementia as long as 10 to 15 years after diagnosis, with Pick's disease from 2 to 15 years, and with Huntington's disease from 10 to 20 years (Butler & Lewis, 1982).

The course of SDAT, the most common organic mental impairment in older persons, is continuous, progressive, and deteriorating. Basically, all mental functions decline while physical strength and health remain unimpaired until very late in the progression of the disease. Once lost, even the most simple mental functions, such as frying an egg, cannot be regained or relearned with our present state of technology. Mental impairment is accompanied by changes in affect and behavior commonly characterized by emotional outbursts, anger, and hostility.

Effect on Family Members

Because most dementias begin slowly and changes are subtle, older persons and their families may experience disruptions in relationships during the early stages of these conditions. Older persons may resort to lies in an attempt to "hide" their failing mental functions, whereas family members may interpret such behaviors as personal rejection. Some spouses of SDAT patients have even sought divorce counseling prior to diagnosis (Chenowith & Spencer, 1986). In general, the diagnosis of dementia leads to a sense of hopelessness and an expectation of increasingly negative and intolerable behaviors as the person grows older (Herr & Weakland, 1984). This follows a period, sometimes extending over years, during which a conclusive diagnosis is not provided, yet during which family relationships are strained and changed.

Zarit, Orr, and Zarit (1985) identified six common problems families experience in the early stages of organic diseases: repetitive questions, denial of memory loss, laziness, accusations, lowered inhibitions, and memory fluctuations. Family members find these behaviors increasingly difficult to cope with as behavior change proves to be significant and long-term (Shomaker, 1987). Increasing dependency of the older person places increasing burdens and stress upon caregivers, usually family members.

Family members who experience anger at relatives for their behaviors prior to diagnosis tend to feel remorseful and guilty when a diagnosis of SDAT or other organic mental impairment is made (Chenowith & Spencer, 1986). It is important for family members to discuss thoroughly with physicians the diagnosis, prognosis, and treatment implications. Even in the best of circumstances, families may be left with a sense of hopelessness and depression.

Needs for information are significant among family members, along with the need to vent feelings of anger, resentment, hostility, and guilt. These needs tend to intensify over time, as the disease progresses and caregiver strain increases. Rabins, Mace, and Lucas (1982) reported that 87% of caregivers experienced chronic fatigue, anger, and depression. The level of depression is directly correlated with the amount of cognitive impairment present in the older relative (Maiden, 1985).

Providing care for an impaired relative in the home has a significant effect on relationships with others. Most families report that friends cease to visit and caregivers become increasingly isolated (Chenowith & Spencer, 1986). Other family members may withdraw support or, in the absence of daily contact with the impaired person, remain critical of the caregiver and question the seriousness of the impairment. Eventually, when care in the home can no longer be provided, the agony of a decision to institutionalize the impaired older person must be made. The most common reasons cited for the decision to institutionalize are:

- 24-hour care was just too difficult and overwhelming (72%);
- caregiver became ill (21%);
- caregiver was unable to cope with behavioral problems such as inability to dress self or leaving kitchen range on (18%);
- incontinence (18%);
- angry and combative outbursts (15%); and
- other reasons, including physician recommendations, wandering (and often getting lost), lack of someone to provide needed care, and financial problems. (Chenowith & Spencer, 1986)

Again, this decision cannot be made without accompanying feelings of guilt, resentment, and even anger on the part of family members.

Watching a loved one change and deteriorate is extremely painful for all concerned, with the spouse being in an especially critical position. Role changes must be made. Rather than relating to one's spouse as a peer, it is necessary to become a caretaker. As the organically impaired older person continues to worsen in a psychological and cognitive sense, a lack of biological and physiological changes can create an incongruence that mocks the loved one in the attempt to provide care. As LaBarge (1981) noted, "there is no 'happy ending' in SDAT . . . it is frustrating to live with . . . [the] emotional losses are tremendous" (p. 139).

Implications for Counselors

The implications for counselors working with older persons who have organic mental impairments are extensive. In reviewing the literature in this area, theoretical and research support focuses almost exclusively on the needs of caregivers. Certainly there is a time, early in the progression of an organic condition, and especially immediately following diagnosis, when the older person is greatly in need of counseling intervention. Given a diagnosis of a disease that has no known cause, no known treatment, no known cure, is progressively fatal, is often described in sensational terms in the media, and that will progressively result in "brain death" while one's body remains healthy—who would not be in need of some means of emotional expression, such as that provided through counseling?

If not told directly by a physician, most persons learn through other channels that they will become increasingly dependent on others for even their most basic daily living needs. Depression is a common response, as is withdrawal from reality into further organic symptomatology. Such withdrawal may be confused with organic, neurological impairment, and is further exacerbated when family members, health care, and other service providers talk *about* the person affected in front of the person. This occurs when the erroneous assumption is made that the withdrawn older person is unable to hear and comprehend.

Milieu therapies have been most successful in treating older persons with organic mental impairments. These typically occur in institutional settings and require the training and involvement of all staff. Chief among the approaches used are reality orientation therapy, remotivation, and resocialization (Butler & Lewis, 1982). Reality orientation is a method to help confused and disoriented persons regain an orientation to time, place, and person. Environmental aids such as calendars and name signs, classes where simplified information is repeated and stressed, and continued attempts by staff to repeat basic information are part of the reality orientation process. Remotivation includes efforts to stimulate activity, social interaction, and involvement among withdrawn older persons. Resocialization has a similar focus in attempting to facilitate interaction among isolated older individuals.

Barnes and Raskind (1984) reviewed environmental and behavioral therapies that caregivers may find useful with older persons who have organic brain impairments. The use of door locks and identification bracelets, for example, can reduce difficulties with wandering and getting lost. Simplifying the home environment and reducing clutter, as well as color coding rooms or providing signs with names and directions, can assist older impaired persons in meeting their daily living needs. Such modifications also reduce stress for the caregiver. Butler (1982) recommended that counselors help caregivers focus on the behaviors that cause the most discomfort or annoyance, and develop behavioral strategies to change the undesirable behaviors in order to reduce stress.

The major treatment recommendations found in the literature are for respite care and support groups to help relieve the stress and burden caregivers experience (Wasow, 1986). Education about the diseases, especially SDAT, forms a major component of such groups. Although groups provide needed support and often an opportunity for expressing negative emotions, reduction of depression, improvement in life satisfaction, and increased coping may not always result (Haley, Brown, & Levine, 1987).

The stigma associated with Alzheimer's disease may prevent caregivers from attending group sessions (Shifflett & Blieszner, 1988). Lack of knowledge about support groups may be an additional barrier. Caregivers' feelings of guilt over leaving the older person alone, or their inability to obtain respite care, may prevent attendance. In some instances, abusive caregivers may fear legal repercussions if they admit to their actions or thoughts. Clearly, awareness of confidentiality is essential for these and other types of group interventions.

Wasow (1986) provided a thorough review of the types and nature of support groups for family members, and key issues for group leaders to consider. The first issue was that of therapy versus support. Many group members are reluctant to engage in therapy or even to delve into a variety of deeply felt, negative emotions. Groups can "conspire" to prevent the expression of grief, anger, or other negative emotions, and focus instead on educational needs and behavioral interventions. The sharing of roles and insights may be minimized. A second issue was whether the focus of the group should be on the disease, coping strategies, or accompanying problems. The third issue raised was a question of whether emotional ventilation would be helpful. As an alternative, groups might provide recreational outlets or encourage the expression of humor and laughter as beneficial emotions.

Wasow further explored the composition of groups, presenting a strong argument for homogeneous membership. Caregivers of persons recently diagnosed as having SDAT would share more common experiences among themselves rather than in combination with caregivers of persons diagnosed with the disease some time ago. Moreover, the latter caregivers could, under the guise of helping, present a picture of a bleak, hopeless, and frightening future to those just learning to cope with organic impairments. Wasow's final suggestion, reflected in writings by Mace and Rabins (1981) and others (Butler, 1982), was for counselors to help caregivers relinquish total care before they are ready to do so. In holding on as long as possible, caregivers attempt to satisfy their emotional needs in providing assistance to a loved one while ignoring personal needs for independence, recreation, and satisfying personal relationships.

Caring for a person with SDAT makes every day a "36 hour day" (Mace & Rabins, 1981). The resultant stress can overwhelm and disable the caregiver. On the other hand, the caregiver may continue in the belief that the emotions resulting from letting-go may be equally overwhelming. In effect, the caregiver is presented with an avoidance-avoidance conflict, or a lose-lose situation. Counselors must help caregivers reframe this situation to achieve a healthy response to best meet the needs of all concerned. Successful outcomes cannot be achieved in the absence of family therapy approaches. Such approaches and the needs of caregivers are discussed further in chapters 3 and 4.

Strategies for Assessment

The difficulty in distinguishing symptoms of dementia from those of other diseases in older persons makes the role of assessment critical if appropriate treatment is to be provided. A thorough assessment will include a lifelong health history, mental status examination, physical examination and laboratory studies, and a home assessment (Whanger & Myers, 1984). Counselors must cooperate with multifunctional medical teams to complete such assessments. Multidimensional functional assessments, discussed in chapter 1, are an important means of assessing the presence of organic brain syndromes and other disorders in frail older persons.

A standard mental status examination to determine orientation to time, place, and person forms an essential part of the assessment of organic dysfunctions. This exam is " . . . an objective observation of the patient's behavior and appearance during the interview . . . the patient should be observed for general appearance, manner, and attitude; psychomotor activity; movements and speech; and mood and affect. Information should be obtained through verbal questioning about intellectual functioning, orientation, and abstract thinking" (Whanger & Myers, 1984, p. 47).

Fabry, Haley, and Cahill (1982) reviewed strategies for assessing organic dysfunctions in older persons. Their recommendations for assessment instruments included several forms of the Mental Status Questionnaire, the Stroop Color and Word

Test, the Bender Background Interference Procedure, and the Wechsler Memory Scale. They also stressed the importance of assessing levels of intelligence and both educational and socio-economic background as part of any mental status examination.

Summary

In this chapter, four critical issues of aging were discussed. These four—depression, suicide, alcohol and drug abuse, and organic brain disorders—were chosen because they are common among older persons, especially old-old persons, they are difficult to diagnose and treat, and the lack of treatment can result in the negative spiral of decreasing functioning described as the social breakdown syndrome. This syndrome, described in chapter 1, can lead to progressive deterioration and eventual death if successful treatment strategies are not implemented. The suggestions for assessment in this chapter, considered to be vital aspects of intervention with older persons, represent only a beginning.

Additional diagnostic and assessment strategies will and must be used with each of the conditions discussed here, and will require counselors to interact with physicians and other health and social service care providers to ensure that needed interventions are provided to meet all the needs of older clients. Family interventions and caregiver support groups will be important in most instances with older persons who are depressed, suicidal, abuse alcohol or drugs, or have any of several organic brain syndromes.

CHAPTER III

DEVELOPMENT AND TRANSITIONS IN MIDDLE AND LATER LIFE

Aging does not occur in a vacuum but rather in a multi-faceted family context. The interaction of developmental tasks and transitions is an important component of family dynamics, thus it is essential to consider the developmental tasks of adult children and how these interact with those of their parents. Psychosocial issues of concern to adult children are explored in this chapter, followed by a review of the literature concerning family relationships in later life. This review includes an overview of family developmental stages and establishes a context for examining some of the important concerns of adult children's interactions with their aging parents. These concerns revolve around common late life transitions and all their potentials for both losses and gains. The major transitions considered are aging and loss, retirement, and grandparenthood. Implications for counselors and strategies for assessment are included.

Psychosocial Concerns of Adult Children

Adult children of aging parents are a diverse group in many ways, not the least of which is age. They can be young, middle-aged, or even old. Troll (1982b) estimated that over 80% of current middle-aged and older persons who have ever married (which is about 90% of the population) are parents of living children. Hence, a majority of persons in the United States are or will be concerned with the aging of their parents. Approximately 10% of persons over age 65 have children who also are over age 65. These children must cope simultaneously with their own aging and the aging of their parents.

Most adult children of aging parents are "middle-aged," which incorporates some 20% of the population between the years of 35 and 55. Such persons have been called the "Command Generation," because they occupy most positions of prestige, authority, and leadership in society. They also have been called the "Sandwich Generation," as their needs are sandwiched between those of their younger children and older parents. They must respond to the needs of adolescents seeking independence and also to older parents who may become increasingly dependent.

The period of "middlescence" is comparable to that of adolescence, but with a major difference: adolescents move toward increased status whereas middle-aged persons move toward decreased status (Fried, cited in Dobson & Dobson, 1985). Most persons in midlife experience a peak in their occupational status, earning capacity, and career mobility. At the same time, middle-aged persons are confronted with their own mortality. There is a shift in perspective of time, so that people begin to see their lives not as time since birth, and hence infinite, but as time remaining until death, and thus finite (Neugarten, 1968). Changes that stimulate a reconsideration of one's lifetime include the physical changes and decline that first become apparent in midlife, recognition of reduced energy levels, and the aging of one's parents.

Buehler (1967) suggested that midlife is a time for self-assessment. It is a time for review and evaluation of one's life, goals, and accomplishments. For some persons, it is a time to make now-or-never changes, to set and begin striving for new goals. Though inappropriately termed the "midlife crisis," the changes of midlife universally prompt a transition marked by taking stock and planning for the future.

Life span developmental theorists have described the midlife years in various ways. Erikson (1963), for example, referred to the central psychosocial crisis of this period as one of generativity versus stagnation. The goal of midlife adults is to leave something of value to the next generation, rather than becoming absorbed in their own concerns. Havighurst (1972) listed seven developmental tasks the person in midlife faces: achieving adult social and civic responsibilities, establishing and maintaining an economic standard of living, assisting teenage children to become responsible adults, developing leisure time pursuits, relating to one's spouse as a person, accepting the physiological changes of middle age, and adjusting to aging parents.

Issues of identity take on renewed significance for women, in particular, with the launching of children from the home and the onset of the empty nest. Many women begin or renew career paths at this time of life. Intimacy issues also emerge as significant, as midlife couples begin once again to relate as individuals without children present. For many couples, this phase of the family life cycle is a challenge, because lack of intimacy in the child-rearing years allowed couples to grow in different directions. Many now find themselves married to someone very different from the person they once knew.

In general, the transitions of midlife include the potential for independence, self-direction, and pursuit of goals postponed during the child-rearing years. New-found freedoms may be abruptly halted, however, when the needs of aging parents increase. Having to be caretakers once again can stimulate a host of negative emotions, including resentment and anger, and reactivate unresolved conflicts with the adult child's family of origin. Furthermore, adult children now may face the "crisis of filial maturity," the onset of which corresponds with the recognition of the fallibility and vulnerability of one's parents. Filial responsibility refers to the feelings of adult children that they *should* help their aging parents (Brubaker, 1985). Filial maturity includes reciprocity in terms of affection and intimacy as well as responsibility, and is a normative component of family development.

The developmental concerns of aging parents, discussed in chapter 1, may be compared to those of adult children. Such comparisons are important because the developmental issues confronting each generation are interactive in nature. Based on the Eriksonian model, both generations turn inward in an attempt to evaluate their lives, assess the extent to which goals have been achieved, and in some way plan for the future. For aging parents, the outcome of this process can be a sense of accomplishment and satisfaction with the lives they have lived.

Alternatively, they may feel dissatisfaction, accompanied by the realization that it is too late to change. At times, feelings about relationships with significant others, especially adult children, may form the focus of the older parents' search for integrity. A desire to make up for past actions and feelings or to right previous wrongs may prevail. On the other hand, aging parents may feel a sense of entitlement for services given to adult children in the past and consider that now it is time to "collect." Increased expectations of and demands on adult children may result from these "score-card" attitudes.

For adult children, the outcome of midlife evaluation may be satisfaction as well, or a desire to make significant changes in planning for the last half of their lives. Desired changes may or may not include a focus on relationships with aging parents. The focus instead may be on relationships with their own children, an integral part of an attempt to achieve the Eriksonian goal of generativity.

Adult children may perceive themselves as having the time and resources to make desired changes, while their aging parents have neither. With the focus of both generations turned inward, there may be little energy left for mutual assistance, or for encouragement of other family members. Alternatively the needs of both generations could bring them closer, with adult children looking to their parents for assistance in their own midlife transitions, transitions their parents have already experienced. Mutual support is more likely to occur in families with a history of healthy interactions and cross-generational respect and support.

Family Relationships and Patterns in Later Life

Morgan (1981) noted that family roles and relationships provide a sense of continuity, personalized interaction, and affection throughout the life span. In addition to understanding the developmental tasks and sequences adult children and aging parents face, an understanding of the dynamics of the family as a developmental unit enables further understanding of individual development and functioning within a family context. Duvall (1971) noted that families "go through predictable stages of development that can be understood in terms of the development of individual family members and of the family as a whole" (p. v).

The conceptual framework of family development includes four major concepts. According to Hill (1971), these are as follows. (1) The family is a system that is relatively closed in nature, causing it to deal with some problems while excluding the environment and with others by allowing environmental inputs. The family system maintains its boundaries, seeks equilibrium, adapts to its environment, and is purposive. (2) The internal functioning of the family may be understood using concepts such as position, roles, and norms. (3) The goal-oriented nature of family functioning facilitates an understanding of task performance of family members. (4) The observation and understanding of family life history require attention to concepts such as stages of development and role sequences.

A variety of stages of family development have been identified and were reviewed by Nichols and Everett (1986). These include Duvall's (1971) eight stages, Howells's (1975) seven stages, and Barnhill and Longo's (1980) description of nine key issues of transitions between family life stages, among others. The various typologies share in common Duvall's definition of family developmental tasks. According to Duvall, family developmental tasks are parallel to those of individuals. They are growth responsibilities that:

> . . . arise at a certain stage in the life of a family, successful completion of which leads to satisfaction and success with later tasks, which failure leads to unhappiness in the family, disapproval by society, and difficulty with later family developmental tasks. Family developmental tasks are those growth responsibilities that must be accomplished by a family at a given stage of development in a way that will satisfy its (1) biological requirements, (2) cultural imperatives, and (3) personal aspirations and values, if the family is to continue to grow as a unit. (pp. 149–150)

Within the family development literature, families with aging members compose the final developmental stage. This is perhaps the least researched aspect of family development. Cherlin (1983) observed that family ties become increasingly important sources of affirmation and meaning for older persons as the variety of social roles available to them decreases. Family bonds of affection and obligation are a primary resource for most persons who need assistance, and aging persons most frequently (and sometimes *only*) turn to their adult children when they need help (Feinauer, Lund, & Miller, 1987; Treas, 1983).

Recent changes in the modern family have resulted in bonds characterized by choice rather than obligation (Hess & Waring, 1978). These changes can have significant implications for older persons, especially those in need of assistance. To help counselors understand the changing nature of family relationships in later life, the information in this section includes a discussion of common myths, a review of common patterns, and a discussion of feelings associated with relationships in families with aging members.

Myths About Older Persons and Their Families

The multigenerational extended family living together in harmony has been exposed as a myth (Treas, 1983). First of all, most persons simply did not live long enough in the past for multiple generations to live together. Second, family members lived together primarily for economic reasons. Twenty years ago only 5% of households included a parent or parent-in-law. Today, fewer than 8% of households include three or more generations (Miller, 1982). Still, today's multigeneration families are pioneers, creating roles without benefit of role models because their own great-grandparents or even grandparents were not alive to serve as role models (Shanas, 1980).

Another commonly believed myth, which is certainly true for some older persons, is that all older persons want to live with their adult children. Most want to live near, not with them (Harris & Associates, 1974). Most older persons live by themselves or with a spouse or other relative. Older women are much more likely than men to be living alone. In the age group 65–74, 38% of older women live alone or with a nonrelative, and 47% are married. This compares to 15% of older men living alone and 78% who are married. For those over age 75, 52% of older women live alone or with nonrelatives compared to 23% of older men. In this age group, 67% of older men are married but only 21% of older women are married (Cox, 1988).

A related myth is that older persons are ignored and neglected by their children (Morgan, 1981). Almost 90% of older persons report having seen one or more of their children in the last month and 75% have at least one child living within a 30-minute drive (Treas, 1983). Hoffman, McManus, and Brackbill (1987) questioned a sample of older persons living in Florida, a state where many older persons move after retirement. They found that 57% of the older persons had weekly contact with their children, and fewer than 17% had less than monthly contact. Daughters, the traditional "kin keepers," were more likely than sons to maintain contact either by telephone or mail.

Despite commonly held misperceptions, it seems clear that aging occurs in a family context, with frequent interactions between adult children and their aging parents. The family remains "the first line of defense" in dealing with the aging population.

Family Patterns in Later Life

Parent-child relationships reflect extremely strong ties. These ties or bonds are shaped both by social roles and the accumulation of years of shared experiences (Moss, Moss, & Moles, 1985). The salience of parents for children persists throughout the life span, and children continue to interact with and learn from their parents (Troll, 1982b). Of interest is the fact that persons in multiple generation families hold multiple roles simultaneously, including those of parent, child, and grandparent. The implications of multiple roles have not been examined (Blieszner, 1986); however, it might be surmised that a positive effect on family ties would be shown. The ability to share common role experiences and expectations can contribute to the development of empathy for other family members. For example, when adult children themselves become parents, they may be more sensitive to and understanding of their aging parents' child-rearing problems, challenges, and limitations, as well as effective parenting activities.

Changing patterns of family life suggest a transition from relationships based on obligation to those characterized by volition or choice (Hess & Waring, 1978). Today's young-old persons tend to be in good physical and psychological health, and like their children, keep their family ties voluntary rather than obligatory (Aldous, 1987). The basis for kin relationships is ascribed rather than chosen, presumably making friendships more important because persons are *chosen* by their friends. Recent research in social gerontology has revealed an apparent absence of a relationship between the emotional well-being of older persons and frequency of contact with their adult children. Morale is increased and loneliness decreased through interactions with neighbors and friends rather than children and grandchildren (Lee & Ishi-Kuntz, 1987). This research is in contrast to most existing studies that support close and satisfying relationships between older persons and their families. Because members of different generations choose not to live together but remain in fairly close contact, the normative kinship patterns that result have been termed "intimacy at a distance" (Treas, 1983).

In general, patterns of reciprocity have been found in studies of relationships between adult children and aging parents. Though financial support and gift giving occur in both directions, aging parents tend to provide financial aid whereas adult children share their energies to assist with housekeeping, chores, and other services when parents are ill. Older parents seem to be selective in their attentions and concentrate on their children who have the greatest need, usually those who are single or divorced and with children (Aldous, 1987). In fact, older persons are more likely to give than to receive both financial and material help from their children (Hoffman, McManus, & Brackbill, 1987).

Most contact between older persons and their families is mediated by adult daughters. Highly reciprocal patterns of exchange of affection have been found in most studies (Blieszner, 1986). Because women are increasingly entering the labor force and are thus less available to their aging parents, these reciprocal patterns may change in the future (Brody, Johnsen, Fulcomer, & Lang, 1983). The decreasing birth rate, postponement of childbearing until later in life, increases in divorces, and increases in the life span may combine to create even more changes in family patterns in the future. One result might be fewer family members to help older persons; another might be increased intimacy among fewer persons and hence a greater potential for family assistance and interaction when needed (Brubaker, 1985).

The family patterns described here reflect primarily normative issues and a positive view of aging. Clearly, other family patterns exist, negative and disrupted relations do occur, and not all families choose to maintain close, caring relationships between adult children and their aging parents. The point is that the norm is toward healthy relationships, particularly when aging parents are young-old and independent. It is when independence is lost or threatened that relationships change, negative emotions can erupt, and dysfunctional patterns are most likely to emerge.

Emotional Issues in Late Life Families

Adult children and their aging parents have had a relationship and some form of communication for many years—as many as 50, 60, or more. Thus, their relationships and the feelings surrounding them are "predictably complex" (Troll, 1982b, p. 44). Where generation gaps exist, they are in the area of values and approaches to life. Norms for interactions within the family specify certain "demilitarized zones," or topics of conflict and confrontation that are avoided through tacit understandings and mutual (silent) consent (Hagestad, 1979). One such area may be roles as family members grow older. Because already established roles are "working," family equilibrium may be disturbed if open suggestions for changes are made.

Mutran and Reitzes (1984) suggested that intergenerational family roles are potential areas for conflict and misunderstanding. They noted that all roles contain some ambiguity, and that this ambiguity is heightened for adult children and aging parents by increased longevity, lack of role models, and uncertainty about filial responsibilities, obligations, and expectations. There is ample evidence to conclude that the quality, rather than the quantity of intergenerational contacts is important to the life satisfaction of all family members, especially aging parents (Lee & Ishi-Kuntz, 1987). Affection and communication seem to determine the quality of intergenerational relationships (Quinn & Keller, 1983). In addition, length of visits is significantly related to the well-being of older family members (Davidson & Cotter, 1982).

Older persons questioned about the satisfactions of having children have noted that children satisfy needs for love, companionship, fun, and stimulation (Hoffman, McManus, & Brackbill, 1987). As persons grow older, children continue to provide these satisfactions, and report feeling good about their parents as long as both generations are in good health and able to remain financially independent (Troll, 1982a). The relationship is reciprocal, however, as satisfaction with one's social supports is an important determinant of self-perceived health (Krause, 1987). Unhappiness with one's children or conflicted family relationships thus can contribute to declining health in aging parents, whereas satisfying relationships can help to mitigate the emotional consequences of physical decline.

Declining health of an older parent combined with the need for caretaking can create or exacerbate family stress (Power & Dell Orto, 1980). As Troll (1982a) noted, it is easier to feel close to an older parent who is not in need. Other researchers have noted a positive correlation between health of the aging parent, attitudes toward aging, and overall affective quality of the adult child-aging parent relationship (Johnson & Bursk, 1977). Reactions to overt or covert conflicts are in part a result of early family experiences that were unsuccessful or hurtful (Boszoromenyi-Nagy, 1980). In the absence of satisfactory resolution, such unresolved family-of-origin issues can interfere with ongoing relationships and needed decision making.

A recent study of multigenerational family issues (Feinauer, Lund, & Miller, 1987) revealed a number of important issues related to adult children and aging parents. Aging parents tended to be unaware of how other family members viewed them and uncertain about family perceptions or acceptance of the aging process. Adult children "experienced the aging process as unfair, unwelcome, and unpleasant, and they were forced to come to grips with their own inevitable aging" (p. 54). Common concerns of adult children involved in multigenerational families include the dependence of their aging parents, feelings of resentment toward noncaretaking family members, and anger, guilt, and irritation with parents who become self-centered and demanding. Aging parents express concerns over their dependence as well, and suffer decreased self-esteem as a result of loss of control in major areas of their lives. Depression and the necessity to grieve multiple losses at the same time can immobilize older family members and result in both mental and physical decline. Role reversals, which occur when children become decision makers and caretakers for their elderly parents, can be awkward as well as painful for members of both generations.

As older persons become less invested in work and community roles, family ties may become increasingly important for them. Some aging parents lean heavily on their adult children for support, to the point of exclusion of an emotional investment in other relationships. Adult children may want to respond to the needs of their parents and at the same time feel pressured and resentful. Despite a seeming potential for other friendships and social contact, adult children report that "Mom (or Dad) *only* wants to be with me!" At times, even the presence of grandchildren or other relatives is not appreciated by the older person, who wants no competition for the attention of his or her adult child. In extreme situations, no amount of attention seems to suffice to meet the demands of an aging parent's needs. Fortunately, such extreme demands usually are not constant, but fluctuate depending on unknown factors, such as the aging parent's feeling of vulnerability, health status, medications, important anniversary dates, and so forth.

Adult children living at a distance from their aging parents, an increasingly common situation in modern times, tend to maintain contact but not always at the level of intensity aging parents desire. Although telephone calls are more personal and interactive, letters can be reread during lonely times and shared with friends and neighbors. Some combination of letters and calls, interspersed with visits, seems to satisfy emotional needs for closeness. Distance, role commitments, and costs mitigate the level and type of long-distance family involvement.

When problems with aging parents arise, the closest or most flexible sibling, usually an adult daughter, is called upon for assistance. The sibling providing care may resent siblings at a distance who are not involved in caregiving. Emotional reactions can contribute to decreased problem-solving ability should the health of an aging parent decline and the need for care increase dramatically. One creative solution helpful to both adult children and aging parents is to select a trusted friend to be legally appointed with a durable power of attorney to assist an older person during times of impairment. The durable power of attorney allows the friend to step in to handle financial matters, such as depositing checks and paying bills, while the older person is incapacitated. This alleviates adult children of the responsibility of traveling to the home of an aging parent in another town or state to assist with financial needs. It also can prevent or forestall sibling arguments over the financial affairs of an older parent. The durable power of attorney is especially helpful for emergency situations or illnesses.

Another common situation for families occurs when either adult children or aging parents relocate. Adult children may want their parents nearby to be able to assist with care and enjoy the development of their grandchildren. Young-old aging parents may prefer to live their own lives in an area that affords leisure opportunities with peers, rather than their adult children and grandchildren. On the other hand, adult children may feel pressured not to relocate when opportunities are available because they consider themselves necessary as care providers for their aging parents. If an adult child turns down an opportunity for a promotion or new job on this basis, feelings of resentment or bitterness toward aging parents may result.

In general, both positive and negative emotional reactions are possible in response to the many and changing situations that confront adult children and their aging parents. The possibility exists for satisfying relationships, especially when mutual independence is maintained. In addition to dealing with family-of-origin issues, relationships between older family members and their adult children can be enhanced through an awareness of common late life transitions and how to resolve them in satisfying ways.

Late Life Transitions: Losses, Gains, Potentials

Schlossberg (1984) defined a transition as " . . .any event or non-event that results in change in relationships, routines, assumptions, and/or roles within the settings of self, work, family, health, and/or economics" (p. 43). Transitions include crises, transformations, and changes. They may be anticipated gains, losses, or alterations of roles that occur in the normal course of the life cycle. Or, they may be unanticipated, unpredictable, unscheduled events unrelated to life cycle transitions. Or, they may be "chronic hassles," continuous, pervasive conflicts or incompatibilities that erode self-confidence and hamper the ability to effect positive change. Transitions are not events but rather processes. They entail a period of emotional confusion, total preoccupation with the transition, and eventual assimilation. Brammer and Abrego (1981) suggested seven stages of the transition process: immobilization, denial or minimization, self-doubt, letting-go, testing out, search for meaning, and integration. Transitions may and often do have positive outcomes, though other types of outcomes may result. There is some evidence that the amount of perceived control over a change is directly related to the ease of adjustment to that change (Keith, 1986). Undesired changes and those over which one has little or no control will require the most difficult adjustments.

Older persons, similar to adults of all ages, experience a number of normative developmental transitions unique to the later periods of the life span. Individual older persons will experience transitions in common with others as well as transitions unique to themselves or only a subgroup of the older population. Each transition will involve a process, and will hold the potential for positive outcomes and growth. Adult children can expect to be observers of transitions, facilitators of transitions, and important parts of the transition process for their aging parents. The reverse is also true.

Several of the transitions older persons commonly experience are discussed in this section. The first include the many changes older persons experience relating to loss. Retirement is a common transition, with tremendous potential for positive as well as negative outcomes. Grandparenthood is another common transition with the potential for positive changes in the lives of older persons and their families.

Aging and Loss

Older persons experience multiple losses; in fact, aging has been described as a time of loss. For example, the aging process is accompanied by inevitable change and decline in all body systems. Though these need not be debilitating, some modification is required to accommodate physiological changes as persons grow older. Retirement (discussed below), itself a loss of occupational role and status, is accompanied by a loss of income. Older persons may lose friends and family members due to death, divorce, and gerographic moves. They may lose a variety of roles, such as that of mother, wife, or worker. Each loss requires an adaptation. Multiple losses require multiple adaptations, often simultaneously.

Two of the most common and major losses of later life are the loss of a spouse and the loss of a home. Both entail the loss of an identity and a way of life, and both occur more commonly for older women than older men. For many of today's older women, the loss of a spouse leaves them alone virtually for the first time in their entire lives. The transition to being single is made singularly more difficult when it is an involuntary change, as often occurs with both widowhood and divorce. Keith (1986) noted that "involuntarily occupying a role or status perceived as unchanging would cause great strain for most persons" (p. 86). Because the potential for older women to remarry is limited, the transition to the single state potentially can be more devastating for women than for men, as it seems to be—and often is—a permanent change.

Both older men and women may experience the loss of a home, though this is more likely to be a transition older women experience. Leaving a long-time family home can be traumatic and represents the loss of memories, status, independence, and a sense of security and stability (Hartwigsen, 1987). Given the relationship of voluntary choice to the resolution of transitions and loss, it is clear that older persons who make a choice to move will adapt more easily than those whose moves are involuntary.

The process of grieving a loss, whether of persons, places, things, or roles, has been described by Kübler-Ross (1969) and others. The process requires a series of phases similar to those required in resolving transitions. There tends to be a period of shock and denial, followed by emotions such as anger, bargaining, and depression. These reactions do not always occur in sequence, and the length of time each is predominant is extremely variable. Eventually, the loss is accepted, the transition accomplished, and a new identity emerges.

This theoretical approach to coping with losses does not take into consideration the dynamics of dealing with multiple losses at the same time, a situation common to older persons. Kastenbaum (1977) described a phenomenon of "bereavement overload," similar to stress or stimulus overload, in which the older person is unable to successfully complete the grieving process for one loss before being challenged to face another loss. The resultant overload situation is a crisis, and the older person may become immobilized by depression, feelings of low self-esteem, and questions concerning the seemingly external nature of their locus of control. Older persons who are self-confident, with an internal locus of control, may seriously question their own self-efficacy when confronted with multiple losses beyond their immediate control.

Older persons tend to be survivors, having lived a long time and having adjusted to numerous changes over their life span. Hence, the potential for positive adjustments in old age is excellent. Counselors can assist in a variety of ways to re-empower older persons and help them re-achieve satisfying independent functioning. Counseling approaches are discussed at the end of the transitions section, including suggestions for adult children to help their aging parents deal with transitions involving loss.

The Retirement Transition

Atchley (1977) defined retirement as being simultaneously a process, an event, and a role. As a process, it involves separation from a job role (or withdrawal), the end of a close relationship between one's life style and one's job, and the acquisition of a "retired" role. Unfortunately, that role is far more ambiguous, has far fewer positive role models, and far less social approval than the role of "worker." As an event, retirement is an informal rite of passage that signifies the end of employment and the beginning of a jobless life. Social status decreases.

As a role, retirement provides the right to an income without working and to autonomy of time management, whether one is prepared or not after 30–60 years of work-regulated time schedules, and whether one is accustomed to decision making or not with respect to one's time. There is an expectation that the retired individual will maintain preretirement modes of interacting with significant others, despite more free time, will automatically increase his or her decision-making capabilities for use of available time, and will manage a retirement income without difficulty or complaint.

All this occurs simultaneously with a loss of identity and consequent loss of a sense of power over one's life and decisions. The ability to determine one's personal directions suffers considerably, expecially if retirement is forced, or, if chosen, the choice was made because of health reasons. A study of retired men in 1963 showed that more than half (53%) retired for health reasons (Atchley, 1977). Of course, health reasons may be used to justify retirement when other factors, such as desires of supervisors or co-workers, may also have contributed to the decision to retire.

For most persons, work serves as a source of income, accomplishment, and identity (Tolbert, 1980). It also provides a sense of status, and is a source of social contacts and self-esteem (Okun, 1984). Work provides an inherent time management structure and a means to stay active and independent. It is rewarding, promotes good health, and contributes to a sense of usefulness and purpose in life. Because of the high value placed on the work role, it is possible to view retirement as a highly significant life event. The loss of employment at retirement can be equally as devastating to the older individual as job loss at *any* time in life. Hayes and Nutman (1981) described job loss as a psychosocial transition. Self-esteem is greatly affected, the individual becomes immobilized and often depressed, and must go through a psychologically painful process of adjustment.

Even for persons who look forward to retirement, the cessation of work presents a "crisis in the meaningful use of time" (Havighurst, in Kleemeier, 1961). Whereas work provides a time managment structure for most persons for most of their lives, the sudden availability of large amounts of free time can be a dramatic shock in the absence of advance planning (McDaniels, 1982). Some aging parents choose to spend their newly found free time with their adult children, developing relationships they simply did not have time to pursue during their work years. At the same time, adult children already may have full lives with their own nuclear family, friends, and employment. Integrating an aging parent into their social life may be difficult, if not undesirable. Hence, adult children may be placed in a position that could be construed as rejection of their aging parent—asking the parent not to call so often, or not to plan to be such an integral component of the lives of their children.

The major factor affecting retirement adjustment of older persons seems to be attitude, with positive attitudes helping to ensure positive adjustment. Most studies reveal the strongest correlate of adjustment to be higher income, with advance planning being the second. Opportunities for counseling, education, discussions, and exposure to news media correlate with more successful retirement transitions. These opportunities share in common ways of broadening the number and types of out-of-work priorities, leading to expansion of nonwork roles and potentially nonwork relationships. Positive adjustments correlate with being male, having adequate income, working in a semi-skilled job, having good health, and having a good education (American Association of Retired Persons [AARP], 1988). Additional correlates of retirement adjustment include the ability to adapt to change, positive expectations, self-satisfaction, and positive family attitudes (AARP, 1986b).

Negative adjustments to retirement are found in greater proportions among women, mid- and upper-level employees, and persons with high work commitments. About one half of retirees have a poor adjustment, and 40% of their problems are related to income. Additional negative correlates include poor health, recent widowhood, and retirement earlier than expected. Forced retirement has been found to have a negative effect on health, longevity, and life satisfaction (Lowry, 1985).

Attitudes toward retirement are further explained by studies of older persons who are working. More than two thirds of men and women report that they work because of the needed income it provides as well as because they enjoy it. Major positive aspects on the job include fellow employees, the organization, the type of work, and the challenge work provides (AARP, 1988). Although more than a third of retirees would like to work, almost 80% find that employer discrimination limits their ability to find jobs (National Alliance for Business, 1985).

Retirement is a naturally occurring event in the occupational life cycle that many older persons eagerly anticipate and choose to pursue. A 20th-century phenomenon, retirement was touted for many years as a desirable time of life. Persons approaching retirement age were lured with promises of the "golden years." Employers initiated retirement incentive programs to encourage older workers to step aside and allow younger workers to enter and advance in occupations. Recent studies have shown many of the alleged virtues of retirement to be a modern myth (Atchley, 1977; Hitchcock, 1984; Kieffer, 1986; Riker & Myers, 1989). However, retirement does offer options for working full- or part-time, pursuing educational and vocational interests set aside during one's primary earning years, and engaging in leisure pursuits limited only by interests, desired companionship, and finances. Counselors and adult children can assist aging parents with the retirement transition, as discussed below.

Grandparenthood

The number of grandparents in the U.S. population is increasing (Sprey & Matthews, 1982), primarily because of a decline in the infant mortality rate that has allowed more people to reach the age of parenthood, thus increasing the potential pool of grandparents. Exact figures on the number of grandparents are not readily available because the national census data (the source of national demographic information) focus on nuclear families and intact households (Hagestad & Lang, 1986). However, recent studies indicate that 75% of all people 65 and over, or 19 million persons, are grandparents (Troll, 1982b). Unfortunately, these figures underrepresent the total number of grandparents because they reflect only the population aged 65 and over.

The age of grandparenthood may range from 30–120, with grandchildren ranging in age from birth to 80 (Troll, 1980). The average age one first becomes a grandparent is during the 40s or 50s, although the increasing number of teen pregnancies has made many individuals grandparents in their 30s. The modal age of first grandparenthood has remained fairly constant during this century at 49–51 for women and 51–53 for men (Cherlin & Furstenberg, 1986).

A large proportion of grandchildren may know most or all of their grandparents now, for the first time in history. A child born in 1900 had a 9 in 10 chance of having two or more grandparents alive and a 1 in 4 chance of having all four grandparents alive. A 15-year-old grandchild in 1900 had a 1 out of 2 chance of having two or more grandparents alive, but only a 1 in 50 chance of having all four grandparents alive. In 1976, the 15-year-old grandchild had a 9 out of 10 chance of having two or more grandparents alive, a 1 out of 2 chance of having three or more living grandparents, and a 1 out of 6 chance of having all four grandparents alive (Cherlin & Furstenberg, 1986). The probability of four- and five-generation families also has increased, thus it is increasingly common for persons to have great-grandparents and great-great-grandparents. In fact, 40% of all people 65 and over are great-grandparents (Troll, Miller, & Atchley, 1979).

A recent national study indicated that 75% of all grandparents had seen at least one grandchild in the past week and 50% had seen one in the last day or two (Harris & Associates, 1974). These figures are particularly significant given the low cohabitation rates of grandparents with grandchildren.

Psychosocial Issues of Grandparenthood

Grandparenthood is a derived status (Johnson, 1985) created by one's children having children. Other than the decision to have a child, a person has no control over conferring grandparent status. The bonding relationship between the grandparent and grandchild, if it occurs, is one of "passive choice" (George, 1980; Troll, 1980). Because it extends over time, it is developmental as well as dynamic in nature (Smyer & Hofland, 1982).

Grandparenthood can claim a part in up to half (or more) of an individual's life span, and consequently is intertwined with a number of developmental stages and tasks. There seems to be a clear distinction in roles between persons who become grandparents in midlife and those who assume this role later in life. Younger grandparents tend to be active in careers and chosen life styles, and the idealized role of the doting grandparent cannot be realized within their constraints of time and priorities. To the great dismay of their adult children, they sometimes take little interest in their grandchildren.

In attempting to establish generativity in midlife, adults link themselves to the future via children, attempting to leave something of value to future generations rather than being totally self-absorbed. Many middle-aged grandparents already have resolved the generativity issue with their own children. They may choose to attend to other life demands, and their grandchildren may not be the focus of their attention.

As part of the search for integrity in later life, relationships and choices become increasingly important. The family emerges or re-emerges as the primary basis of security for older adults (Feinauer, 1983). Freed from work tasks, older grandparents may have both the time and inclination to establish strong relationships with grandchildren. Kivnick (1982) suggested that the grandparent role facilitates the individual's psychosocial development throughout the life cycle, especially in old age.

Older persons may have an innate need to establish an "alpha-omega chain" (beginning to end to new beginning) to link the generations (Troll, 1980). The grandparent role allows many older persons to feel a sense of biological renewal (Neugarten & Weinstein, 1964). Timberlake (1980) found that over 80% of grandparents viewed their grandchildren as an expansion of themselves beyond their own lifetime. The ambiguity of the grandparent role, or the lack of explicit role definition and expectations, can interfere with meeting these basic needs.

Grandparenting is voluntary (Johnson, 1985), and differs depending on whether the link is through a son or a daughter. Because women are more deeply involved in kin networks, maternal grandparents have a greater likelihood of being involved with their grandchildren (Cherlin & Furstenberg, 1986). Kivnick (1981) discussed the nature of perceived helplessness in the grandparent role, concluding that active attention to the role is important to avoid depression that may accompany perceived lack of control in such an important life arena.

Schaie and Geiwitz (1982) suggested that older persons who interact with their grandchildren know more about and are more interested in a broad range of life events. They tend to be more lenient and accepting of their grandchildren's behaviors and have the privilege of avoiding discussing sensitive issues. In contrast, parents do not have this luxury, and must discuss some issues with their children that may lead to conflicts or arguments. Grandparents are "required" not to take sides in disputes between parents and grandchildren, and must disagree covertly rather than openly (Johnson, 1985). They cannot take sides with grandchildren.

Grandparenting is viewed by most as an easier role than parenting. Robertson (1977) found that over 40% of grandparents enjoyed grandparenting more than parenting. Kivett (1985) found that the grandfather role seems to be less important than that of grandmother; however, it seems that grandparenthood is beneficial to most (if not all) midlife and older adults and also to grandchildren. In general, the transition to grandparenthood offers a new, vital role for older persons to supplement or replace roles lost through retirement or other life changes. The challenge is to achieve a sense of congruence between the needs of adult children, grandparents, and grandchildren with respect to time and resources devoted to sharing in each other's lives.

Helping Responses: Implications for Counselors

Adult children and their aging parents both can benefit from helping interventions aimed at assisting members of each generation to successfully cope with developmental tasks and transitions. In addition, family interventions can enhance the abilities of family members to assist each other in coping with these changes. From the work of developmental family theorists, some of the key issues for counselors working with families with older members include: (1) understanding family boundaries and rules for confronting problem situations, and when it is acceptable to seek or receive outside assistance; (2) understanding the position and roles of family members and how the aging of parents affects those roles; (3) understanding how each member of the family functions to maintain the family system and family goals; and (4) understanding the family history of coping with transitions and changes for individual family members as a model for coping with the transitions surrounding aging parents.

Family members may be expected to have emotional reactions to their own developmental tasks and transitions as well as to the transitions of their parents and children. In this section, some suggestions are made for helping adult children and aging parents cope with transitions in general, as well as with the specific transitions relating to loss, retirement, and grandparenthood.

Coping With Transitions

When questioned, adult children of aging parents can readily identify transitions in the lives of their parents that require a family response or assistance. The major transitions identified include divorce, widowhood, retirement, and grandparenthood (Remnet, 1987). Although older persons experience transitions as individuals, family involvement in each transition occurs to a greater or lesser extent. Individual counseling approaches always may be helpful, but because families are part of any transition, some intervention with the entire family system will yield the greatest potential for successful resolution of problems and actualization of positive potentials. Parents have always maintained a sense of responsibility for the welfare of their children, yet it is only recently that middle-aged adults are expected to be responsive to the needs of their parents (Johnson & Spence, 1982).

Remnet (1987) noted that adult children have a number of needs that must be met if they are to assist their aging parents in coping with transitions. These include the need for information in three content areas: communication skills, normal and abnormal aging, and available community resources. In addition, adult children prefer to obtain information in ways that fit easily into their busy schedules, such as through reading of journals and magazines, meetings of professional or social service clubs, and radio and television. Midlife women, the primary kin-keepers, are most in need of these types of information.

Myers (1988b) suggested three primary strategies for interventions to meet the needs of adults and their aging parents. These include individual and group counseling, education and workshops, and use of resource materials. Aging parents may not respond to counseling labeled as such because of primary generational values of independence and a pervasive stigma surrounding mental health care (Waters, 1984). Adult children may not have time for counseling. Hence, when multiple generations are brought together it is important to maximize the available time and opportunity for interventions. Dobson and Dobson (1985) suggested a combination of approaches, including providing information as well as opportunities to process attitudes, emotions, and feelings. A multimodal approach would best meet the identified needs of busy adults in midlife.

Coping with transitions entails an understanding of the transitional process. In helping adult children and aging parents understand the nature of transitions, counselors can both facilitate successful coping with current transitions and set the stage for success in future transitional situations. Furthermore, an understanding of the transitional process can help adults set goals toward achieving desired changes. Thus, counselors can focus on providing an atmosphere to talk, explore feelings, develop an understanding of transitional processes, and plan needed actions. Either adult children or their aging parents, or preferably both, can be included in sessions.

One of the most important factors to consider in working with persons in transition is how choice affects the outcomes of the transitional process. It is clear that transitions that are chosen are easier to cope with than those that are imposed. Counselors can assist both adult children and aging parents in developing positive attitudes regarding any transition, whether chosen or not. Once given the opportunity to explore feelings, doubts, fears, and concerns, what remains is a choice of attitudes and plans for the future. A sense of filial maturity will prompt adult children to assist their aging parents in setting goals and plans. Counseling can help them sort through their own conflicting feelings to determine just how much assistance they can reasonably provide to aging parents in transitional situations while still meeting their own needs for independence and developmental growth and change.

Coping With Loss

Aging is accompanied by many losses over which older persons have little or no control. The loss of important persons, places, and things can affect self-esteem and lead to a sense of loneliness and isolation. Loneliness, in turn, is related to poor psychological adjustment and dissatisfaction with family and social relationships (Hansson, Jones, Carpenter, & Remondet, 1986). Lonely persons exhibit poor social skills and the cycle of isolation becomes self-perpetuating. Where possible, dating is a hedge against loneliness for older persons (Bulcroft & O'-Connor, 1986). When adult children resent the entry of a new partner into the lives of their widowed or divorced parents, they foster the cycle of isolation, loneliness, and low self-esteem. Counseling with all family members can help them to explore the meaning of lost partners/parents and help each accept the need for and presence of new significant others in the lives of older parents. Of course, the reverse also is true, in that aging parents must be helped to accept divorce, remarriage, and blended family relationships of their adult children. For many of today's older persons, values placed on marriage may inhibit their acceptance of divorces and blended families among their children.

The greatest need of single older persons seems to be for companionship. Adult children can meet this need partially. Setting limits on the amount of intergenerational interaction may become necessary when adult children find themselves the major social outlet for their parents' feelings of loneliness. Aging parents often have more available free time than their middle-aged children. They may have difficulty understanding why their children can see them sometimes but not as often as they would like. Adult children, on the other hand, need to accept being able to spend *some* time with their parents while not feeling overwhelmed by the need to spend *all* of their free time with older relatives.

Counseling groups are an effective strategy for overcoming feelings of loneliness in older persons (Honore, 1984). Selection of group members is important. Including a number of older persons who are isolated may result in the development of friendships in the group that may extend beyond the group meetings. Including persons with active and happy social lives may be useful and stimulating for some older persons, but may further depress other members of the group who feel their situation is hopeless.

Another area where groups may be an effective strategy is in helping older persons cope with the loss of a home. This loss, like many of the others of later life, may be anticipated and thus plans for a transition made well in advance of the event itself. Adult children often have difficulty understanding why their aging mother (usually) will not leave a large house that she can no longer care for adequately. The large house was necessary during the child-rearing years but now can be burdensome. On the other hand, aging parents may have difficulty understanding how it is that their children do *not* understand their desire to stay in a family home. The house is more than an object. It is an accumulation of memories, often a lifetime of memories. The house is full of objects, each with a story or meaning behind it. The yard may be a source of pleasure developed over years of effort. The house and the yard may be integral components of the older person's sense of identity and esteem. To take away the memories is equivalent to destroying a part of the person. To move into a smaller dwelling will require an extensive effort of sorting through a lifetime of memories to choose only those objects one can take along, and to decide how to dispose of the rest.

Adult children can assist their aging parents in moving to a smaller, more manageable setting, but only after the decision to do so has been made. Sometimes reframing the situation can be helpful. If older persons can consider a move in a positive sense, as evidence of plans for continued control of their lives, the move may be made easier. Rather than discussing the loss, the need to move to a smaller home can be compared to the need, when younger, to move to a larger home. Placed in the context of reacting to the changing circumstances of life, rather than in a context of need (e.g., "You *can't* keep living in that house!") can restore a sense of control and make a decision to move far easier for the older person. It is helpful to all concerned if such moves can be made while the aging parent is in relatively good health and with adequate reserves of energy to accomplish the monumental tasks of paring down a lifetime of possessions. Unfortunately, healthy older persons may fail to see the need for making changes, especially if their major leisure time pursuits center around care of the house and yard. It is critical that activities be developed to fill the time that will become available when home care activities are no longer necessary or available.

Both family interventions and other groups with older persons can help all involved in coping with losses surrounding a move. Educational groups can help families explore options for retirement housing, which can range from full independent housing to apartment or shared living situations, with or without available daily living assistance or health care. Anticipated grief reactions can be shared and expressed. Even after a move, older persons can meet with others in similar situations to discuss their reactions. A facilitator can encourage the expression of emotions of loss, and help older persons focus on what they have gained as a result of taking control of an important area of their lives and daily needs.

Helping interventions for persons coping with losses are described in numerous available sources (e.g., Worden, 1982; Wrenn, 1979). It is helpful for counselors to recall that persons who are grieving need an opportunity to express their feelings toward lost objects and persons. Too often adult children attempt to protect their parents from the pain of remembering. Encouragement to talk about their loss can help older persons and adult children understand how, to the extent possible, to develop new interests, friendships, or activities necessary to successfully resolve transitions involving losses.

Coping With the Retirement Transition

The retirement transition presents unique challenges and opportunities for older persons. Considered in one way, it represents a loss of monumental proportions—the loss of identity, status, and a sense of meaning and purpose in one's life. When work is viewed as a primary source of status, the loss of the work role results in a significant drop in self-esteem. Considered another way, retirement presents a new freedom from the responsibilities and time constraints of the working years. Older persons have a unique opportunity to design and create lives of fulfillment, using an unlimited variety of leisure roles and even work roles. Faced with an abundance of time to fill with new activities, some older persons decide to make up for lost time in family relationships. Adult children, however, busy with their own lives, may be unable to integrate parents to the extent either may desire or require for life satisfaction.

To ease the retirement transition, the primary strategy that has been shown to be effective is prior planning. Persons who adjust best to retirement are those who have actively planned for the event. Planning includes attention to basic aspects of living such as where (geographically) one will live, what type of housing one will choose, what leisure activities one will pursue and with whom, and how a retirement life style will be financed. Leisure activities include all activities chosen to fill one's time, including educational pursuits, volunteer or paid work, gardening, watching television, traveling, visiting with family and friends, or reading, to name a few. Leisure pursuits can be as varied as the persons who engage in them.

On the other hand, failure to plan for retirement tends to result in a lack of satisfaction with the retirement transition. The old cliché that "those who fail to plan are planning to fail" is relevant here. In the absence of plans, retirement can be a depressing time. Because the retirement years constitute up to one fourth or more of the average person's life, the importance of planning cannot be overemphasized.

Adult children can assist parents in planning for their retirement by taking the time to talk with them about their future. Asking parents to consider where and how they will live and how they will fill their time can help adult children as well in planning for the retirement of their parents. If it seems that adult children will become a primary source of companionship for their parents, planning ahead will ease this particular transition for all concerned. If adult children would prefer their parents to develop a social life of their own, advance planning and open communication will help ensure this outcome. This is particularly important when parents move to live near their adult children when they retire. Open communication *before* the move is essential to avoid conflicts, unmet expectations of shared time, and feelings of rejection and loneliness *after* a move.

Preretirement and retirement planning and counseling are increasingly available through business, industry, military, government, and other occupational settings. But, such programs can only help if persons choose to participate in them. Those who say, "It's not for me; I'm going to go fishing," can count on disappointments anywhere from 2 weeks to 6 months into their retirement years. Adult children can encourage their aging parents to take advantage of retirement planning programs and opportunities for retirement counseling. Both structured and unstructured programs are available to help older persons complete the retirement transition successfully (Riker & Myers, 1989).

Coping With the Transition to Grandparenthood

The transition to grandparenthood, although being one over which older persons have virtually no control, holds the potential for positive outcomes. Grandparenthood is a new role for many older persons, one with few role models or expectations, and one that offers the potential for creativity and satisfaction. The grandparent role can take the place of other roles lost as persons grow older, and thus it can serve as a source of esteem and status within the family and community.

There is a void of informational or educational support programs for persons making the transition to grandparenthood (Strom & Strom, 1987). There are no "how-to" books and few articles. Adult children may have unrealistic expectations of how their parents can or should perform in this new role. The cookie-baking grandmother and skills-teaching grandfather may be unrealistic role models for many modern families. Grandparents can offer companionship, friendship, support, encouragement, and a listening ear to their grandchildren. When freed from the necessity of providing discipline, grandparents can form unique bonds of friendship that tie the generations together. Because grandparents often assist with care of grandchildren, they are not always freed from the role of disciplinarian.

The frequency of divorce and blending of families may make grandparenting a singularly difficult role for many older persons. Kinship patterns typically reflect associations through women, and women usually gain custody of children in divorce proceedings. Thus, maternal grandparents are more likely to have access to their grandchildren, and single mothers are more likely to need and want their assistance with child care and child rearing. Paternal grandparents may be denied access to visitation with their grandchildren. Parents trying to blend families may find that their attempts to relate to older relatives can cause difficulties. Including the maternal and paternal grandparents in a child's kin network allows for potentially eight persons for a child to relate to, *if* none of the grandparents have divorced and remarried, which of course would raise the number. When families are blended, step-grandparents may form a part of the extended kin network. Both maternal and paternal grandparents, and maternal and paternal step-grandparents, may have an interest in relating to younger children. Parents are left to mediate involvement in the grandparent role, sometimes making no one happy, including themselves, their spouse, their children, and all sets of grandparents.

Counselors and other helping professionals can facilitate the transition to grandparenthood by encouraging adult children and their aging parents to discuss expectations for the grandparent role before grandchildren are born. Adult children can be helped to understand that investment in the grandparent role is developmental. Some older persons will spend little time with their first grandchildren, who arrive while the grandparents are still active and employed, and more time with later grandchildren, who arrive after grandparents have retired and have more free time. Such differential affections toward grandchildren can activate or reactivate unresolved conflicts and sibling rivalries in adult children.

In general, the success of the retirement transition depends to a great extent on communication between the generations. Expectations and concerns will change over time; however, a clear understanding of perceptions prior to the birth of grandchildren is a start toward dealing with changing needs as adult children, grandchildren, and grandparents cope with the myriad other transitions and changes in their lives.

Strategies for Assessment

Much of the assessment required to help adult children and aging parents with transitions will be based on interview data, both structured and unstructured. A careful history of life transitions and coping techniques used will be helpful in determining how members of each generation may be expected to cope with age-related changes. The clinical tools of using genograms, Early Recollections, and life review are discussed in chapter 5 as means for assisting adult children and aging parents in identifying and coping with the transitions and circumstances that result when parents grow old. In this section, suggestions for assessment related to loss, retirement, and grandparenthood are provided.

The PERI Life Events Scale mentioned in chapter 2 (assessment of depression) is a useful tool for helping older persons analyze the changes in their lives that may become areas for counseling intervention. Assessments of well-being, life satisfaction, anxiety, and depression can be useful tools to determine reactions to loss and possible avenues for helping interventions. The Geriatric Hopelessness Scale, also discussed in chapter 2, can reveal whether the losses of aging have resulted in a sense of hopelessness about the future, and hence what counselors might focus on to assist older persons in coping effectively with losses.

Most retirement preparation programs include some variety of checklists for assessing retirement readiness. These include a review of major concerns such as choice of housing, options for employment, and ensuring adequacy of support networks (Riker & Myers, 1989). Johnson (1982) developed the Retirement Maturity Index to assess preparation for retirement. This instrument includes 14 variables that have been demonstrated to have an effect on life satisfaction among older persons.

The importance of planning for constructive use of leisure time as part of the retirement transition cannot be overemphasized. Although leisure plans and needs can be assessed in interview situations, a number of instruments have been developed to assess leisure preferences and styles. McDowell and Clark (1982) reviewed these instruments and evaluated them within the context of the construct of leisure wellness. Some of the more commonly used instruments these authors reviewed are the Mirenda Leisure Interest Finder, the Leisure Activities Blank, Constructive Leisure Activity Survey, and the Leisure Well-Being Inventory. A brief description of each instrument is found in the appendix.

Some older persons may want or need to work, and may need assistance with vocational planning and placement. Instruments such as the Career Assessment Inventory, Skills Card Sort, and the Self-Directed Search have been used successfully to help older persons with planning for second careers and either full- or part-time employment in later life (Sommerstein, 1986). An added advantage of using career planning and interest inventories is that identified interests may be used in planning leisure as well as work activities.

The dynamics of the transition to grandparenthood may best be assessed through a series of questions that both adult children and aging parents could review and discuss. These questions would center around perceptions of the roles of grandparents, images of the "ideal" grandparent, expectations for grandparenting involvement in rearing or taking care of grandchildren (including babysitting), and so forth. Young grandparents who state that they cannot see themselves in the grandparent role can be helped to explore the meaning of grandparenthood based on age, and whether they anticipate that their feelings will change as they grow older.

Some examples of questions for families to consider in preparing for (or adjusting to) the grandparent transition are as follows:

For adult children:

- How would you define the "perfect" grandparent?
- What do you see as common roles for grandparents?
- How do you see your parents functioning as grandparents?
- What types of activities would you like to see your children and parents share?
- What are your parents' feelings about being grandparents?
- How much time would you like your children to spend with their grandparents?
- Do you consider discipline a function of grandparents?
- What are your expectations for grandparents as babysitters for your children?

For aging parents:

- How would you define the "perfect" grandparent?
- What do you see as common roles for grandparents?
- How do you see yourself functioning as a grandparent?
- In what ways do you see yourself changing over time in terms of your reactions to being a grandparent?
- What are your children's feelings and expectations about what you will be (or are) like as a grandparent?
- How much time would you like to spend with your grandchildren?
- What kinds of activities would you like to share with your grandchildren?
- Does the age of grandchildren make a difference in the time and activities you would like to share with them? In what ways?

Summary

In this chapter, psychosocial concerns of adult children were explored, based on developmental theories and knowledge of common transitions that occur in midlife. Family relationships and patterns in later life were discussed, including attention to the emotional issues that are activated or reactivated as parents grow older. Three common late life transitions were explored, including the various losses older persons experience, retirement, and the transition to grandparenthood. Suggestions were made for counseling with adult children and aging parents based on common individual and familial developmental and transition issues, along with strategies for assessing needs as part of developing intervention plans.

CHAPTER IV

FAMILY STRESS SITUATIONS AND HELPING RESPONSES

A number of family stress situations and responses involving older family members are important to consider. Some of these are more common and potentially more serious than others. In this chapter, four common stress situations and responses many families experience are discussed. These include caregiving, elder abuse (often a response to caregiving), institutionalization, and death and dying. The dynamics of each situation and the effect on the family are described. Implications for counselors and helping professionals, as well as strategies for assessment, are included at the end of each section.

Caregiving

"Families are the first and often the only resource turned to by many elderly. With the changing economic climate over the past five years, it is likely that increasing numbers of elderly will continue to move into the homes of their adult children. The transitions required and stresses that occur may be very disruptive to the family" (Feinauer, Lund, & Miller, 1987, p. 52). "We live in a time when you could spend more years caring for your aging parent than you did caring for your children" (Johnson, 1988, p. 4). Parent care has been defined as a modern-day normative family stress (Brody, 1985). In this section, several aspects of parent care are discussed. These include precipitating factors, a profile of caregivers, and the effect of caregiving on aging parents and their adult children.

Precipitating Factors

Older persons universally report fearing physical decline and dependence. They want to maintain their independence in personal care as well as in living arrangements. The decision to enter a multigeneration household, never an easy decision, is made for various reasons, including widowhood and ill health (Mines, Rockwell, & Hull, 1980). In fact, there is a direct relationship between the health of the older person and the probability of living in the same household as an adult child: the poorer the health of the parent, the greater the likelihood of cohabitation.

Children respond to the needs of their parents based on family history, with familial obligation (filial maturity), reciprocity, and affection being the most likely antecedents of a decision to provide care (Horowitz & Shindelman, 1981). Children provide more assistance when the dependence needs of their parents increase, when their sense of filial responsibility is greater, when the children live closer, and when the adult child is a daughter (Cicirelli, 1983b).

A Profile of Caregivers

A national profile of caregivers completed recently revealed that they are predominantly women and one third are over age 65 (and are also vulnerable themselves). Competing demands for caregivers' time include child care responsibilities (21%), the need to quit jobs to provide care (9%), and work conflicts (20%) (Stone, Cafferata, & Sangl, 1987). A minority of care providers use formal services or purchase services, with most formal services being provided when daughters work outside the home and are thus unable to provide assistance (Brody & Schoonover, 1986). The hours of assistance vary according to the level of parental impairment, presence of the older parent's spouse, and the competing demands on the adult child's time (Stoller, 1983).

Structural features of families, primarily size and sex ratios, are important determinants of the patterns of care (Matthews, 1987). Working daughters are able to provide fewer hours of help and less personal care and cooking; however, they tend to coordinate whatever care is needed. Sons are likely to become caregivers only in the absence of a female sibling or spouse to provide care. Sons provide less overall assistance, especially personal care, and report experiencing less stress in the caregiving role (Horowitz, 1985). Overall, almost 80% of caregivers are women. Almost half of caregivers are daughters (45%), 11% are adult sons, and 11% are adult siblings (Pastorello, 1986).

A national survey conducted by the American Association of Retired Persons revealed that a high percentage of people who work are involved in providing care to older relatives. Out of 1,338 respondents, 24% provided care for a relative who lived with the worker, alone, or in a nursing home. Caregiving activities ranged from shopping assistance to care for a bedridden or homebound person. The care recipient usually was a woman between the ages of 71 and 90, and the typical caregiver was a woman in her mid-50s. Some 63% of the caregivers had been providing care only within the last 5 years, 66% received no outside or family help with their caregiving responsibilities, and 86% used no paid assistance. In general, these women did not lose time from work, and one fourth reported having no one to talk to about their concerns (Caregivers in the Workplace, 1988).

The Effect of Caregiving on Aging Parents and Adult Children

Most older persons do not enjoy being in a dependent position. In fact, the strongest predictor of psychological well-being and family adjustment of aged persons has been shown to be health (Quinn, 1983). As older persons' health declines and their dependence increases, so too will their level of frustration and the resentment of their caretakers. When family relations already are strained, illness will cause additional stress (Mines, Rockwell, & Hull, 1980).

Feinauer, Lund, and Miller (1987) reviewed some of the feelings aging parents may experience in response to needing care. These include lowered self-esteem, fear, withdrawal, depression, grief, and anger. Some aging parents develop a demanding, self-centered manner of communicating, perhaps in an attempt to gain some control over their environment or assert the authority they once had. Adult children may respond with their own anger and resentment, guilt over their negative emotions, and a feeling of being trapped and in a situation over which they have little or no control. Coping with the role reversal required when one begins to take care of a former caregiver can be especially difficult and painful (Jacobsen, 1988). When interpersonal conflict is present, both caregivers and care receivers experience high levels of strain and negative affect (Sheehan & Nuttall, 1988).

On the other hand, when families have a history of healthy and mutually supportive interactions, the caregiving process may be less stressful—though never without any stresses. There are some positive benefits to the caregiving process (Horne, 1985). These include the possibility of developing closer relationships with aging parents and closer relationships with siblings as part of sharing caregiving duties.

The tasks involved in providing care to an aging, infirm relative most often result in caregiver strain, stress, or burden. This includes the multiple role strain that results when adult children attempt to meet simultaneously all of their responsibilities as parent, child, worker, spouse, and so forth (Cantor, 1983). Adult children may see no end in sight and only a bleak future for their relationship with aging parents (Rakowski & Clark, 1985). They also may become very tired when faced with increasing responsibilities rather than the anticipated decreasing burdens in midlife. Cicirelli (1983c) noted that the most frequently reported negative feelings of caregivers included feeling physically worn out, feeling emotionally exhausted, feeling that nothing they said or did would satisfy their aging parent, and feeling frustrated, irritated, and impatient. These and other consequences of caregiving, particularly for women, are described using case examples in a recent book by Sommers and Shields (1987).

It is clear that caregivers are persons "at risk." They are more likely to experience physical or emotional illness, premature aging, and a host of negative emotions leading to low levels of life satisfaction (Johnson, 1988). They may undergo severe psychological, physical, and financial stress (Selan & Schuenke, 1982). Furthermore, the need to provide care, combined with the stigma of illness placed on many older persons, results in reduced social participation. Friends and other family

members cease to visit, leaving the caregiver increasingly isolated and subject to reduced support and opportunities for
intimacy (Masciocchi, 1985). In fact, the lack of social supports
rather than behavioral problems of the older person are most
predictive of caregiver burden (Zarit, 1980, 1981).

The greatest strain seems to occur when older persons have
organic brain impairments or dementias (Gwynther & George,
1986). Family caregivers in these situations are most apt to
experience isolation, loneliness, depression, anger, grief, and
guilt (Kramer, 1984). The emotional consequences of isolation
are intensified as the social interactions of the caregiver increasingly are limited to an impaired older person with limited
capacity for effective cognitive and affective interactions (Masciocchi, 1985). Social supports and respite care offer the greatest
relief to these caregivers.

Family caregivers tend to be very committed and have strong
bonds of attachment and filial responsibility. Aging parents may
openly express fear or dread of long-term care placements. For
any number of reasons, caretakers may hold on to caregiving
responsibilities far beyond the time when decisions to institutionalize an aging parent may be best for all concerned (La-
Barge, 1981).

Implications for Counselors

The difficulties that arise in regard to caring for an aging
parent usually start long before the care begins. At some point
a decision to provide care is made. Sometimes the decision
occurs after a period of increasing need on the part of the aging
parent and increasing care provision by relatives; at some point
living in the same household may become necessary to continue
the provision of care. At other times, the need for care is sudden, following an illness or condition of sudden onset, as in the
case of a stroke. At times, the provision of care may start as a
temporary situation in response to a need, and escalate into a
more permanent situation. Sometimes it seems that there is no
decision to be made, or perhaps no choices. At other times,
decisions are made so gradually that there seems to be an absence of choice.

Clearly, a major role for counselors is to help family members discuss the dynamics of caregiving, consider the needs of
all involved, and make choices among the available options and

alternatives. Making a decision that is satisfying to all concerned may be difficult at best, particularly because values concerning caregiving may differ among members of the family (Mines, Rockwell, & Hull, 1980). Techniques such as genograms, discussed in chapter 5, can be useful to help family members better understand their differing values.

At times it may seem to family members that there are no options to providing care for an aging parent, or that there are no *good* options. Older persons fear a time when institutionalization may be required. When this fear is communicated to adult children, feelings of guilt may cloud the issue and prevent even cursory consideration of other options. Long-term care in nursing homes is not the only alternative. Older persons who are ambulatory and semi-independent can live in companion, congregate, or assisted-living environments. Only the most seriously impaired need utilize nursing homes. Assisted-living settings allow older persons to remain as independent as possible for as long as possible. Even when a choice is made for multiple generations to live together, personal care can be purchased rather than directly provided by family members. When possible, add-on housing units or separate apartments attached to a family home can help both older parents and family members maintain a sense of independent living.

In the last few years, several books have been published that provide extended discussions of living options and in-depth reviews of issues related to caregiving (e.g., Hooyman & Lustbader, 1986; Horne, 1985; Jacobsen, 1988; Johnson, 1987; Kenny & Spicer, 1984; Mace & Rabins, 1981; Sommers & Shields, 1987). One issue is the decision to provide care to an older relative. The dynamics of the decision include a consideration of other familial and community resources and whether the relative is a parent or parent-in-law. The decision should not be made hastily or on impulse, but rather after an extended discussion that considers all possible options with all persons involved.

It is important to involve the aging parent in these discussions for several reasons. Open communication can help aging parents deal realistically with their losses, maintain a sense of control in determining the course of their lives, understand the concerns of relatives, and plan ways to cope with their own needs as well as the needs of their adult children. It is also important to involve minor children who may face the challenges of sharing their home with an aging, infirm relative.

Dysfunctional family patterns of relating will become apparent in discussions surrounding caregiving issues, providing a focus for current and future family counseling sessions.

It is critical that all family members understand and agree that any decision to provide care can be reversed. Caregiving can be construed as a life sentence, a rather depressing thought to many adult children. Both adult children and aging parents must be helped to understand that the needs and circumstances of each will change. Caregiving is not a static situation, and continual reevaluation is necessary once the caregiving decision is made. To encourage this process, goals, plans, and timetables can be set that specify times and places when the family will meet to reconsider the needs of all family members and the advisability of continuing care of an aging parent. Again, the aging parent must feel a part of the planning and evaluation process. After all, it is the parent's life that is being considered.

Once caregiving begins, support programs for both adult children and aging parents have proven to be helpful in reducing feelings of stress and burden. Most such programs focus on the needs of caregivers rather than those of disabled parents. Aging parents placed in a dependent position may expect to feel angry, resentful, and fearful about their future. When adult children divorce, feelings of fear over who will provide the care they need may be exacerbated. Compassion and concern for the needs of adult children also are evident when divorces occur. Even if dependent, aging parents may be expected to continue a lifelong pattern of concern for their child's welfare.

It is important to consider counseling for aging parents, as well as caregivers, to assist them in exploring and dealing with the many negative emotions that result from being old, sick or infirm, and dependent. Even with older persons suffering from organic brain diseases such as Alzheimer's, therapeutic group methods can help slow behavioral deterioration and maximize daily functioning (Shoham & Neuschatz, 1985; Winoground, Fisk, Kirsling, & Keyes, 1987).

Counselors should be prepared to help adult children in assessing the negative effects of caregiving and evaluating how to cope with these effects. It is equally important to help them examine the positive outcomes of the caregiving process. The motivation for caregiving needs to be explored, including filial behaviors and the meaning of filial responsibility. Johnson (1988) offered a number of suggestions for helping adult children examine their caregiving attitudes. When adult children try to be perfect in pleasing their parents, chastise themselves for failing to do the impossible, and focus on all that they "should" do for their relatives, the stress of caregiving is multiplied. They can benefit from a supportive environment that allows them to express and examine their need to provide care, receive feedback from others in similar situations, and have an opportunity to discuss their feelings and concerns about their aging parents.

Unfortunately, groups are not always effective. For example, in a study of group interventions for caregivers of persons with dementia, Haley, Brown, and Levine (1987) found that the participants rated groups as helpful but other measures of effectiveness showed no change. Caregivers did not show improvement on measures of depression, life satisfaction, social support, or coping resources.

Support groups for caregivers to older persons offer adult children an opportunity to learn about their needs and the needs of their parents, the medical implications of various diseases, other options for care, and techniques for providing care. Participants in such groups can express and normalize their feelings and develop peer support (Kramer, 1984). Some of the benefits of caregiver support groups include an increased awareness of community resources, enhanced ability to set limits, lower levels of frustration with and greater understanding of the behaviors of mentally impaired parents, better time and resource management skills, and improved family relationships (Selan & Schuenke, 1982). Groups can help caregivers understand the importance of socialization, respite care, and the need to take time for other roles and family relationships.

Groups that include family members have the potential to help each person understand how to help the others to relieve role strains and the stresses of providing care for a disabled relative. Though many of the same benefits can be gained through individual therapy, it is clear that caregiving includes and affects the entire family system. Hence, the need for family therapy is paramount when caregiving is required. Family therapy is discussed in more detail in chapter 5.

Strategies for Assessment

Brubaker (1985) offered a list of questions about important caregiving decisions that counselors can use to facilitate discussion among family members. The major categories of concern for adult children include getting to know the family and how its members deal with situations and interactions, getting to know the situation and what caregiving would mean physically and emotionally, and becoming familiar with community resources that can assist with caregiving responsibilities. Both adult children and aging parents will benefit from exploring these concerns before a decision to provide care has been concluded.

Simonton and Haugland (1986) developed a brief questionnaire to assess information needs of caregivers. The questions include causes and treatment of the older person's symptoms, prognosis, behavioral management, family decision making, activity levels of the older person, and the possibility of institutionalization. The results from administering this questionnaire reveal primary needs in the area of prognosis to assist families in planning for the future.

Another important area for assessment is that of caregiver stress. Techniques in this area are discussed at the end of the section on elder abuse in this chapter, because an excess of stress or burden is known to increase the potential for abuse of older, dependent individuals.

Institutionalization

Placement of an older person in a nursing home is a major life transition with significant effects on both the older person and the family. Although only 5% of older persons reside in nursing homes at any one time, the risk of such placements and the anticipation of incapacitating illness are a source of fear for many older persons. Notwithstanding the fact that many persons leave nursing homes for less restrictive settings, the view of nursing homes as halfway houses—halfway between society and the cemetery (Butler, 1975)—remains a powerful and negative motivator.

In this section, some of the known data concerning nursing home placements are considered, along with alternatives to nursing home care. Factors surrounding the decision for placements are considered, followed by a discussion of emotional reactions of older persons and their families and implications for counselors.

Incidence

There are over one million persons currently residing in nursing homes in the United States, and over two thirds of them are women. Though only 5% of older persons reside in nursing homes at any one time, between 20% and 30% of the older population can expect to spend some time in a long-term care facility (National Institute on Aging, 1986). The risk of institutionalization among older persons has been about one in four during the 1980s, and is expected to increase to about one in three before the end of the century because of increases in the size of the older population (Kart & Palmer, 1987).

Of the persons in nursing homes, 90% are over age 65. Over 20% of residents are age 85 or older. About 85% have no living spouse and many have no living relatives at all. An estimated 60% of nursing home residents have a psychiatric diagnosis in addition to physical declines related to aging (National Conference on Social Welfare, 1981).

Alternatives to Institutionalization

Though institutionalization is usually the choice of last resort, many families are unaware of alternatives that could prevent or postpone this choice. Community service alternatives to institutional care include several options. First is family caregiving, discussed earlier, which may entail the older person's living in his or her own home or in the home of relatives. Older persons living independently in the community are eligible for a number of home-delivered services through agencies funded under the Older Americans Act. These services include transportation, home-delivered meals, shopping and chore assistance, escort service, and others. Each community in the United States is served by an area agency on aging responsible for planning and coordinating services to older persons, and also providing information and referral for needed services.

Residential care facilities provide room and board and frequently offer social or recreational programs. For families caring for older persons in their homes, many communities sponsor *day-care or respite* programs that offer both relief to family members and rehabilitative services for older persons. *Continuing care communities* and *assisted living settings* provide help with daily living needs but allow older persons to continue living somewhat independently in an apartment or rooming-house environment. *Intermediate care facilities* (ICFs) are nursing homes that provide nursing, rehabilitative, and social and personal care services. ICFs typically house older persons who have mobility limitations but who do not need full nursing care. *Skilled nursing facilities* (SNFs) are the choice for persons who require 24-hour medical supervision and care. Medical maintenance, not acute medical care, is provided, along with rehabilitative services to maintain or enhance functioning.

All services older persons need could be provided in a home environment, including skilled nursing care, but the costs are prohibitive for most persons. Medicare and Medicaid cover some of the costs of nursing home care, but not enough to prevent signficant expenditures of family resources. Costs for nursing home care, which are continually increasing, are estimated at $1,200–$2,000 per month for intermediate care facilities.

The Institutionalization Decision

Zweibel (1984) estimated that families consider at least six alternatives prior to the decision for institutionalization. These include long-term care, in-the-home companion services, supportive congregate housing, counseling, in-home services, and independent housing. Her data indicated that only 25% of families were unable to locate their preferred alternatives, and 35% reported cost as a barrier to services. Several respondents in this study indicated that their older relatives refused placements that adult children considered to be viable, and over 60% indicated that conflict between the older relative and the caregiver hindered the decision-making process.

It seems clear that the decision for institutionalization is usually not the first choice. Typically this decision is made to remove the older person from a potentially harmful situation or to relieve the family of the burden of care (Zarit, 1983). Many families feel trapped by the decision they must make, reporting that there was nothing else to do (Smallegan, 1985). The relative placed in an institution typically is in poor health and requires many hours of nursing care, the family is unable to provide the level of care needed, and community supports to keep the older person in the home are unavailable (American Health Care Association, undated, a).

There are several positive aspects to nursing home placement that affect the decision-making process. The needs of the
older person for nursing care in a supportive environment can
be better met. Consistent and adequate nutrition can be provided. Social and rehabilitative support may be available, thus
helping the older person to regain or maintain levels of physical
and psychological functioning and avoid isolation and loneliness
(American Health Care Association, undated, b).

Butler and Lewis (1982) recommended that the decision
to institutionalize be made "conservatively and with care to fully
prepare and cushion the individual against inevitable shock"
(p. 284). They also provided a list of considerations about the
older person that influence decisions to institutionalize. These
factors, taken from Lowenthal (1964), include disturbances in
thinking and feeling (i.e., delusions, depression), physical illness, potentially harmful behavior, actual harmful behavior,
incapacity, and environmental factors such as the unavailability
of care.

Once the decision has been made, family members must
face the task of choosing from among available alternatives for
placement. It is helpful if one or more members of the family
visit several facilities and talk with both staff and residents.
Several organizations have prepared booklets and survey forms
to assist family members in asking relevant questions when considering which facility to choose (American Health Care Association, undated, c; U.S. Department of Health, Education
and Welfare, 1973; Falck & Kane, 1978). The U.S. Health Care
Financing Administration (HCFA) has developed a guide for
consumers with state-by-state guides to the quality of care in
more than 15,000 federally certified nursing homes. In addition, the guide, available from the U.S. Government Printing
Office in Washington, DC, includes 32 standards that have been
"met" or "not met" by each home. One important consideration
in choosing a home is the presence of a resident council supported by the staff and administration. The function of such
councils is to ensure that residents are able to share in the tasks
of managing and controlling their lives and the decisions concerning their daily care.

Many families are hesitant to consider institutional care and
postpone the decision until excessive physical and financial strain
forces them to stop providing care to aging relatives. One result
is that most families have little time available for planning, and
the decision becomes just one more component of an over-

whelming series of events. The existing myths about nursing homes, untrue of most homes but true of some, perpetuate fears about placements. These myths include the following (American Health Care Association, undated, a): nursing homes are like hospitals; everyone in a nursing home is senile; there is no privacy in a nursing home; staff of nursing homes are cruel and abusive; nursing home admission is one way only—people never get to go home again; nursing homes smell; residents of nursing homes are neglected; all persons in nursing homes are women; food in homes is terrible; people are tied down and drugged in nursing homes; and families and friends abandon older persons in nursing homes.

Family members do, in fact, visit relatives in nursing homes. Results of recent studies reveal that most visitors are children and grandchildren, most residents (96%) receive visits from families at least monthly, and visits do not drop off after the first year (Brubaker, 1985). Still, the negative perceptions of nursing homes persist, making the transition to long-term care one of the most difficult of life's decisions for older persons and their families (Dye & Richards, 1980).

Emotional Reactions to Institutionalization

Both older persons and their families experience emotional reactions to institutionalization. Both may focus only on what they have lost, not on any potential gains. Unfortunately, negative expectations may become self-fulfilling prophecies. Improvement in the functioning of older persons and relief of family stress seem to be related to attitudes, with the most improvement shown in families having expectations for positive outcomes. Such expectations are more often associated with foster home care than nursing home care (Braun & Rose, 1987). Older persons who seem to make better transitions are those who have achieved ego integrity. Persons with low ego integrity tend to be more fearful of death and more dependent upon external supports to achieve high levels of life satisfaction (Goebel & Boeck, 1987). Such supports may be less available in long-term care environments.

Older persons experience significant losses upon entry into nursing homes, being unable to take with them such meaningful possessions as their homes, most of their furniture and memorabilia, pets, gardens, family members, and so forth. Under the circumstances, feelings of loss of control are common. The effect of institutionalization is so pervasive and common that many authors have described an "institutionalization syndrome." This syndrome includes depression, dispair, fear, passivity, lower life satisfaction, increased mortality, uncooperativeness, lack of social alertness, and preoccupation with death (Supiano, 1980). Older persons in institutional settings quickly develop a sense of learned helplessness. Faced with a major blow to their self-concept, institutionalized persons experience numerous adverse reactions. They may become confused, disoriented, and increasingly preoccupied with their bodily functions and less responsive emotionally. Women in particular may react by feeling rejected and unloved (Dye & Richards, 1980).

Berkowitz (1978) summed up the feelings of many older persons in citing the findings of a Michigan court that " . . .the effect of long-term institutionalization is to strip the individual of the support that permits him (sic) to maintain his (sic) sense of self-worth and the value of his (sic) own physical and mental integrity" (p. 239). Family members can help to alleviate these effects by helping older persons prepare for the transition to a long-term care environment (for example, helping them choose what personal possessions to take along), accompanying them on moving day to lessen the shock and trauma that may ensue, and visiting on a frequent basis to assure the older parent that someone in the family still cares (National Institute on Aging, 1986).

Family members who have been providing care for aging parents may feel a tremendous sense of relief when parents are institutionalized, and a fair amount of guilt as a result. Because the decision was made based on the inability of the family to provide care, and because the health of the older person may have declined prior to institutional care, a frequent occurrence is an improvement in functioning soon after admission to a facility providing 24-hour care. Family members may then be inclined to question whether their decision was too hasty.

In general, family satisfaction with nursing home placements seems to be related to the adjustment of the older relative, satisfaction with the level of care received, information provided by staff of the facility, programs and activities in the facility, and continued family contact with the older person (Hatch & Franken, 1984). At the same time, anger over the need to make the decision, guilt over doing so, and feelings of failure are common reactions. The decision reflects a crisis and may reawaken many unresolved issues concerning family relationships, not just those with the aging parent (Troll, 1982b). Family members who were uninvolved with caregiving may communicate resentment over what has happened, and angry feelings between family members may result.

Implications for Counselors

Given the critical nature of decisions regarding institutionalization, counseling for all family members is a need, one that is too often not met or inadequately met. Assistance with decision making needs to take place long before the situation reaches crisis proportions. Both caregiving and noncaregiving family members should be involved in counseling sessions in addition to the older relatives receiving or needing care. Because institutionalization is a family crisis, if this is the first time a family is seen in counseling, crisis intervention techniques will be useful. Families with dysfunctional patterns of relating may be expected to be at their worst during crisis situations, further complicating the decisions to be made and the emotional implications of various choices.

Counseling interventions are needed to help ease the decision process. Some useful strategies are to help all family members clarify their values (including religious values) regarding caregiving, institutions, and responsibilities of children in regard to their aging parents (Mines, Rockwell, & Hull, 1980). All family members should be encouraged to express their concerns, questions, fears, doubts, and feelings. It may be necessary to schedule individual as well as group counseling sessions to provide the assistance various family members need. Additional suggestions for interventions may be gained through a review of factors associated with caregiving and family responses (see Horne, 1985; Hooyman & Lustbader, 1986; Kenny & Spicer, 1984; Sommers & Shields, 1987).

Although many institutionalized older persons maintain a dream of returning home, such goals often are not realistic and result in further despair when they are not realized. Counselors can help older persons and their families set realistic goals and work toward achieving them. For example, improvements in memory and control over one's environment can be realistic goals, provided that gains are measured in small increments. Allowing older persons to effect even minor changes in their environment such as deciding what to wear, when to open the curtains, or how to solve minor problems can help to restore a sense of independence and control, and thus enhance self-esteem.

Counselors can assist adult children and aging parents in adjusting to institutionalization by encouraging them to express their feelings and focus on the positive nature of the institutionalization decision. Affirming their feelings and fears as normal is important. Many family members will benefit from books, articles, and other resources that provide information about nursing homes and nusing home life. Family members can be encouraged to volunteer their services or otherwise become involved in the life of the home, so that the facility becomes an extension of the family and thus more acceptable to all concerned. When family members can accept that the decision they made was the best they could have made, considering all possible alternatives, the adjustment of all concerned will be made easier.

Strategies for Assessment

Macione (1979) noted the need for a valid, reliable, and sensitive instrument that would measure change over time in functional capacity related to independent living of older persons in the community. Such an instrument would be useful in helping older persons and their families determine when institutionalization is needed and should be considered. She developed the Macione Physical and Mental Competence for Independent Living in the Aged Scale (MACPAMCILAS) to meet this need. The scale assesses activities of daily living, such as eating, transfer (moving independently from bed to wheelchair, etc.), walking, stair climbing, mobility, toileting, dressing, and bathing, and provides both subscale and overall scores in each area. The information this assessment provides can help adult children and health care providers determine the feasibility and appropriateness of institutional care.

Other strategies for helping with the institutionalization decision include the multidimensional functional assessments discussed in chapter 1. Once a person has been institutionalized, continuing assessment of functional abilities is important to determine emotional and physical status and evaluate gains or declines. In addition, the needs of nursing home residents can be assessed and services and programs instituted to meet both physical and psychological needs, such as the need for recreation and involvement (Wilhite & Teaff, 1986).

Elder Abuse

Once family caregiving has begun, decisions to discontinue caregiving or to institutionalize an older person are extremely difficult to make. At the same time, the stress of caregiving may increase continually. When caregivers' efforts to cope are unsuccessful, abuse of aging parents may result. Most, though not all, such instances are unintentional and unrecognized by care providers. They result from an accumulation of stresses, lack of respite care, inadequate support for the caregiver, and lack of access to resources (Hooyman & Lustbader, 1986).

In this section, abuse of older persons by family care providers is discussed. Abuse also occurs in institutional settings and by nonfamily members in community settings for many of the same reasons as it occurs within families. The following discussion includes a review of the definition and incidence of abuse, a profile of typical abused persons and abusers, contributing factors, and suggested interventions, including strategies for assessment.

Definition and Incidence

Several typologies have been proposed to define elder abuse. One of the most widely used incorporates four categories: physical abuse, psychological abuse, material abuse, and violation of rights (Franklin Research Center, 1980). Physical abuse can take the passive form of withholding needed food and medication as well as more active means such as hitting or sexually mistreating an older person. Psychological abuse may include isolation, neglect, and ignoring the older person's needs or pleas, as well as humiliating, threatening, insulting, or otherwise actively demeaning the older person's sense of dignity and worth. Material abuse includes theft or misuse of money or materials. Violation of rights may include attempts to seek adjudication of an older person as incompetent when that is not the case, or eviction from a primary residence and relocation.

It has been estimated that 4%, or one million older persons per year are victims of abuse. Though the frequency of elder abuse is only slightly lower than that of child abuse, one in three cases of child abuse are reported compared to only one in six cases (or fewer) of elder abuse. It is possible that as many as 1 in 10 older persons living with family members are abused (Giordano & Giordano, 1984).

Most studies have found that more than half of all abused older persons experience psychological abuse, including verbal assaults, fear, and isolation. One half also suffer financial abuse and one fourth, physical abuse (Sengstock, Barrett, & Graham, 1984). Moreover, most instances of abuse are recurring rather than isolated instances (Select Committee on Aging, 1981).

A Profile of Abused Older Persons and Their Abusers

Victims of elder abuse are likely to be women, aged 75 or older, White, middle-class, and dependent on an adult child for care and protection (Select Committee on Aging, 1981). The incidence of abuse correlates with an increase in age and disability. The so-called "frail elderly," older persons with physical or emotional limitations, are most likely to be abused. Older persons with organic brain syndromes are especially at risk for abuse by caregivers (Wisniewski & Cohen, 1984).

Because adult women in midlife are the primary caregivers for aging parents, it follows that the typical abuser is an adult female child in midlife who is a caretaker for a dependent aging parent. Again, the abuse may not be intentional, but the result of an overload of caregiving stress combined with a lack of available resources for respite and support.

Factors Contributing to Elder Abuse

Many of the factors contributing to elder abuse are the same factors that contribute to family violence in general. Causes of elder abuse have been identified in one of four major categories: personal characteristics of the abuser and victim, interpersonal factors of the relationship between the abuser and victim, situational factors that increase the likelihood of abuse, and sociocultural factors that are related to the acceptable use of violence (Henton, Cate, & Emory, 1984).

The "cycle of violence" explanation of abuse implies that abuse of aging parents is more likely in families where children learn abusive behaviors as a means of reducing stress. Steinmetz (1979) found that 1 in 400 children reared nonviolently will abuse their parents later in life, whereas 1 in 2 children who were abused are likely to respond similarly to caregiving stress. Older persons who act out in a physically or emotionally violent manner, common in some types of organic brain syndromes, are more likely to be abused, as are older persons with mental health problems (Steinmetz & Amsden, 1983).

Past unresolved conflicts between adult children and aging parents can contribute to abuse (Pillemer, Wolf, & Gwynther, 1987). Such conflicts may involve power struggles (Henton et al., 1984), failure to resolve the filial crisis (Block & Sinnott, 1979), or even a caregiver's concern that sufficient appreciation for caregiving efforts is not shown by the aging parent (Giordano & Giordano, 1984).

Situational factors contributing to abuse include the role conflicts and strains many caregiving adults face in midlife. Disappointment over not being able to pursue a long-postponed career, unemployment, decreased income, or lack of time to engage in educational or leisure pursuits may be expressed as anger at the aging parent. Substance abuse, marital problems, medical complications, or conflicts between adolescent children and older persons can lead to abuse, as can the stress of providing constant care without adequate relief (Bergman, 1981; Pierce & Trotta, 1986).

Sociocultural factors that contribute to abuse include the negative attitudes toward older persons that place them in a position of low status and hence vulnerability. Lowered self-esteem of frail older persons makes them more susceptible to victimization and less capable of self-advocacy. Additional factors that contribute to abuse include geographic separation of families and the trend toward smaller families, both of which place greater strain on the available persons who do provide caregiving assistance.

Implications for Counselors

Myers and Shelton (1987) reviewed the literature on elder abuse and strategies for intervention. They specified the lack of knowledge on the part of caregivers as a primary factor leading to stress. Information caregivers need includes knowledge of the aging process, medical aspects of aging parents' diseases and disabilities, medication management and effects, community resources, and stress reduction techniques. This information could be provided through support groups for caregivers, with the added advantages that such groups can provide. Caregivers could develop peer support, experience an outlet for emotional tension, fears, resentment, and anger, and learn new coping strategies through sharing and modeling.

An added benefit of support groups for abusive caregivers is the opportunity to talk about their actions in a safe, supportive environment. Once assured of confidentiality, they may be more inclined to talk about abuse to strangers than to family members or close friends. Group members and counselors can help abusers understand the reasons for their actions and teach them that many times the abuse was not intentional or malicious but the result of physical exhaustion or ignorance (Hooyman & Lustbader, 1986). Groups can be an important resource for teaching as well as providing a means for expanding the caregiver's support network.

One of the frustrations counselors may experience is the lack of willingness of abused older persons and caregivers to change their circumstances or even to end the abuse. Home care, even abusive care, may be preferable to institutionalization or dependence on nonfamily members. Familiar surroundings often are preferable to a change of environment. If the adult child has moved into the home of the aging parent, this may be an even more significant factor. Aging parents can feel trapped—not wanting the abuse to continue but seeing no other viable options for remaining in their own homes and receiving needed assistance with daily living.

Caregivers, in turn, may feel a strong sense of commitment in taking care of aging parents. They may feel that they "owe" their parents for earlier care received, and at the same time perceive that this is their last chance to make up for any past transgressions in dealing with their parents. In anticipation of a parent's death, caregiving can become a last-resort option to tackle *or* to avoid unfinished business. As a result, adult children also can become trapped, feeling that they *must* care for aging parents as no other viable options exist.

Sometimes an adult child terminates employment in order to care for an aging parent. The adult child may or may not have enjoyed working, and may or may not have used the aging parent as an excuse to quit working. At other times, an unemployed adult child may move in with an aging parent who needs assistance. It is important to assess the potential independence and both emotional and financial needs of these caregivers. Although caregivers may resent their duties, or may be abusive, the experience of caregiving and its secondary gains—room, board, etc.—are chosen to meet certain of the caregiver's needs. These caregivers are perhaps least likely to seek counseling assistance through support groups.

In addition to caregiver support groups, support groups for abused aging parents, or even aging parents in care-receiving situations, could be implemented. There are few (if any) articles in the professional literature suggesting such groups. To some extent, many aging parents contribute to abusive situations through abrasive, demanding, hostile, or other unpleasant behaviors. Through support groups they could be provided an opportunity to discuss their fears and feelings of vulnerability that often lead to these negative behaviors.

Individual counseling with aging parents or adult children can help each express concerns and emotions affecting their relationships. Family interventions also can be helpful, especially if non-care providing relatives can be included. Family members could be encouraged to provide needed respite care, explore other options for caregiving, and work through feelings of resentment or anger between those who provide care and those who do not. Bibliotherapy, discussed in chapter 5, could be used to encourage family members to learn more about aging parents, caregiving stress, community resources, and options for caregiving. Of course, any number of unfinished business issues can change the focus of therapy from relationships with and about adult children and aging parents to relationships between adult children.

Counselors and other helping professionals need to know when and how to intervene, because abuse of any kind is a sensitive and potentially volatile issue. Too much too soon can cause abusive caregivers to become defensive and withdraw, and also may result in retribution against and further abuse of the aging parent. Abusive caregivers may be at once unaware of their actions or so closed, resistant, or suspicious that they are unable to admit to any type of abuse. In rare instances, the abuse may be carefully planned to achieve certain ends, such as control of financial resources. To expect an open admission of abuse under these circumstances would be futile. In these cases, outside intervention through legal means may be advisable or necessary. When the abuse is physical it may be more easily documented, despite the aging parent's refusal to admit that there is a problem. Financial abuse, neglect, or violation of rights may be much more difficult, if not impossible, to assess or prove. Abusive caregivers may be reluctant to participate in support groups or other counseling for fear of legal reprisals. Assurances of confidentiality may be helpful in their decision to participate; however, counselors must be aware of elder abuse laws in their state and requirements for mandatory reporting of abuse before undertaking caregiver support groups.

At some point in counseling, the question of whether caregiving should be continued undoubtedly will arise. In fact, this question will arise repeatedly. One of the options for finding answers lies in accurate assessment of the needs of adult children and aging parents, along with an awareness of available community resources.

Strategies for Assessment

Hooyman and Lustbader (1986) noted that "... professionals encountering abuse within families need to recognize that they can easily make the situation worse if they cannot offer better alternatives. . . .To be beneficial, interventions must be preceded by a careful attempt to understand why the abuse is occurring, why it is tolerated, and what alternatives can be provided" (pp. 102–103). Counselors should convey an attitude of helpfulness and a desire to improve care, rather than appearing confrontational and on a fact-finding hunt when talking with aging parents and caregivers suspected of abuse. It is important to assess the long-term nature of family relationships, the familial history of abuse and violence, and acceptable means within the family for coping with stress.

Because family circumstances unrelated to caregiving may affect perceived levels of stress and caregivers' reactions, counselors should be prepared to assess current life problems and counseling needs of caregivers and other family members. It is also important to assess changes in the family since the onset of caregiving, changes in the older person that necessitated caregiving, and changes in all family members' needs since caregiving was initiated.

The Hwalek-Sengstock Elder Abuse Screening Protocol (Hwalek & Sengstock, 1986) is perhaps the only available instrument to screen families for possible elder abuse. It includes seven categories of items: physical abuse, physical neglect, psychological abuse, psychological neglect, material abuse, violation of personal rights, and risk indicators. The last category of items do not assess abuse directly but are predictive of the presence or absence of abuse.

Death and Dying

Death is a universal fact of life and has been described as the final stage of growth (Kübler-Ross, 1975). For persons in midlife, death may be a remote and seldom considered possibility—until the inevitable changes of the midlife period confront persons with their own mortality. These changes, which combine to create an awareness that life is finite, include a shift in time perspective from time since birth to time remaining before death (Neugarten, 1968), physiological changes and the awareness of physiological declines, and the death of parents.

For older persons, death is a certainty that can no longer be totally ignored. The nearness of death functions as a stimulus to the process of life review and the search for ego integrity. For adult children, a central task of midlife is to adjust to the changes that signify the inevitability of death. For many this is a difficult task, and avoidance of death issues is a more comfortable stance. Thus, whereas older persons need and want to talk about death and dying, adult children find it difficult and even offensive to discuss these issues with their parents. In reviewing the literature, it is clear that the death concerns of older persons and their adult children are seldom studied at the same time, but rather treated as distinct concerns.

To be most effective in helping adult children and aging parents to cope with death and dying, counselors must be aware of general perspectives on these issues and of areas of concern to members of each generation. In this section, psychosocial aspects of death and dying are reviewed as they affect persons of any age, particularly older persons. Bereavement, mourning, and grief are discussed in general and in terms of specific concerns for aging parents and their adult children. Special concerns of adult children when aging parents die are considered, followed by implications for counselors and some strategies for assessment in relation to death, dying, and grieving.

Psychosocial Aspects of Death and Dying

Psychosocial aspects of death and dying may be summarized and discussed in terms of talking about death, death fears and correlates, dynamics of the dying process, and attitudes toward death (Wass & Myers, 1982). In this section, these aspects are reviewed as they apply to death and dying in general. The objective is to provide an overview of information that may be useful to counselors working with either adult children or aging parents. Considering that 80% of persons who die in any one year are age 65 or older (Butler, 1980), the following information may be most useful in understanding the needs and concerns of older persons.

Talking About Death

It is clear from the available literature that adult children find it difficult to discuss death with their aging parents (Wass & Myers, 1984). The reasons given for avoiding talking about death include fears that it would upset the older person and considering such discussions morbid. Thus, family members operate in a conspiracy of silence that can have negative consequences. Older persons may become extremely ill or incompetent and thus unable to assist in making important decisions and plans, or they may be denied the right to maintain control over their lives to the extent possible by being excluded from participating even in making their own funeral arrangements.

Some older persons might want to express feelings about prolonging life through artificial means if only family members would listen. Preparing wills and making arrangements for what will transpire after death can help an older person achieve a sense of peace and readiness, a sense that can be denied aging parents in the absence of family support. The myriad concerns that follow a death may be made easier for survivors who have assisted in planning the affairs of aging relatives.

It seems that health care personnel also avoid dying persons (Bowers, Jackson, Knight, & LeShan, 1975). Visits to those who are terminally ill, whether living at home or in institutional settings, decrease as death nears. Thus, older persons are deprived of the support necessary to help them cope with one of life's most universal and significant transitions. Interestingly, numerous studies have led to the conclusion that older persons think about and talk readily about death (Wass, 1977). Although they often are unable to discuss their concerns with relatives, and though they obtain little support from interpersonal interactions, both terminally ill and healthy older persons may welcome the opportunity to talk about and prepare for dying and death (Wass & Myers, 1982).

Death Fears and Anxieties

Butler and Lewis (1982) noted that the fear of death is a part of human experience, yet older persons fear death less than younger persons and are more concerned with the death of loved ones than their own death. May (1958) provided a definition of existential anxiety as "an individual's becoming aware that his (sic) existence can become destroyed" (p. 50). It seems to be a normal process of development, then, for older persons to become aware of the finiteness of existence. By implication, those who deny this awareness may be more inclined to experience feelings of anxiety about death.

Wass and Myers (1982) reviewed studies of death fear and anxiety and concluded that the research on correlates of death fears is as yet inconclusive. Most researchers have found that younger persons experience greater death anxiety than do older persons. In some studies women have evidenced greater anxieties than men, whereas in others differences have been insignificant. Black older persons seem to have a greater death concern than White older persons. Higher levels of death fear have been associated with older persons in poor health, whereas older persons living in the community—who tend to be healthier—have reported lower death concerns. Comparisons of religious beliefs with death concerns have produced conflicting results, though many authors maintain that strong religious or philosophical convictions facilitate acceptance of death and thus lower death fears (Butler & Lewis, 1982; Johnson, 1987).

Kübler-Ross (1969) noted that fears of death revolve around the concern that one will die before one is finished living, or with unfinished business. Older persons may fear being helpless or dependent, taking a long time to die, or making loved ones unhappy (Stricherz & Cunnington, 1982). Particularly when a terminal illness is present, older persons may even want to die (Kastenbaum, 1971).

The Dying Process

More than half of all deaths occur in institutional settings, yet four out of five persons would prefer to die at home (Hine, 1979–80). Within these settings, the emphasis is on physical rather than emotional concerns. Hence, the dying process is made more difficult (Butler & Lewis, 1982).

The psychological process associated with dying was identified by Kübler-Ross (1969) as a stepwise progression through five stages. These include denial, anger, bargaining, depression, and acceptance. Of course, this process is not simple, nor is it linear. The five stages may occur in or out of sequence, and progress through some may be circular rather than linear. Despite criticisms and alternate models, the stages Kübler-Ross proposed maintain their validity and offer a useful framework for understanding psychological reactions to terminal illness and the dying process.

Denial in this process is a healthy means of coping. An inititial state of numbness allows the individual and family members time to assimilate the news of impending death. Anger over the ultimate loss, the loss of one's life, is another normal response that allows the dying person to mobilize his or her resources to fight. Unfortunately, anger is often expressed at the nearest and most convenient sources: medical personnel and family members. Eventually, anger at God may result. Bargaining may be attempted with God or with medical personnel.

Depression ensues when the dying person realizes that bargaining will not work. Expressions of depression may range from total hopelessness to extreme apathy to angry withdrawal, any of which may alienate friends and helpers. Support can faciliate progress through the stage of depression and assist dying persons to accept the inevitability of their future. The stage of acceptance, although providing a comforting sense of peace to the dying individual, may be disconcerting for loved ones (Johnson, 1987).

Attitudes Toward Death

Wass and Myers (1982) noted that "some old people may not experience a great deal of fear about death but no one has a neutral attitude toward it" (p. 133). Older persons cannot avoid confronting their personal death, though younger persons often manage to do so. Younger people tend to have negative attitudes toward death and consider it inconceivable that anyone could have a positive attitude. In general, death remains a taboo subject that many in our society actively avoid thinking about or discussing. Ethical issues surrounding right to life, prolonging medical treatment for the terminally ill, and euthanasia evoke highly emotional responses in many. When these issues are personalized, attitudes and values make necessary choices difficult at best.

Bereavement, Mourning, and Grief

Bereavement refers to a loss through death and is a survivorship status. Mourning refers to culturally accepted behaviors to express responses to death. Grief refers to a survivor's state of distress (Kastenbaum & Costa, 1977). This section focuses on the process and emotional reactions associated with grief and aspects of the grieving process that may differ for adult children and aging parents.

Bereaved persons are expected to grieve; however, social limitations are placed on the length of acceptable expressions of sadness and loss. A number of grief reactions have been identified, including both normal and pathological grief and anticipatory grief.

Lindemann (1944) described a typical pattern of grief that exists regardless of age. This pattern is similar to the stages postulated by Kübler-Ross to explain the dying process. An initial stage of shock, numbness, and denial is followed, usually within 2 weeks, by a stage of awareness. At this time a plethora of emotional reactions may occur, including sadness, guilt, hopelessness, and helplessness. These are accompanied by somatic responses (sleep disturbances, sighing respiration, lack of strength, exhaustion, loss of appetite), cognitive reactions (difficulty sleeping or concentrating), and affective components (anger, crying, hostility, resentment, agitation, identification with the lost person).

The duration and intensity of these reactions depend on many factors, such as the suddenness of the loss, preparation for the loss, and significance to the bereaved person of the one who died. Although Lindemann (1944) indicated that normal grief lasts only 8 to 10 weeks, contemporary researchers have suggested that it may last 1 to 2 years (Glick, Weiss, & Parkes, 1974; Lynch, 1977). Some authors have questioned whether a significant loss can ever fully be resolved (Raphael, 1983; Worden, 1982). Myers (1986) noted that bereavement is in some ways the cost of emotional commitment. Although everyone grieves, the process is self-limiting and usually resolves itself without outside intervention.

Abnormal or pathological grief is a distortion of the grief process in terms of intensity as well as length. Severe grief reactions lasting beyond 8 to 10 weeks typically have been considered abnormal. Symptoms would include general ill health, psychosomatic, psychiatric, and psychosocial disorders, depression, altered relationships, anniversary reactions, increased vulnerability to stress, and death (Raphael, 1983). A significant number of widowed persons die within one year of bereavement (Williams & Polak, 1979), perhaps because grief serves as a bridge or mediating response between the loss of a spouse and subsequent death (Jacobs & Douglas, 1979). Persons seeking help for pathological grief reactions have been found to have "significantly more intense and frequent stress-specific symptoms, such as intrusive thoughts and feelings, as well as more anxiety and depression" (Horowitz et al., 1984, p. 383). They also tend to be women rather than men and single more often than married.

Anticipatory grief refers to participation in the grieving process prior to the time of bereavement or actual loss (Rando, 1986). It typically occurs following the diagnosis of a terminal illness and also occurs with the aging and expected death of parents. The period of anticipatory grief permits persons to work through unfinished business and offers the potential for more rapid and successful recovery after a loss. However, no matter how well prepared one may be, the death of someone close is always a shock for which we are never quite prepared (Myers, 1986).

There is some evidence that grief reactions differ for older and younger persons. Raphael (1983) suggested that the grief of older persons is more diffuse and pervasive, and that agitation, irritability, depression, and hallucinatory experiences are more common. Gallagher and Thompson (1982) stated that the death of a spouse is the singular most stressful event in the life of an older person. Old persons lose family members and friends, among other losses, and may become chronic grievers, a state which for them is normal and not pathological (Wass & Myers, 1984). High socioeconomic status and strong social supports correlate with adjustment of older persons to losses (Glick, Weiss, & Parkes, 1974).

Johnson (1987) discussed stages of emotional responses that adult children and other family members experience in reaction to the loss of aging parents. The first stage involves learning about the illness or sickness, while maintaining an emotional aloofness to keep the reality of death "out-of-reach" (p. 96). The second stage involves recognition of one's feelings and the experience of the full emotional effect of the loss. Depression soon follows the common emotional responses of frustration and guilt, and eventually one finds hope when the depression begins to lift. The final stage, compassion, provides strength and determination to allow family members to cope effectively with their loss.

When Aging Parents Die

Five percent of the U.S. population loses a parent within any given year—about 12 million persons per year. According to Myers (1986), the loss of a parent is the single most common form of bereavement in our culture. At the same time, the prevalent attitude is one of diminishing or denying the importance of emotions following parental loss. Despite a societal tendency to deny the significance of all deaths, the loss of parents seems to be:

> . . .even more thoroughly neglected than other losses . . . .
> It's not as if people purposefully neglect your grief for
> your parent. Rather, they just don't consider it to be
> significant. The unstated message is that when a parent
> is middle-aged or elderly, the death is somehow less of
> a loss than other losses. The message is that grief for a
> dead parent isn't entirely appropriate. (Myers, 1986,
> p. 5)

Adult children facing the tasks of grief and mourning after parents die may be expected to experience the "normal" responses to loss described above. In addition, there are certain qualities or characteristics related to the loss of parents that are unique and thus engender unique grief responses. At the same time, societal expectations to minimize expressions of loss—

after all, aging parents have lived a full life, so who can begrudge an *on-time* death?—can create conflicts during what is actually a time of extreme vulnerability.

Myers (1986) researched the topic of parental loss in depth and summarized his findings in the book *When Parents Die: A Guide for Adults*. One of his most important findings was that there are significant patterns to what adults experience following the death of a parent. These include overwhelming feelings of loss, vulnerability, and grief that can "strip off decades of confidence and competence in a few seconds" (p. 2). One possible explanation is that loss of parents signifies, for many adults, the loss of the only source of unconditional love in their lives. Even when relationships with parents are conflicted, the fact remains that those relationships have existed for many years—for virtually all of the adult child's life. And, the effect of parental bonds continues beyond the time of death (Moss & Moss, 1983).

Though the loss of either parent is significant, the loss of the second parent takes on added meaning. Adults report feeling orphaned and yet not understanding how the feelings of loss can be so strong, especially when their support system includes a spouse and children. The death of parents removes a buffer between adult children and the world in general, including their own aging and eventual death. Adult children become the older generation, the aging parents; whatever family roles their own parents filled now become theirs by right of accession. The confrontation with personal mortality and the existential concern for the meaning of life can be troublesome and frightening.

It is known that as persons grow older they become more like themselves and less like other persons. Thus, the population of midlife and especially older persons is extremely heterogeneous. Not surprisingly, reactions to parental loss are extremely variable. The loss can be both regretted and accepted at the same time, and both feelings may last as long as one lives.

Guilt is one of the more common emotional reactions. Raphael (1983) noted that the prevalence of guilt is related to the imperfection of human relationships. Kushner (1981) suggested that guilt arises from our need to make sense of the world and to find a cause and effect for every occurrence. Furthermore, in times of stress we revert to childhood patterns of omnipotence in an attempt to explain what is happening. The loss of a parent heightens adult children's awareness of the innumerable instances of nurturance and care received over their lifetime. At the same time, feelings of guilt arise over possibly (or actually) not having expressed enough appreciation or done enough in return.

It is helpful to remember that there will *always* be more, or different, things that an adult child could have said or done while an aging parent was alive. The mere fact of the loss is a stimulus to such feelings, without the complication of the reality that things *could* have been different. During the grieving process it can be difficult to remember that one can never repay parents for their influence, care, or effect on one's life. Therefore energy invested in "keeping score" can be destructive, or at least emotionally draining. Even taking care of parents for the same number of years they raised a child can never equal the circumstances of a child nurtured, raised, molded, or abused from birth to adulthood through parental actions and influence.

There is some indication that grief reactions differ for men and women, and also differ in relation to the loss of a mother or a father. The death of a father functions as a mortality shock for sons, partly because fathers are such strong role models for the development of male children. The death of a mother seems to be more difficult for both sons and daughters because mothers have been the primary source of nurturance and support (Myers, 1986).

The type of relationship between adult children and aging parents is an important determinant of the nature of the grief response. Circumstances that affect reactions include the cause of death and the manner in which the survivor learns about the death. Suicides and homicides are more difficult to accept. Sudden deaths leave a sense of uncertainty and unreality, and the need to come to terms with unknown or shocking circumstances.

On the other hand, some adult children experience parental death as an event with limited emotional significance. These persons seem to share one of the following circumstances: " . . . (a) advanced age of the parent, (b) institutionalization of the parent, (c) loss of functioning of the parent, (d) substantial disengagement from social interaction with the parent, and (e) same sex of surviving child and deceased parent (Owen, Fulton, & Markusen, 1982, p. 215). Myers (1986) summarized the polarities of responses when he noted that "sudden death hits like an explosion, knocking you flat, [while] . . . slow decline arrives more like a glacier, massive and unstoppable, grinding you down" (p. 83).

Whatever the cause of death, the aftermath of the death of the second parent brings siblings together to settle an estate. The process of settling an estate can create tensions and resentments among siblings and prolong the grieving process for each. Myers (1986) estimated that only about half of all families settle estates amicably. Families with dysfunctional patterns of relating may be expected to experience serious disruptions during the time an estate is being settled, particularly if one of the siblings is named as executrix or executor. The appointment of an heir to this position is actually a conflict of interest.

The relationships of family members to one another are altered by the death of parents. The outcome can be positive, and the experience of shared grieving can be a time for growth for all concerned.

Implications for Counselors

Both adult children and aging parents can benefit from counseling in relation to the many issues surrounding death and dying. The involvement of counselors may be with members of either generation separately or together. The information provided above can serve as a starting point for counseling involvement; however, the issues each family and situation presents may be expected to vary tremendously. Hence, the role of the counselor needs to remain open and flexible to facilitate responses to the varying needs of family members.

Because family members sometimes have difficulty talking about death whereas older persons experience a need to do so, counselors can encourage discussion of this topic. It is necessary first to determine *who* is uncomfortable with the subject. Older persons who are nearing death can be given the opportunity to discuss their anticipations and fears, hopes, and plans for funerals as well as estates. Adult children who are able, through counseling, to discuss the death of parents with them will be better able to assist their parents in adjusting to death as well as in planning the necessary arrangements. In the absence of prior discussion, post-death actions may occur that are at once contrary to the wishes of the parent and destructive of family ties for survivors.

Older persons who are terminally ill or otherwise close to death may be experiencing any of the stages Kübler-Ross (1969) identified. Counselors can assist adult children in understanding the dying process and help them find ways to assist their parents in dealing with this final challenge. It is important to help persons who have lived a life of independence to continue to feel a sense of control at the end of their lives. Taking the time to discuss their fears, anxieties, needs, wishes, concerns, and desires can be an important means of helping aging parents to reach the final stage of acceptance.

Although counselors can facilitate this process, the involvement and active participation of adult children can be helpful to all family members. Rather than being bound by "deathbed" wishes, adult children can become aware of parental desires and have the time to work through any that seem unreasonable or difficult to accomplish. When all the adult children are involved, the parents' wishes are more likely to be implemented than if only one hears and interprets parental desires. The latter situation is more likely to lead to disrupted family relationships than one in which communication is open and reciprocal.

Because adult children also experience a series of stages of acceptance when the death of parents is imminent, the availability of counseling also can assist them in recognizing and working through their emotional reactions. Understanding that their feelings are normal and that other persons have had similar experiences can be helpful. At the same time, aging parents can assist their children in working through the stages of anticipatory grief, if they understand the grieving process.

Counselors can assist all family members in preparing for death and anticipating and responding to emotional reactions. Providing a safe climate for exploring and clarifying family roles and role expectations is important. Techniques such as life review can help older persons prepare for and accept the reality of death. This technique can be used with families to review a lifetime of shared experiences. It can be used with adult children to assist them in identifying past coping methods so these can be mobilized to deal with reactions to the death of parents. Counselors can help all family members, but especially older persons, recognize the importance of death as the final stage of growth.

Regardless of the circumstances, coming to terms with the death of a parent requires accepting that unfinished business always will remain unfinished. Counselors can assist survivors

in coping with their losses, working through the stages of grieving, and reaching the stage of acceptance. A reminder that
acceptance is not the same as an end of sad feelings over their
loss can be helpful. Some persons may benefit from planning
activities to assist the grieving process during significant anniversary dates and events.

Wrenn (1979) reviewed a number of strategies counselors
can employ to provide caring responses to persons who are
dying or grieving. He stressed the importance of the counselor's
building a positive view of death and a belief that life after
death is joyous. (Of course, the belief in an afterlife is an artifact
of certain religious beliefs and not a universally held assumption.) Taking the time to visit with persons who are dying or
grieving and to ask questions that facilitate discussion of the
concerns they have and feelings they are experiencing can be
helpful. He emphasized that caring means listening, and sometimes just being there so the person will not be alone. Just as
there are no set patterns for grieving, there are no set patterns
for grief counseling. Rather, caring, sharing, touching, and encouraging grieving persons to express their feelings, in their
own way and in their own time, is what is important. After a
loss, it can be helpful to allow time for the grieving person to
talk about their parent and review the good times as well as any
bad times. Catharsis is an essential part of healthy grieving and
acceptance of losses.

Williams and Polack (1979) stressed the fact that grief is
always a crisis. It is the result of a significant loss and begins
with a sense of dismay and unreality. Horowitz (1985) concluded that the death of parents is a serious life event that leads
to measurable symptomatic distress. Grieving persons may in
fact be suffering from a diagnosable adjustment reaction.

When parents die, the nature of the grief process is determined in part by the meaning the parent held for the survivors. One function of counselors is to assist adult children in
exploring that meaning. Encouraging them to talk about parents, review their relationships, and express concerns about
unfinished business, guilt, frustration, and any other emotional
reactions will be useful.

When counselors are involved during the dying process,
they may be expected to share the survivors' sense of loss and
also to grieve. They may need time and assistance to work
through their own feelings and reactions, both in terms of the
specific loss and in terms of their job that engenders such vul-

nerability. Therefore, support networks for counselors, especially those working with terminally ill and dying persons, are important.

Counselors also may be called upon to work with survivors. The tasks involved in probate and settling of estates, as mentioned earlier, may be made easier with advance planning. Talking to parents about their desires for funeral arrangements or their financial circumstances can be difficult for adult children. Parents themselves may resist such discussions. One technique for facilitating discussions is a checklist of preparedness developed by Pathfinders, a counseling and planning service agency in New York (Subak-Sharpe & MacLean, 1988). Other techniques as well as information about community agencies to assist adult children and aging parents is available from Children of Aging Parents (CAPS), a nationwide referral agency (2761 Trenton Rd., Levittown, PA 19056).

A final technique that can be helpful to families as well as counselors, reviewed in chapter 5, is bibliotherapy. Asking adult children and aging parents to read and discuss their reactions to various books can be helpful. Suggested books to facilitate talking about death, dying, and grieving would be *Freddie the Leaf* (Buscaglia, 1982), *A Death in the Family* (Agee, 1967), *The Precious Present* (Johnson, 1984), and *The Giving Tree* (Silverstein, 1961).

Strategies for Assessment

Wass and Forfar (1982) reviewed instruments for assessing attitudes toward death and dying. These included the Lester Fear of Death Scale (Lester, 1966), the Templer Death Anxiety Scale (Templer, 1970), the Dickstein Death Concern Scale (Dickstein, 1972), and the Hoelter Multidimensional Fear of Death Scale (Hoelter, 1979), among others. Two additional instruments dealing with life and death issues they reviewed were The Threat Index (Krieger, Epting, & Leitner, 1974), which measures the degree to which a person is threatened with death, and The Purpose in Life Test (Crumbaugh & Maholick, 1969), which examines existential concepts of purpose and meaning in life. These authors stressed the need for a comprehensive, individualized assessment including physical as well as psychological components.

Each of the instruments mentioned above can be used with adult children or aging parents, individually or in groups. These instruments can assist in the identification and discussion of death fears and anxieties, acceptance of death, and evaluation of purpose in life. Projective techniques, such as the Thematic Apperception Test, also may be used. Scoring would involve analysis of death-related themes and responses.

Summary

In this chapter, four major family stress situations were examined. These included caregiving, institutionalization, elder abuse, and death and dying. Caring for an impaired older person can have both positive and negative implications. On the positive side, adult children can express feelings of affection, nurturance, love, appreciation, and filial maturity through caregiving. When excessive demands are placed on caregivers, however, stress and burdens result. Multiple role conflicts and lack of respite care contribute to stress, which in extreme situations may lead to to elder abuse. Once begun, the caregiving commitment tends to continue, often beyond the time when an institutionalization decision might have been made. Such decisions are among the most difficult that families have to face.

Concerns related to death and dying arise for aging parents as well as adult children. Grief reactions may occur in anticipation as well as in reaction to major losses. Adult children can assist aging parents in dealing with their concerns about death through open communication and willingness to talk about death concerns and issues.

Implications for counselors in each of the four areas reviewed were explored, with emphasis on the need to provide opportunities for counseling for both adult children and their aging parents, separately as well as in family therapy situations. Strategies for assessment and available instruments for use with adult children and aging parents also were discussed for each stress situation.

CHAPTER V

COUNSELING ADULT CHILDREN AND AGING PARENTS

A number of important issues counselors may encounter in working with adult children and aging parents were addressed in the first four chapters of this book. For each of these issues, some implications for counselors were raised and strategies for assessment were discussed. In this chapter, a few additional considerations for counselors are reviewed that may be of help in working with adult children and aging parents. The focus of the chapter is on *building and maintaining healthy and positive relationships* for members of each generation. Some ideas for encouraging intergenerational communication and improving relationships are reviewed in the first section.

A brief overview of family counseling and assessment is provided, as applied to work with families with aging parents. Several selected counseling methods that can be used with adult children and aging parents, separately or collectively, are described. These include bibliotherapy, life review therapy, genograms, and early recollections. Community resources to assist in meeting the needs of both adult children and their aging parents are discussed. The chapter concludes with some final comments on relationship building between adult children and their aging parents.

Building and Maintaining Healthy Relationships Between Adult Children and Aging Parents

Ideally, a lifetime of relating can result in healthy, positive, and satisfying relationships between adult children and aging parents. Many people are able to approximate and enjoy this type of relationship as parents grow older. Other adults are able to enjoy happy relationships as long as parents remain relatively healthy and independent. The other end of the spectrum includes adult children who *never* really had satisfying relationships with their parents during childhood and are unable to enjoy healthy relationships later in life. Counselors working with adult children will encounter relationships of both types and anywhere in between as well.

Aging parents, on the other hand, may have both satisfying and not-so-satisfying relationships with their adult children. It is predictable that the intensity and quality of relationships with each child in the family will be different. It is also reasonable to assume that aging parents, having done what they considered to be their best (at the time and with their existing resources) at the task of child rearing, still will have their regrets and ideas on things they could have done differently. In the search for ego integrity, a desire to right previous wrongs may result. At the same time, adult children may be unwilling to admit or may not be open to realizing that their parents have "changed." Trapped in typical patterns of relating, adult children may miss important opportunities for developing closer, more intimate relationships with their aging parents, relationships that both adult children and their parents increasingly may desire but not know how to promote in the later years. Stated another way, everyone may *want* to change, but no one knows quite *how* to change.

An example of this phenomenon that occurred with one aging parent may help to clarify this point. In one particular dysfunctional family, the norm for relating was to deny or negate feelings, especially negative ones, with some spillover that prevented the open, appropriate expression of *any* feelings, including positive ones. Physical contact and terms of endearment were few. The adult daughter, while visiting her widowed mother, was distressed to see many visible "signs of aging" that had not been evident on previous visits. While her mother napped, the daughter assembled a kitchen cart that the two had purchased and placed some dishes on it she thought her mother would prefer, as a surprise. Indeed it was a surprise! When her mother saw the cart, she was overwhelmed with emotion and reached out for her daughter in tears, exclaiming that no one ever did such nice things for her. The daughter, unused to such emotional displays from her mother, withdrew and minimized the feelings, reacting exactly as she had been taught to do. She missed the opportunity for intimacy and the joy of receiving a hug denoting a genuine feeling of appreciation and caring from her mother. The mother was denied acceptance and comfort for her expression of love, and the opportunity to receive a hug and love in return.

In fact, as may other examples could show, recognizing the aging and increasing vulnerability of parents is a painful realization that adult children consciously or unconsciously try to avoid. This avoidance comes out in many ways: refusing to discuss wills and funeral arrangements or other "morbid" subjects, becoming impatient or angry with a parent's hesitation or failing memory, refusing to accept a parent's needs for assistance, or blaming any complaint or change in behavior or affect on "aging," rather than trying to understand what that change may imply. Mom or Dad does not suddenly become "a cranky old person." There is always some precipitating factor or combination of factors—retirement, declining health, loss of a sense of worth—that, if understood, can suggest a path to more positive behaviors. Some adult children overreact to signs of aging in their parents and become more protective than is warranted. Many aging parents complain, jokingly, but with a hint of seriousness, that their adult children try to "parent" them entirely too much.

Regardless of the types of relationships adult children have experienced with aging parents throughout their lives, the circumstances of later life can evoke crises. As explained by Chinese symbolism, crises entail both danger and opportunity. The danger for adult children and aging parents lies in uncontrolled expressions of negative emotions, and failure to use the later years to develop and enhance close relationships. The opportunities, on the other hand, are almost unlimited in terms of developing satisfying and mutually supportive relationships. Even, and especially *before* crises occur, family members can prepare themselves to react in healthy ways. Families with a strong foundation of caring and mutual support will be better prepared to cope with the crises of aging. So, prevention is an important strategy for coping.

Even more important, however, is the knowledge that all human relationships can be improved and that the process of doing so is continual. Adult children and aging parents whose relationships are unsatisfactory in important ways can be helped to develop better relationships. And, even *good* relationships between adult children and aging parents can get better.

Some ways in which counselors can help adult children and aging parents develop better relationships are discussed in this section. These include taking the time and effort to develop an understanding of each other's needs, analyzing mutual support networks to determine who, and who *else*, is available to provided needed care, focusing on helping children and their parents recognize conflicts and set limits, learning how to become friends and remain friends, and learning how to recognize and adjust attitudes that hinder the development and maintenance of healthy, positive relationships when parents grow old.

Understanding Each Other

Adult children and aging parents face similar as well as distinct developmental challenges and life transitions. One way counselors can assist each generation in understanding the other is to develop an awareness of developmental issues and life transitions. Once adult children and aging parents are able to understand and empathize with one another, the next step can be to help each other respond to the various issues and transitions.

For example, knowing that a central task of later life is to achieve ego integrity, family members can concentrate on ways to help older parents review their lives. Through careful listening and sharing of memories, as discussed later in this chapter, older persons can be helped to achieve a sense of integrity. At the same time, family members can benefit from a rich store of family history that is not available from other sources.

On the other hand, aging parents can be helped to understand (or even remember) the task of generativity that faces persons in midlife, or the developmental challenges that accompany the midlife reevaluation period. Parents, too, can learn to listen, encourage, and assist adult children in coping successfully with the tasks and transitions of midlife.

Another way to help adult children and aging parents better understand one another's needs is through focusing on life arenas and tasks within each arena. Johnson (1987) discussed issues for adult children and aging parents related to career, leisure, intimacy, family, inner life, and spiritual arenas. Everyone functions simultaneously in each life arena, though the salient concerns at various times of life may be different. The concept of life arenas offers a structure for examining and clarifying values, expectations, and role conflicts and demands at any particular point in life.

What is needed, of course, is assistance to adult children and aging parents in developing empathic listening skills. Rather than telling each other what is best to do, members of both generations can concentrate on listening and trying to understand from the other's frame of reference. It may be that simply trying to understand, learning to be nonjudgmental, and communicating that one is trying will help to improve relationships. Setting aside a lifetime of role expectations and demands can be difficult, but the rewards are well worth the effort.

If either adult children or aging parents take the responsibility for changing their own behavior and typical modes of interacting or reacting to the other, positive changes may be anticipated. It is desirable but not necessary that *both* sides work on becoming more empathic and caring. In fact, it is often the case that adult children must initiate change if positive relationships are to result. What is important is to break the cycle of actions or statements and responses. By making an effort, often seemingly an impossible one, to break the typical cycle of interaction, new and more positive patterns of relating may be established. Of course, those who try to change may find themselves frustrated in the beginning, but eventually changed relationships will provide the rewards and incentives to keep trying. It is important in this process that adult children be willing to accept small, incremental changes over time.

In families where open expression of positive emotions was discouraged, for example, adult children can be encouraged to end each visit or conversation with an aging parent with a hug and and "I love you." At first aging parents may react with surprise, or not at all, and without reciprocation. However, repeated demonstrations of affection eventually may lead to some pleasant surprises for all concerned. Aging parents who initiate such changes also must be prepared for an initial reaction of surprise. It may be helpful for adult children as well as aging parents, if they are the initiators of this process, to remember an old adage attributed to Kierkegaard: Just because the message was not received doesn't mean it wasn't worth sending.

Analyzing Support Networks

A helpful exercise for persons at any time in life is to analyze their support networks. For persons with strong support systems, this can be a strength-bombardment type of activity. For those with limited support systems, including older persons who have lost important supports and have not yet found replacements, this exercise can be painful. The focus needs to be on identifying strengths as well as weak areas, and developing strategies for filling in existing gaps.

Several different techniques for analyzing support systems have been developed (e.g., Salmon, 1981; Waters, Weaver, & White, 1980). Most of these involve listing supports and defining whether they are strong, weak, or conflicted in nature. Both formal (agency or institutional) and informal (family, friends, and neighbors) supports should be included. Hobbies, daily passtimes such as walking or watching television, and other activities that are sources of support should also be detailed. Favorite pets and favorite places or objects, such as a family home or mementos, are important to many older persons and also should be included. The goal is to identify all of the people, activities, places, and things that make people feel good and provide help to them when needed.

When supports are missing or conflicted, counselors can assist adult children and aging parents in developing new supports as well as resolving existing conflicts when possible. By discussing their support systems together, adult children and aging parents can develop a greater understanding of one another. Making assumptions ahead of time that one knows all about the other can lead to some surprises for everyone involved.

Recognizing Conflicts, Setting Limits

Johnson (1987) suggested that adult children have a difficult time saying "no" to their parents because of a fear that something awful might happen. It is hard to say no to the needs of aging parents when adult children remember how much nurturing and care parents once provided to them. The care came when the children were small and vulnerable, and for many the nurturance and assistance of parents continued throughout the adult years during their times of need. It is difficult to sort out what, if anything, is "owed" to parents for care that they willingly provided when needed.

The phenomenon of role reversal, when adult children find themselves having to be caretakers for aging parents, heightens the conflict and confusion over when, how, and even *if* to say no to needs or demands. The awareness of behaviors described as "parenting one's parents" can be disconcerting, frustrating, and frightening. The care provided by aging parents seemingly had a "natural" end as adult children became increasingly independent with age. The future with respect to aging parents seems to be the opposite, so that caretaking proceeds in the direction of increased rather than decreased need. Often the onset of these reversals and involvement in caretaking occur gradually over a period of time, so that the adult children seem to have established firm patterns of helping before they even begin to consider doing otherwise. At that point, the expectations of aging parents for continued care, along with their expressed appreciation for the help, can further confuse adult children and heighten their awareness of the issue of filial responsibility.

Counselors can help adult children reframe these situations and recognize that role reversals most often are and need be physical circumstances only. Aging parents may require caretaking for material needs, but still remain vital individuals worthy of continued caring and respect. This perspective allows adult children to cope with seeming role reversals in a more positive manner (R. Johnson, 1988, personal communication).

Counselors can assist adult children and aging parents in recognizing conflicts and also in becoming aware of the need to set limits. The process of setting limits on adult childrens' (or aging parents') caregiving or shared time together requires first building an awareness of other role constraints and demands. Other persons who are important in the lives of adult children, such as their spouse and children, should be involved in discussions to help potential caregivers clarify and set priorities on their role expectations. Aging parents need to be included in these discussions. Ideally, all family members can reach tentative agreements about time and resources devoted to care. It is helpful for everyone to remember that relationships, circumstances, and needs will continually change. Thus, it is important to set specific times for reevaluation of needs and priorities as well as resources for meeting those needs. Just knowing that everyone will be meeting to discuss any changes can be a relief to those experiencing caregiving burden and stress.

Caregiving is not the only situation that adult children and aging parents will experience where setting limits can be helpful. For example, the retirement transition for older persons may represent a new opportunity to get to know their adult children on a different level. Aging parents may express a desire to spend a lot of time with their children or grandchildren— perhaps too much time in relation to the life demands of adult children and their families. Setting limits on the "fun" times for socialization, odd as it may sound at first, may become necessary for some families.

On the other hand, adult children may find that their young-old, active aging parents are busy and involved with their own lives and not available to socialize, or to babysit grandchildren. Aging parents may be the ones to set limits, to explain that they do not have time for caretaking. Again, open communication of role expectations, careful listening, and understanding of each other's needs can help to alleviate conflicts. There is always *some* time that can be spent together. The important point is to focus on the quality rather than the quantity of shared time.

Becoming Friends, Staying Friends

In addition to saying "no," some adult children and aging parents need to learn to say "yes." One of the unique possibilities for adult children is to become friends with their aging parents. Friends are people we feel close to, experience a fondness for, and respect. McGinnis (1979) noted that friendship "is the model for all intimate encounters" (p. 9). Somehow, many persons separate their friends from their family. Often fewer demands or expectations are placed on friends, and their imperfections are more easily accepted than those of family members, particularly parents.

The guidelines we employ for cultivating friendships and intimacy can be used effectively to become friends with family members, though overcoming role expectations may make the process more difficult. McGinnis (1979) offered a number of suggestions for building and maintaining friendships, such as learning to listen, self-disclose, communicate warmth and caring, touch, and provide positive affirmations. At the same time, the ability to forgive and to overlook flaws in others contributes to the development and maintenance of intimacy.

Carnegie (1936), in his classic book *How To Win Friends and Influence People*, proposed numerous suggestions to help people be friends. One of the most important concepts is to avoid being critical of others, even when they are wrong. He noted that criticism engenders resentment and still does not correct the situation. It is often difficult for adult children and aging parents to avoid being critical of each other, yet the benefits of learning to react to one another as they would to friends can be vastly rewarding to all concerned. Someone needs to take the risk if behaviors and patterns of relating are to be changed, and counselors can facilitate the change process.

Attitude Adjustment

One of the adages often heard in relation to football and other sports is that "the best defense is a good offense." Rather than dwelling on how bad things are, adult children and aging parents can develop a positive perspective on things each can do to build stronger, more satisfying relationships. Breaking out of a negative cycle of expectations and reactions can be extremely difficult. As one older woman said, " . . . if I told my children I love them they'd probably fall over dead!" Certainly the children might be surprised at such a "new" statement, but soon they would learn to reciprocate both the statements and the feelings. Furthermore, they would most likely be relieved and pleased to be able to do so. Attitude adjustment can begin with a change in behavior patterns, but someone has to initiate the change. Someone has to take time out from old patterns before new ones can be attempted.

Sometimes instead of rehashing old resentments, especially on a foundation of poor relationships, attitudes can be adjusted by taking positive steps to change how parents and children relate. Small increments or changes may yield large benefits. By reacting in new ways to old situations, both adult children and aging parents can set the stage for new and more satisfying types of interactions.

Part of the process of building and maintaining friendships involves taking an interest in each other's interests. Adult children and aging parents need to make the time and also the effort to find out what is really important and enjoyable to each other. Making plans for time to be spent together at home or on vacation is something that everyone can enjoy. Especially for older persons living alone, having a visit or trip planned with relatives can be a focal point to look forward to for weeks at a time.

Many aging parents benefit from regular contact they can count on. Regular visits or calls at specified times can become almost family rituals that everyone looks forward to and enjoys. Letters are important, because they can be reread. Older persons living alone may especially appreciate something they can pull out and review during lonely times to reaffirm that they are loved. Letters need not be long. Even a few lines can communicate the main message that someone cares and is thinking about you. Also, the letters can be shared with friends and neighbors as evidence and affirmation of family ties and support.

Knowledge is an important key to attitude change. For example, rather than reacting with disgust to a change in an older person's behavior, adult children can talk with physicians, learn about medical aspects of parents' illnesses, and check their medications to determine possible side effects and interactions. Some helpful resources in this regard were discussed in chapter 2. By encouraging independence, rather than assuming that declines are inevitable, adult children *can* assist aging parents in coping successfully with the changes that may accompany the aging process. By helping parents remain independent, adult children can foster positive role models of aging for them-selves and their own children. Adult children and aging parents have a unique opportunity to help each other overcome neg-ative stereotypes and fears of aging, and develop positive atti-tudes and relationships that will enhance the life satisfaction of all family members. Some of the ways counselors can help are discussed in the following section.

Family Counseling and Assessment

Proponents of family therapy stress the importance of "considering the environmental context when attempting to implement therapeutic intervention strategies" (Baruth & Huber, 1984, p. 242). As discussed in chapter 3, aging occurs in a family context, and an understanding of developmental family history can be useful in understanding the concerns of aging clients. In this section, the family is examined as a system and further described in a developmental context. A brief overview of dysfunctional family behavior patterns and family counseling is provided, along with some suggestions for family assessment. The information provided here is meant to supplement the available family therapy literature, and to highlight points for consideration by counselors working with adult children and aging parents.

Family Systems

Families may be defined as systems with specific properties. These properties include rules and roles for communication, negotiation, and problem solving, and are designed to ensure the smooth functioning of the total system. Several rules of systems have been defined that are applicable in family counseling (Baruth & Huber, 1984).

The principle of wholeness is based on the assumption that members of the family can be understood only within the family context. It is important to consider individual behaviors, but only in the context of the family functioning as a whole. Any family system is greater than the sum of its parts.

Furthermore, subsystems exist within each family system, and the family itself is a subsystem of an extended family, community, and other higher order systems. Hierarchical organization is characteristic of families, with the existing power base defined by coalitions, generational differences, external systems, or some other factor. The principle of "equifinality" as applied to families means that the family reaches the same final state regardless of the conditions and circumstances. This is because families are goal-oriented systems governed by rules, both overt and covert, that circumscribe the behavior of family members. Overt rules define daily living tasks whereas covert rules define psychological interactions between family members (Jackson, 1965).

Another principle of family functioning is that of homeostasis, which suggests that the family functions to maintain itself in a steady state, even if that steady state is dysfunctional. Through the use of "feedback loops," families behave so as to maintain the family unit (Minuchin, 1974). When families experience stress, homeostatic mechanisms are activated to reduce the stress. These mechanisms consist of behaviors by various family members that may seem maladaptive when the individual is considered, yet they are "necessary" to maintain the family system.

In terms of systems theory, older persons can be understood best within the context of their family as a whole, including adult children. Aging parents may compose a subsystem of their own that is nonproblematic for the whole family system until one of the parents becomes incapacitated or dies. At that point the subsystem of the older generation needs to become more closely allied or integrated with some other component of the family. Thus, the balance of family functioning or equilibrium is disturbed.

On the other hand, older persons may represent the existing power base in a family. When that power base erodes through the increasing illness, frailty, or dependence of the aging parent, the equilibrium of the family is disturbed and rules may need to be renegotiated. What worked to maintain the family equilibrium under one power base may not work under another. Stated another way, when Dad (or Mom) controlled family interactions, certain constraints may have been placed on sibling interactions. In the absence of Dad (or Mom), the covert rules of interaction may no longer be observed, leading to renewed sibling rivalries, overt or covert power plays, or any number of dysfunctional behaviors until a new power base becomes established and accepted. If Mom (or Dad) becomes ill and requires care, the role reversal that may result is difficult to accept because it violates the basic covert rules of family functioning.

When family systems are stressed by the needs of aging parents, some homeostatic mechanism will occur to reduce the level of stress. This could consist of seeming martyr behavior by a caretaking child, abuse of the older person by a caretaker, sibling arguments, or any number of behaviors that can be understood only within the context of the functioning of an individual family unit. Knowledge of the developmental history of the family is essential to an understanding of family interaction patterns and homeostatic mechanisms. Hence, family counseling with adult children and aging parents is often necessary.

Family Development

Duvall's (1971) concept of family developmental stages was discussed in chapter 3. The basic tenet of this approach is that a longitudinal frame of reference is best for understanding families because it provides clues to understanding how each family developed its unique rules and patterns of interaction. Haley (1973) further suggested that family dysfunctions occur when the natural sequence of family development is interrupted. He proposed that difficulties in mastering family life cycle stages were the basis for symptomatic dysfunctional behaviors. It is necessary for families to change, grow, and develop in response to developmental changes, just as individuals must do. Families that fail to adapt to normative developmental tasks experience increasing difficulty with later stages and tasks.

The stress that results from caregiving needs for aging parents is one example of a natural developmental task of aging families. Those families that have experienced success in adapting to change, through the stages of marriage, childbearing, preschool and teenage child rearing, launching of children, and the postparental stage are most apt to experience success in coping with the needs of aging parents. Families that developed dysfunctional patterns in earlier years may be expected to experience serious difficulties in dealing with the needs of parents as they age.

Family life stages may be encountered more than once, in contrast to individual developmental stages. This occurs when a family member leaves one family and enters another, blended family. The potential for such changes to isolate an older family member is readily seen when genograms (discussed below) are constructed. Dysfunctional patterns between adult children and aging parents also can subvert attempts at creating blended families for adult children.

Dysfunctional Family Patterns

Symptomatic behaviors and problems arise when families that lack effective means of coping with stress are confronted by crises. Baruth and Huber (1984) summarized the research on three common dysfunctional behaviors: pathological communications, unclear boundaries, and scapegoating.

Clear communications refers to the sending and receiving of clear messages within the family. Communications that are unclear result from making assumptions about the feelings of other family members, overgeneralizing, talking in abstract rather than concrete terms, and relying on covert meanings or symbolizations. Congruent, or direct communications facilitate problem solving and effective family functioning, whereas incongruent communications result in dysfunction (Satir, 1974).

Satir (1974) described four patterns of incongruent communication that family members might use under stress. These four patterns may be typical of various sibling responses to the increasing needs of aging parents. One response is to placate, or agree, acquiesce, and so forth to "keep the peace." Another is to blame, accuse, or find fault with others, thus putting them on the defensive. A third pattern is to remain detached, reasonable, and calm to express the feeling that the situation is really not serious but is manageable. The final pattern is to distract, or act unaware and uninvolved, as if the situation did not exist.

These patterns and their various combinations limit effective communication and problem solving for families with aging parents. It is easy to imagine a caretaking adult child acquiescing to the demands of an aging parent while internally building resentments. A noncaretaking, out-of-town sibling may blame the caretaking child for not doing enough to prevent the decline of the aging parent. Yet another sibling, removed from the situation, may express to the caretaker that she is making much ado about nothing, or may refuse to be involved in the situation at all. When a crisis occurs, such as a decision for institutionalization or increased needs for caretaking because of illness or operations, the family that communicates with these dysfunctional patterns is unable to make considered, rational, cooperative decisions.

Unclear boundaries are a second major dysfunction in some families. Healthy families maintain clear boundaries between "I" and "we," and each member maintains an individual as well as a family identity. At one extreme, boundaries may become blurred and families enmeshed; at the other extreme, rigid boundaries contribute to disengagement of family members. Enmeshed families are characterized by "an inappropriate lack of privacy as family members intrude on each other's thoughts and feelings, ever alert to signs of distress in one another. Family belongingness dominates all else, at the expense of each member developing a separate sense of self" (Baruth & Huber, 1984, p. 253). In such families, care for aging relatives may be provided at the expense of the individual development of one or more siblings. In fact, the rapidity with which caretaking is assumed may overshadow serious problems in relating. Enmeshed families are characterized by excessive speed and intensity of responses to stress (Minuchin, 1974). Respite care may be unwelcome, and available community resources may not be utilized, even if caregiving stress leads to abuse.

Family disengagement, on the other hand, results in little sense of family belongingness. Mutual support is lacking. In times of stress, such as when an aging parent becomes ill, the family may seem not to respond at all.

Families that are unable to develop effective means of maintaining homeostasis may "scapegoat" one member who then carries the disturbance for the entire family. The focus of stress is put on "the black sheep." The scapegoating process is mutual, the victimized member participating in the process. It is important that different family members may take on the scapegoat role as family needs change and different crises are encountered. Older family members can become scapegoats for other family problems, such as marital disturbances among adult children. This role effectively blocks the older parent's needs for growth and possibly services to maintain independent living. Similarly, an adult child may become a scapegoat to draw attention away from the increasing needs of an aging parent, thus keeping the family from developing a healthy response to the older person's needs.

Other dysfunctional patterns of relating have been identified, all of which may inhibit the development and maintenance of healthy relationships between adult children and their aging parents. It is important to assess these patterns within families as part of the process of providing family counseling.

Family Counseling

Herr and Weakland (1979) provided an extensive discussion of counseling for older persons and their families. Their primary focus was on understanding the family system and mobilizing families to become effective problem solvers. Key elements of their approach include involving all family members, after first determining the extent of the family system. Non-blood-related kin, including neighbors, service providers, and physicians, can be important persons to include. Such individuals may have influence on the decisions families make. It is important to understand the family rules, and in particular how those rules or compromises may be upset when an older relative moves in with adult children and their families. In effect, the latter situation represents a type of blended family. Inflexible family rules will inhibit successful cohabitation among members of different generations.

Additional concerns in understanding families include the need to know the power base of family members, what solutions they have attempted to resolve existing problems, and how those solutions perpetuate the problems. An important point Herr and Weakland (1979) made is that good intentions can create problems for all concerned: " . . . middle-aged persons struggling to behave like 'good children' often create disastrous problems by applying dysfunctional solutions to what were initially nonproblems or, at most, ordinary life difficulties of their elders" (p. 144).

Sterns, Weis, and Perkins (1984) reviewed the literature and developed a conceptual approach to counseling older persons and their families. In applying this approach, the authors cautioned that families must be treated individually, regardless of what is known about the processes of "normal" aging or "normative" family development. Accurate information about each family member must be obtained, including attention to their feelings, responses, and perceptions of family relationships.

The Sterns et al. (1984) model posited five levels of individual effectiveness, with the same five levels applying to family effectiveness. Selection of a treatment modality is contingent upon the level of individual and family effectiveness as assessed by the counselor. The five levels, from healthy to nonhealthy functioning, are mastery, coping, striving, inertia, and panic. Interventions, arranged in the same order, are educational, peer support, group counseling, family therapy, and individual counseling. Each therapy modality applies to three levels, with the exception of individual counseling, which is recommended only for the lowest level of individual and family functioning (panic). Family therapy, for example, would be used with families in panic, inertia, or striving, whereas group counseling would be used with families who were inert, striving, or coping.

Family counseling approaches are designed to help families become aware of and change their dysfunctional patterns of relating. The goals have been variously stated, but incorporate both long- and short-term objectives. Long-term goals are reflective of the counselor's theoretical orientation, but basically refer to development of healthy family patterns of relating. Short-term goals may include getting to know the family and assessing characteristic relationship patterns. An important short-term goal is to determine who the participants in family therapy will be (Baruth & Huber, 1984). This is especially true when older persons are involved, because their family of origin may be dead whereas children and grandchildren or other relatives may be an important part of their family constellation (Herr & Weakland, 1979).

Family Assessment

Regardless of the conceptual model chosen, all family counseling requires some type of clinical assessment. When working with older persons, this assessment is made in addition to and does not replace individual assessment, including multidimensional functional assessment. The focus of family assessment is explaining behavior on the basis of transactions within the family system. A search for solutions involves all members of the family and perhaps other supra-systems as well. Assessment may or may not lead to family therapy (Nichols & Everett, 1986).

Family assessment is an ongoing process, undertaken continually as a basis for understanding the family and determining appropriate interventions. Nichols and Everett (1986) provided a list of 10 questions that counselors can use as a basis for assessing families. Some of the major areas to consider are: how the family member who called represents the family system, how the presenting problem or individual is connected to the family system, what recent event(s) prompted the referral, whether the dysfunction represents an acute or chronic pattern of functioning, how amenable the system will be to therapy, whether the system is enmeshing or disengaging, and whether there is any immediate evidence of significant intergenerational influences.

West (1988) reviewed available inventories to measure dimensions of family systems. These included self-report inventories for couples, nuclear families, and families of origin. Perhaps the most useful of these for working with adult children and aging parents would be the Family-of-Origin Scale (FOS) (Hovestadt, Anderson, Piercy, Cochran, & Fine, 1985) and the Personal Authority in the Family System questionnaire (PAFS) (Bray, Williamson, & Malone, 1984). The FOS is designed to measure health in the family of origin, whereas the PAFS is designed to assess relationships in three-generational families. Both instruments are described briefly in the appendix.

In addition to clinical and formal assessments, genograms are used in family counseling to evaluate family relationships and patterns. The use of genograms is discussed in detail in the next section. One of the many things genograms can illuminate is the influence of out-of-town family members on decision making in regard to aging parents. Though not a part of the counseling process itself, failure to include consideration of family members wielding decision-making power, or having frequent contact with the aging parent or adult child in counseling, will inhibit the overall success of counseling efforts. Triangulation, for example, could be the basis of problems with aging parents that could be overlooked in the absence of assessment of geographically separate family members who form part of the triangle (Herr & Weakland, 1979).

Selected Counseling Methods

Four selected counseling methods are discussed in this section: bibliotherapy, life review therapy, genograms, and early recollections. These are not the only techiques that can be used successfully with adult children and aging parents. They were chosen because each has been used with either younger or older persons, each has empirical support for its effectiveness, and each offers the potential for helping adult children and their aging parents, individually and collectively, to achieve more satisfying lives and intergenerational relationships.

Bibliotherapy

Hynes and Hynes-Berry (1986) explained bibliotherapy as literally what the Latin root words imply: *biblio* meaning books, and *therapy* meaning to heal. Thus, bibliotherapy has come to mean the use of literature to promote mental health (Wedl,

1982). Audiovisual materials (films, movies, songs, etc.) may be incorporated into a broad definition of literature. Hynes further defined bibliotherapy as an interpersonal or interrelational process in which a facilitator uses guided discussion of literature to clarify and mold values, character, and personality. The process may be conducted on a one-to-one or group basis. Clinical bibliotherapy is an extension of this process to work with emotionally disturbed persons. Bibliotherapy may be used alone or in combination with other therapeutic approaches.

Ryan (1957) identified several goals for the use of bibliotherapy in counseling. These included: to show persons that they are not the first to encounter the problems they face, that there is more than one possible choice of action, that there are underlying motivations to behavior, that there are values involved in human experiences, and that they can face their situation realistically and develop a plan to achieve desired outcomes. Menninger (1961) listed several additional goals of bibliotherapy: achieving insight through emotional and intellectual understanding of one's condition, assisting in verbalization of problems through providing an objective focus for discussion, externalizing problems to enlarge one's sphere of interests and achieve an external reality, identifying with a character or experience so a subsequent abreaction may be achieved, and thinking more constructively as one learns more about oneself.

Bibliotherapy is basically a projective technique. Clients are provided a stimulus in the form of literature and are asked to discuss their reactions. Presumably, their interpretations will be based on their own experiences and understandings. Carefully selected tools for use in bibliotherapy can provide adult children and aging parents with positive role models and a wealth of ideas for discussion and implementation in their own lives. Talking about their reactions to literature can provide meaningful opportunities for getting to know and understand each other. Insights and empathic understanding may be gained through this process.

Several books were recommended earlier that could be useful to families in coping with death and dying. Other books that may be useful to assist families in coping with the aging process are listed below, along with some of the major themes contained in each. Many of these are short and may be found in the children's section of bookstores; however, the nature of the content is for children "of all ages." The list provided is by no means meant to be exhaustive of all possibilities, rather, this

list is included to serve as a starting point for gathering bibliotherapy tools. Many of today's older persons enjoy poetry, and
counselors are encouraged to develop poetry resources for use
in bibliotherapy. It is essential that counselors using any literary
sources first be familiar with them before assigning them to
adult children and aging parents to read.

The Giving Tree (Silverstein, 1961)—life span development;
relationships between parents and children across the life
span.

Man's Search for Meaning (Frankl, 1965)—importance of
having a purpose in life regardless of circumstances; importance of attitude in determining reactions to circumstances.

Illusions (Bach, 1977)—importance of attitude in determining outlook and reactions to life circumstances; emphasizes that each person is free to choose his or her
reactions and attitudes.

The Little Prince (de Saint-Exupéry, 1943)—nature and
meaning of friendships, life, and death.

The Velveteen Rabbit (Williams, 1983)—what it means to grow
old; how people become more special as they get older.

The Precious Present (Johnson, 1984)—the importance of
living, being, and becoming in the present moment.

Enjoy Old Age: A Program of Self-Management (Skinner &
Vaughn, 1983)—tips and techniques for adapting to and
enjoying the later years of life.

Transitions: Making Sense of Life's Changes (Bridges, 1983)—
explains the nature of transitions and strategies for coping with changes in life.

Hope for the Flowers (Paulus, 1972)—the importance of relationships; evaluation of striving for achievement versus
living life in a more balanced manner.

Unconditional Love (Powell, 1978)—examines the nature and
manifestations of love, especially unconditional love.

Fully Human, Fully Alive (Powell, 1976)—explains why change
is frightening and how to go about developing and achieving a new vision of oneself; based in cognitive therapies.

Life is Tremendous (Jones, 1981)—maintains that a positive
view of life may be enjoyed by anyone who invests in
positive attitudes.

Some feature-length films (about 90 minutes each) that
may be useful in bibliotherapy and are available for rental at

video stores include the following (again, no attempt is made to include all possibilities):

On Golden Pond is a story of the relationship between a woman in midlife and her parents. A history of conflict with her father is successfully resolved when each learns to value and respect the other as a unique human being. Family relationship themes are prominent.

Harry and Tonto is a story of an older man who is widowed and lives with a pet cat. Evicted from his home when the building is condemned, he travels across the country visiting his children and enjoying a series of adventures. Major themes include relationships with adult children and achieving ego integrity in later life.

Cocoon is about a group of older persons living in a nursing home who discover a secret to eternal youth. Some want it and some do not. Relationships between older persons as well as intergenerational relationships are featured. The meaning of life and old age is another theme that could be discussed.

The Trip to Bountiful is an award-winning film about an older woman living with her son and daughter-in-law. The daughter-in-law and she do not get along. The older woman wants to make one last trip to her family home before she dies. Ego integrity, reminiscence, and family relationships are some of the themes that could be discussed.

Harold and Maude is a story about a young man who meets an older woman doing something that both enjoy—visiting funerals. Death and dying are prominent themes. Relationships between older women and younger men could be discussed as well.

The Four Seasons is a story of three couples in midlife who are long-time friends and how they cope with the divorce and remarriage of one of the couples. Can be useful in raising the topic of how adult childrens' divorces affect aging parents.

I Never Sang for My Father is an award-winning film about a family with a controlling father and handicapped mother; when mother dies, the son and daughter are left with their father and a history of painful and manipulative relationships to resolve.

Although bibliotherapy can be a valuable and useful tool in counseling with adult children and aging parents, several suggestions may enhance the usefulness of this technique. First, as mentioned above, counselors must themselves be familiar with a resource before assigning it. Second, maximum benefit may be obtained if both adult children and aging parents use a resource and discuss their reactions together. Finally, counselors should allow participants to express their reactions and encourage exploration of the meaning of the reading, film, and so forth. Simple evaluative statements about likes or dislikes will provide only superficial reactions. When adult children and aging parents "miss" messages that counselors consider to be important, some means of identifying those themes for discussion needs to be developed.

Life Review Therapy

Butler (1963) identified life review as a "naturally occurring, universal mental process characterized by the progressive return to consciousness of past experience . . . prompted by the realization of approaching dissolution and death, and the inability to maintain one's sense of personal invulnerability" (p. 66). Prior to the definition of life review as a normal and necessary process, reminiscence was viewed as a negative aspect of old age. Old persons who reminisced or constantly told stories about the "old days" were considered to be living in the past and losing touch with reality (Kiernat, 1984). Actually, *the process of life review is normal* for persons of any age and can be useful therapeutically with anyone, especially those who are going through transitions. It has been studied more with older persons because it tends to occur most commonly with this population. In effect, the story telling of older persons is done with a purpose, hence it should be encouraged and even facilitated.

According to Butler (1963), life review involves the return to consciousness of past experiences and particularly past conflicts. The awareness of death initiates the process of life review, which essentially is a process of taking stock of oneself and one's life. The successful outcome of the life review process is a sense of satisfaction with the self and a sense of pride and accomplishment. The feeling that the life one has lived was the best that one could have lived results in what Erikson (1963) termed *ego integrity*. Older persons who fail to achieve a sense of integrity in reviewing past accomplishments and conflicts and focus instead on what they could have done differently may experience regret, depression, or even despair. The recognition that time to make changes is limited or nonexistent, or that persons with whom one would like to reconcile are no longer living or accessible, makes unfinished business extremely painful.

Life review can result in increased self-awareness, flexibility, and wisdom. It offers an opportunity for vulnerable older persons to experience reinforced self-identity, grief resolution, and increased awareness of successful coping mechanisms. It can result in an ability to relinquish what has been lost and to create a new identity with one's remaining personal and interpersonal resources (Molinari & Reichlin, 1985). The life review process may be a natural defense mechanism that helps older persons overcome the threats to their self-esteem from the many losses of aging. Rather than viewing their circumstances in terms of loss of competence, older persons can identify with past accomplishments that serve to enhance ego strength (Kiernat, 1984).

On the other hand, guilt, agitation, and excessive rumination may result when the focus is on past conflicts, regretted choices, or perceived failures. Older persons whose life reviews have a negative focus can be assisted through counseling to reframe their experiences in more positive terms. Though helping interventions usually are not required, life review therapies offer the potential for stimulating and enhancing the normal review process and helping alleviate negative outcomes.

Gerfo (1980) defined three forms of reminiscence among older persons: informative, evaluative, and obsessive. Informative reminiscence refers to memories of factual experiences that are recalled for the purposes of enhancing self-esteem. This is a nonproblematic form of reminiscing that provides pleasure through awareness of one's longevity, memory, and reevaluation of one's life history. It offers the opportunity to revive past interests and to develop new ones.

Evaluative reminiscence is seen as an attempt to come to terms with old guilts, conflicts, or defeats, and to find meaning in one's accomplishments in life. When older persons are unable to accept the past and come to terms with what has occurred, obsessive reminiscence may result. This type of reminiscence may be precipitated by stress or significant life changes. It can lead to severe depression or suicidal behaviors. Rather than life review therapy, obsessive reminiscence may result in full concentration on the unhappy memories or experiences. Psychodrama or Gestalt techniques have been useful in helping older persons express emotions and feelings stored up over a lifetime. Techniques that encourage emotional expression are needed.

Life review therapies are useful in both group and individual settings, with group sessions being particularly helpful as a means of sharing and validating experiences. Group approaches have been particularly helpful with institutionalized older persons as a means of stimulating conversation and interest and improving attention span and memory (Kiernat, 1984). Other benefits include greater self-acceptance, lower anxiety, more positive view of others, and more social connectedness (Reedy & Birren, 1980).

Life review may be facilitated in a number of ways. Structured life review techniques focus the attention of older persons on specific events, topics, or phases of life in an attempt to assess the psychological effect on the individual (Westcott, 1983). These techniques facilitate recall of experiences that include unresolved conflicts as well as many pleasant memories. Some common ways of structuring life reviews include writing journals and autobiographies and taping oral histories. Within individual or group counseling sessions, older persons can be asked to reflect on certain periods of life or life events, such as their 20s, 30s, 40s and so forth, or the Depression years, war years, and other periods. Common issues such as work, leisure, or family relationships can be a focus of reviews. Aids to the life review process can include sharing of music common to a particular era, photographs, diaries, or other memorabilia designed to evoke memories the older person can discuss and review.

Kaminsky (1984) provided a compendium of creative approaches to life review therapy, including plays, workshops, and poems. Waters and Weaver (1981) provided several additional techniques for facilitating the review process, including work sheets asking persons to recall past educational, vocational, and leisure activities, and to note what they liked or disliked about each activity. Persons are then encouraged to examine the skills learned through each activity identified and the values each represents.

R. Johnson (1986) developed a life review game called "Generations . . . the Game." It uses the six life arenas (career, leisure, intimacy, family, inner life, spirituality) as a structure. The game offers 16 separate, developmental task-oriented questions for each decade: 0–10, 11–20, 21–30. . . .70+, in each of the six life arenas for a total of 768 life review questions.

A spinner is used to add an element of fun and a "chance" dimension to the game. Johnson recommends using the game with family members to enhance intergenerational understanding.

Life review activities can be a meaningful way to enhance intergenerational family relationships. Collison (B. Collison, personal comunication, 1988) used the creative idea of writing a book for his grandchildren entitled "I Was a Little Boy Once, Too!" The book includes a recounting of childhood experiences and significant events when the author was the age of his grandchildren. The book will be given as a Christmas present to be enjoyed for years to come.

In summary, the normal process of life review offers a unique opportunity for adult children to interact with aging parents and learn about their own family history while assisting aging parents to achieve ego integrity. Unfortunately, the life review process has the potential for other than positive outcomes, particularly when the focus is on previous conflicts and unfinished business. The potential for successful outcomes may be enhanced when counseling assistance is available or when adult children facilitate the life review process through their willingness to listen to a recounting of their aging parent's past experiences and memories.

Genograms

Aging parents represent a rich source of family history, often the only such source. One activity that could be used to stimulate the sharing of memories is the development of genograms or family trees. Brief biographies of each family member could be developed and included in a text for distribution to other family members. Used in this manner, genograms can be a developmental technique for enhancing family relationships and intimacy. Another common use of this technique is for clinical assessment in family therapy.

According to McGoldrick and Gerson (1985), a genogram is " . . . a format for drawing a family tree that records information about family members and their relationships over at least three generations. Genograms display family information graphically in a way that provides a quick gestalt of complex family patterns and a rich source of hypotheses about how a clinical problem may be connected to the family context and the evolution of both problem and context over time" (p. 1). Genograms are concrete, tangible, and facilitate clear mapping of family structures. They provide a lot of information in a short amount of time, beginning with the first counseling session.

Genograms are subjective, clinical self-report measures that the clinician interprets and from which it is possible to draw hypotheses about the functioning of the family system. Repetitive family patterns over the generations may be viewed through use of the genogram in combination with a chronological family history of events. Interpretation places the family in an interpretive role with the counselor, and helps family members see themselves in new ways, as part of a functioning family system.

Bowen's (1978) family systems theory is the one most closely associated with the development of genograms. The structural and strategic family therapists (e.g., Haley, Minuchin) have stressed current emotional relationships in the immediate family, whereas genograms can "highlight both current and historical family patterns to illustrate these and other dysfunctional family structures" (McGoldrick & Gerson, 1985, p. 4).

The creation of genograms involves three basic tasks: (1) mapping the family structure, (2) recording family information, and (3) delineating family relationships. Until recently, there was no standard set of symbols or methodology for drawing the family map. McGoldrick and Gerson's (1985) book on genograms in family assessment developed such a standard.

The family map or structure shows different family members in relation to one another. Each family member is identified by either a box (men) or a circle (women). Lines are doubled around the identified patient, or symptomatic individual, and an "X" is placed inside the figure for someone who is dead. Dates of birth and death are written above each symbol. Specified symbols are used to identify marriages, divorces, pregnancies, cohabitation, natural and adopted children, blended families, and other relevant details. Family relationships are shown as close, very close or fused, poor or conflicted, estranged, fused and conflictual, or distant using combinations of lines.

Clearly, genograms used clinically can become very complex, particularly once the basic map or family tree has been established and family members begin to provide information about each family member and relationships between family members. Demographic information is provided for each person, as well as information related to their medical, emotional, and behavioral functioning (Lawson & Gaushell, 1988). Family myths, rules, roles, and typical patterns of relating emerge as the genogram is detailed and explained.

The American Association of Retired Persons (AARP), the U.S. Postal Service, and the U.S. Genealogical Service recently joined forces in an effort to encourage children and grandparents to exchange letters about family roots and family history. Titled the "Plant a Family Tree" campaign, the project is designed to encourage intergenerational interactions in our mobile society. Posters announcing the campaign and free fill-in-the-blank family tree charts are now available in post offices and AARP offices nationwide. The blanks are relatively simple and would have limited use with blended families.

Early Recollections

The use of Early Recollections (ERs) is an Adlerian technique that can build upon the normative life review process as it provides an opportunity for structured reminiscence. This technique can assist older persons in achieving ego integrity and also help them live "more satisfying and effective lives on a daily basis" (Sweeney & Myers, 1986, p. 3). ERs have only recently been used with older persons, and are best understood within the context of Adlerian life-style assessment.

Sweeney (1989) noted that ERs typically are generated and recorded as part of an overall life-style assessment process that includes a description of one's family constellation and memories of relationships with parents and siblings while one was a child. The life-style assessment process makes certain assumptions about people that are the foundations of Adlerian theory. As detailed in an article by Sweeney and Myers (1986), these assumptions include the following major concepts:

1. Behavior is purposive—we act to achieve goals we believe are important to us in solving the process of living.
2. Behavior is best understood in a social context—persons strive to be "somebody" in relation to everyone else, to make their place. If we observe behavior and listen for the private logic in how others expect to achieve their

place, then we will be able to anticipate future responses to related life tasks.

3. Behavior is understood best in an holistic context—all thoughts, feelings, attitudes, and values are an expression of an underlying theme of how individuals make their place. The influence of body, family, environment, and so forth are all important influences, but none is more significant than the selective meaning persons give to their experiences.

4. Each person creates a private logic as to how to cope with life. This perspective does not change over time so long as it goes unexamined or the person continues to believe that it is useful in meeting life's demands.

5. Memory of early childhood experiences is selective and serves the function of helping us to be unconsciously guided by "rules" about life, ourselves, and other people.

In effect, ERs are "cues for understanding present behavior" (Sweeney, 1989, p. 122). They present a way to examine the meaning each person gives to life and the coping mechanisms they employ to deal with life's circumstances. The use and interpretation of ERs, combined with encouragement and evaluation of life styles, is a way to help older persons better understand themselves and use their self-awareness to achieve a sense of ego integrity. Stated another way, ERs help clients understand the motivations for their behaviors and their own personal power over the events in their lives.

ERs are specific events recalled prior to the age of 8 or 9. They differ from reports, in that reports refer to routines or frequent interactions rather then specific events. For example, a memory that one's family had a picnic each weekend would be a report. A statement of one specific weekend picnic and the events that occurred on that day is a recollection (Sweeney, 1989). The difference is that recollections are specific and focus attention on particular past incidents. It is not necessary to interpretation that the incident actually did, in fact, happen; rather, it is only necessary that it be recalled as such.

Though life themes may become evident through one recollection, the usual process of life-style assessment involves recording several different recollections. Through analysis of the various recollections, typical mechanisms of coping may be identified. In addition, fundamental beliefs or private logic about self, others, and life in general may be determined. This private logic determines how a person approaches life and copes with circumstances and other persons.

The method for using ERs begins, as mentioned, as part of a life-style assessment. However, using ERs alone without family constellation information can be useful in gaining insights about older persons and helping them identify coping resources and styles. The process involves asking the older person to remember as far back as possible and recall specific events. They should be asked to give their age and describe the incident, which should be recorded verbatim because the choice of words is significant in identifying one's private logic. The behavior and feeling reactions of the person to the events when they occurred is an essential component. The interviewer may ask "What did you do then?" and "How did you feel?" in response to a stated remembered event.

An example of the use of ERs with older persons may be taken from a recent training videotape completed as part of a national project on gerontological counselor preparation (Myers, 1988a; Sweeney & Myers, 1988). In a group counseling session led by Sweeney, one older woman indicated that she had recently remarried after being widowed for a number of years. Shortly after the marriage, her second husband had a heart attack and she was now in a caretaker role. When asked about her earliest recollections, she reported that her family had a pony that she used to ride. One day while she was riding, the pony became frightened and took off running. She was unable to control the pony and just held on for dear life. When asked how she reacted, she stated that she "just held on!" When asked how she felt, she indicated she was "really scared."

One possible interpretation of the ER was that she was not comfortable in situations in which she was not in control. The older woman rejected that possible interpretation, but gave a smile of recognition and nod of assent when one of the group leaders asked, "Could it be. . . . that you expected it to be one way, and it wasn't at all. You expected the pony to be gentle, and instead it took off and you barely were able to hold on. And you don't like it when you expect one thing to happen and something else occurs!" The follow-up to this explanation involved making a parallel interpretation to her current situation. She had remarried expecting one thing to happen, and something else happened instead—and it threw her. Sweeney then turned the focus of the interpretation onto the *meaning* of the recollection in terms of her typical methods of coping. The client nodded assent when reminded that she did not fall off the pony, and volunteered that that was just what would happen in her current situation. She would hold on and get through it successfully.

Although many other examples of the use of ERs could be provided, the point to be made here is that this technique offers a positive perspective from which to view the reminiscences and coping styles of older persons. Though examples make ERs seem deceptively simple, like the life review process they can have less than optimum outcomes when used by persons without training. In the case of ERs, some knowledge of and training in Adlerian theory and life-style assessment techniques is important to influence successful outcomes. For more information, the reader is referred to Sweeney (1981, 1989) and Sweeney and Myers (1986).

Community Resources

Counselors working with adult children and aging parents must be knowledgeable about community resources available to assist in meeting tangible, identified needs, especially the needs of older persons. Some of the most salient resources are those provided through the Aging Network. This network, authorized by the Older Americans Act as it was first passed in 1965 and subsequently amended, begins at the federal level with the U.S. Administration on Aging. Ten regional offices exist to coordinate the efforts of 50 state and 6 territorial offices on aging. Within each state, area agencies on aging are designated as planning and service areas to coordinate and plan all service programs for older persons in a specified geographical area. Among the social service programs provided through the Older Americans Act are congregate and home-delivered meals, transportation, shopping and escort assistance, chore service, health screening, and numerous other services designed to assist older Americans in living independently in their own homes as long as possible.

One of the mandated services of the Older Americans Act is information and referral (I & R). I & R services maintain directories of service programs for and service providers to older persons in a specific geographical area. Knowing the number to call to find out where needed services are available is important for adult children, aging parents, and helping professionals. I & R services also may maintain lists of geriatric physicians in a particular area. Another federally mandated resource is an ombudsman position available in all state offices on aging to assist older persons and their families in dealing with issues related to long-term care.

In addition to the federal aging network, a wide variety of national, state, and local service organizations and associations exist to provide information and services to older persons, their families, and professional helpers. These include organizations such as the American Association of Retired Persons, the National Association of Area Agencies on Aging, the National Council on Black Americans, and so forth. A recent listing of such agencies is provided by Myers (1988a).

One of the major services some older persons need is adult day care. Montgomery and Still (1984) provided an extensive bibliography on adult day care that includes listings of available services. Day care services provide respite for family caregivers to allow them to maintain employment or other activities in the community during the daytime, yet continue to care for aging relatives in their own homes. Despite all the services available, 80% of older persons continue to receive needed care from family members. The informal network—family, friends, and neighbors—continues to be the major resource for assistance to older persons.

Mental health services are available to older persons and their families through private practitioners as well as community agencies. State and county operated community mental health centers often have specialists available who have been trained in gerontological counseling and are aware of services and resources to assist older persons in their community. At present, the need for services exceeds the availability of trained practitioners. The reluctance of older persons to seek or receive mental health services, combined with the reluctance of some practitioners to work with them, contributes to the present state of underservice to this population.

Some agencies that adult children and aging parents may find helpful, particularly when caregiving is involved, are:

Children of Aging Parents
2761 Trenton Road
Levitown, PA 19056
(215) 547-1000

Older Women's League (OWL)
730 11th Street, Suite 300
Washington, DC 20001
(202) 783-6686

American Association of Retired Persons
1909 K St. N.W.
Washington, DC 20049
(202) 728-4300

U.S. Administration on Aging
330 Independence Avenue
Washington, DC 20201
(202) 245-0724

Some Final Comments

The variety of issues that may arise to challenge adult children and aging parents may seem unlimited. It seems that most problems exist when aging parents are in poor health and need a lot of assistance. The onset of poor health typically is gradual, thus the onset of problems is itself gradual in nature. It is entirely possible and often likely that problem situations build without the conscious awareness of family members. By the time anyone talks about the situation, a crisis is in effect. Taking the time and making the effort to build healthy relationships while aging parents are themselves healthy can provide a useful buffer against the problems that can ensue. It is important to remember, however, that not all adult children and aging parents experience illnesses or conflict. So, the benefits of building healthy relationships may only be positive, satisfying memories of special types of intimacy between adult children and their adult, aging parents.

Professional helpers have important roles to play in prevention as well as remediation of problem situations between adult children and aging parents. When issues of competence are involved, counselors will need full awareness of ethical issues, principles, and guidelines to ensure that older persons maintain their rights in dealing with families, agencies, and institutions. When faced with conflict situations, it can be easy for counselors to become confused over who actually is their client—the adult child or the aging parent? Rather than taking sides, counselors must remain open to the needs of members of all generations, and focus their efforts on assisting all family members in achieving and maintaining satisfying relationships. A lifetime of dysfunctional patterns within family systems can seem to be an insurmountable situation. The good news is that positive relationships *can*, in fact, occur between adult children and aging parents for the first time when parents grow old. Our challenge as helpers is to facilitate building and maintaining such relationships.

Summary

In this chapter, suggestions were made for building and maintaining healthy relationships between adult children and aging parents. Family counseling methods were discussed and four approaches to counseling were explained, including bibliotherapy, life review, genograms, and the use of early recollections. Community resources that help adult children and aging parents were discussed.

Though the later years of life can be accompanied by many challenges for older persons and their families, the potential for satisfying relationships remains and should be optimized.

APPENDIX

ANNOTATED LIST OF ASSESSMENT INSTRUMENTS

Affect Balance Scale (ABS): A short, 10-question test designed to assess the affective status of the general population. It is administered in an interview where subjects respond to five questions tapping positive affect and five questions tapping negative affect. May be considered as a general screening tool. See Bradburn, N.M. (1969). *The structure of psychological well-being*. Chicago: University of Chicago Press.

Beck Depression Inventory (BDI): Consists of 21 sets of statements written to reflect feelings such as mood, pessimism, guilt, irritability, fatigability, and loss of libido. The statements are read to the subjects, who choose the one in each set that best describes their affect. See Beck, A.T., Ward, C., Mendelsohn, M., Mock, J., & Erbaugh, J. (1961). An inventory for measuring depression. *Archives of General Psychiatry, 4,* 53–63.

Bender Background Interference Procedure (BIP): Used for assessing main dysfunction, this instrument consists of 9 Wertheimer Figures that subjects copy as accurately as possible, with no time limits. The subjects are then asked to reproduce the figures on special paper that provides visual interference. The administrator then scores the extent of the subject's brain impairment. Contact Arthur Canter, Western Psychological Services, 12031 Wilshire Boulevard, Los Angeles, CA 90025.

Career Assessment Inventory (CAI): Two versions of this 300 + item instrument are available and provide occupational interest scores based on the Holland themes. Administration requires 30–40 minutes. Mail-in computer scoring is available through the test publisher. Contact National Computer Systems, Professional Assessment Services, P.O. Box 1416, Minneapolis, MN 55440.

Constructive Leisure Activity Survey (CLAS): A comprehensive inventory consisting of over 300 items in which respondents indicate past and future leisure likes and dislikes. See Edwards, P.B. (1979). *Leisure counseling techniques: Individual and group counseling step-by-step.* Los Angeles: University Publishers.

Death Anxiety Scale (DAS): The most widely used death anxiety scale, this 15-item true-false inventory instructs subjects to respond to personal death-related questions. Contact Dr. Donald Templer, The California School of Professional Psychology, 1350 "M" Street, Fresno, CA 93721.

Death Concern Scale (DCS): 30 Likert-type scaled items assess respondents' "conscious contemplation" and "negative evaluation" of death. Contact Dr. Louis Dickstein, Department of Psychology, Wellesley College, Wellesley, MA 62181.

Facts on Aging Quiz (FAQ): The 25 items of this instrument cover information documented by empirical research about basic physical, mental, and social facts about aging. Common misperceptions of aging are incorporated as well. The FAQ, which can be self-scored, has been found to be useful as a stimulus for group discussion. See Palmore, E. (1981). The facts on aging quiz: Part II. *The Gerontologist, 21*, 427–431.

Family-of-Origin Scale (FOS): This is a 40-item self-report instrument designed to measure perceptions of health in the family of origin. A total score for perceived health is provided along with subscale scores indicating degree of autonomy and intimacy in the family of origin. See Hoverstadt, A.J., Anderson, W.T., Piercy, F.P., Cochran., S.W., & Fine, M. (1985). A family-of-origin scale. *Journal of Marital and Family Therapy, 11*, 287–297.

Fear of Death Scale (FODS): 21 death-related statements compose this instrument. Subjects' responses yield fear of death and inconsistency scores. Contact Dr. David Lester, Richard Stockton State College, Pomona, NJ 08240.

General Aptitude Test Battery (GATB): Developed by the United States Employment Service for use in counseling and job referral of individuals. Subscales assess general learning ability (vocabulary, arithmetic reasoning, three-dimensional space), verbal aptitude, numerical aptitude, spatial aptitude, form perception, clerical perception, motor coordination, finger dexterity, and manual dexterity. Administration of the entire battery requires 2 1/2 hours. Contact U.S. Employment Service, Division of Program Planning and Operations, Employment and Training Administration, U.S. Department of Labor, 601 D Street, N.W., Washington, DC 20213.

Geriatric Depression Scale (GDS): A self-rating format of 30 items, this scale can be administered in oral or in written form. Designed to tap affective, cognitive, and behavioral symptoms of depression, this is often used as a screening instrument and discriminates between nondepressed and mildly to severely depressed persons. See Brink, T.L., Yesavage, J.A., Lum, O., Heersma, P., Adey, M., & Rose, T.L. (1982). Screening test for geriatric depression. *Clinical Gerontologist, 1,* 37–43.

Geriatric Hopelessness Scale (GHS): 30 true-false items indicate a subject's degree of hopelessness defined as negative expectancies toward oneself and toward the future. The scale was developed to assess hopelessness in both high-depression and low-depression older persons. See Fry, P.S. (1984). Development of a gertiatric scale for counseling and intervention with the depressed elderly. *Journal of Counseling Psychology, 31,* 322–331.

Geriatric Scale of Recent Life Events (GSRLE): This 50-item inventory is a revision of the Holmes/Rahe Recent Life Events Schedule and is reported to be more appropriate for changes older persons experience. Subjects are asked to indicate whether they've experienced various life events within the past 3 months, and an index of stressful events is calculated. See Kiyak, A., Kiang, J., & Kahana, E. (1976). *Methodological inquiry into the schedule of recent life events.* Paper presented at the American Psychological Association Meeting, New York.

Hamilton Psychiatric Rating Scale for Depression (HAMD): Consists of 17 items rated by an observer and designed to identify and diagnose clinical depression. The instrument covers affective disorders and somatic symptoms including depressed mood, hypochondriasis, insomnia, retardation, loss of insight, and loss of weight. See Hamilton, M. (1960). A rating scale for depression. *Journal of Neurology, Neurosurgery, and Psychiatry, 23,* 56–62.

Hwalek-Sengstock Elder Abuse Screening Protocol (HWEASP): A 16-item dichotomous (yes/no) response inventory designed to screen subjects for elder abuse. Authors are still collecting validity data for the instrument. See Hwalek, M., & Sengstock, M. (1986). Assessing the probability of abuse of the elderly: Toward development of a clinical screening instrument. *Journal of Applied Gerontology, 5,* 153–173.

LaCrosse Wellness Inventory (LWI): A two-part self-administered inventory used to assess the current level of respondent wellness. Contact Paula Silha, LaCrosse Wellness Project, 203 Mitchell Hall, UW-LC, LaCrosse, WI 54601.

Leisure Activities Blank (LAB): The most standardized instrument in the field of leisure wellness, this 120-item inventory measures past and future leisure involvements. Past interest subscales are: mechanics, crafts, intellectual, slow living, sports, and glamor sports. Future interest subscales include: adventure, mechanics, crafts, easy living, intellectual, ego recognition, slow living, and clean living. See McKechnie, G.E. (1974). *The leisure activities blank manual.* Palo Alto, CA: Consulting Psychologists Press.

Leisure Well-Being Inventory (LWBI): 125 yes-no items survey the subject's breadth of leisure wellness. This instrument has been widely used and researched because it goes beyond measuring simple leisure interests and assesses four aspects: coping, awareness-understanding, knowledge, and assertion. See McDowell, C.F. (1978). *Leisure well-being inventory.* Eugene, OR: Leisure Lifestyle Consultants.

Life Satisfaction Index A (LSIA): A 13-item scale derived from the basic Life Satisfaction Ratings. Respondents check statements with an "agree, uncertain, disagree" response format according to self-perceptions of life satisfaction. See Wood, V., Wylie, M.L., & Shaefer, B. (1969). An analysis of a short self-report measure of life satisfaction. *Journal of Gerontology, 24,* 465–469.

Mascione Physical and Mental Competence for Independent Living in the Aged Scale (MPMCILAS): A brief instrument developed to assess changes over time in functional capacity in independent living for noninstitutionalized frail older persons. Factors assessed include activities for daily living, mental functioning, physical functioning, and continence. See Macione, A.

(1979). *Macione Physical and Mental Competence for Independent Living in the Aged Scale.* Paper presented at the Seventh Annual Nursing Research Conference, Tucson, AZ.

Mental Status Questionnaire (MSQ): An inventory of 10 items including the day of the week, the name of the president, and the current year. Both awareness of current events and memory of more distant events are measured. See Kahn, R.L., Goldfarb, A.I., Pollack, M., & Peck, A. (1960). Brief objective measures for the determination of mental status in the aged. *American Journal of Psychiatry, 117,* 326–328.

Mirenda Leisure Interest Finder (MLIF): Using the column format for checking off leisure interests and needs, this 90-item instrument has been computerized and is widely used for assessing leisure interests. The items were selected from the nine categories of leisure activities on the Avocational Activities Inventory. See Wilson, G.T., & Mirenda, J.J. (1975). The Milwaukee Leisure Counseling Model. *Counseling and Values, 20,* 42–46.

Multidimensional Fear of Death Scale (MDFODS): Eight subscales are assessed by 42 items of this instrument. Subscales measured are: fear of the dying process, fear of the dead, fear of being destroyed, fear for significant others, fear of the unknown, fear of conscious death, fear for the body after death, and fear of premature death. Contact: Dr. John W. Hoelter, Department of Sociology, University of Cincinnati, Cincinnati, OH 45221.

Multilevel Assessment Instrument (MAI): Developed by the Philadelphia Geriatric Center, this instrument incorporates work from the OARS to assess well-being [competence] in the areas of health, activities of daily living, cognition, time use, social interaction, and perceptions of the objective environment. Designed to be administered in about 50 minutes, the MAI has been shown to have utility for assessment and research of older persons. See Lawton, M.P., Moss, M., Fulcomer, M., & Kleban, J. (1982). A research and service oriented multilevel assessment instrument. *Journal of Gerontology, 37,* 91–99.

Older Americans Research and Service Center Instrument (OARS): This 105-question instrument requires approximately 1 hour to administer and measures functional activity in five areas: social resources, economic resources, mental health, physical health, and the capacity to perform activities of daily living. A trained rater judges the functional status in the five domains of individuals along a continuum ranging from excellent functioning to totally impaired. See Pfeiffer, E. (1970). *Multidimensional functional assessment: The OARS methodology.* Durham, NC: Duke University, Center of the Study of Aging and Human Development.

Older Persons Counseling Needs Survey (OPCNS): A 54-item Likert-type scale instrument designed to identify a wide range of needs of older persons. Designed for group, individual, or self-administration, the inventory identifies four primary areas of concern or need—personal, interpersonal, activity, and environmental. Contact Dr. Jane Myers, Counselor Education Department, 1215 Norman Hall, University of Florida, Gainesville, FL 32611.

Personal Authority in the Family System (PAFS): The PAFS is a 132-item self-report scale using a five-point Likert response format. Designed to assess relationships in three-generational family systems, the instrument includes five intergenerational scales (discussed in chapter 5). See Bray, J.H., Williamson, D.S., & Malone, P.E. (1984). Personal authority in the family system: Development of a questionnaire to measure personal authority in intergenerational family processes. *Journal of Marital and Family Therapy, 10,* 167–168.

Philadelphia Geriatric Center Morale Scale (PGCMS): A revision in 1975 of this scale highlighted three factors—agitation, attitude toward own aging, and lonely dissatisfaction—as salient in this measure of subjective well-being. This instrument is reported to be usable with marginally comprehending individuals (i.e., persons who lack cognitive ability or who have poor reading skills). See Lawton, M.P. (1975). The Philadelphia Geriatric Center Morale Scale: A revision. *Journal of Gerontology, 30,* 85–89.

PERI Life Events Scale (PERI) (Psychiatric Epidemiology Research Interview): 102 life events were selected to represent both positive and negative life experiences. Respondents note whether they've experienced each event, which are grouped into 11 areas (e.g., health, finances, family, love and marriage). See Dohrenwend, B.S., Krasnoff, L., Askenasy, A., & Dohrenwend, B.P. (1978). Exemplification of a method for scaling life events: The PERI Life Events Scale. *Journal of Health and Social Behavior, 19,* 205–229.

Retirement Maturity Index (RMI): 59 items that can be self-administered or by structured interview measure 14 variables shown to effect preparation for retirement or life satisfaction in retirement. Responses on a 10-point Likert-type scale create a composite retirement maturity score. See Johnson, R.P., & Riker, H.C. (1981). Retirement maturity: A valuable concept for preretirement counselors. *Personnel and Guidance Journal, 59,* 291–295.

Salamon-Conte Life Satisfaction in the Elderly Scale (SCLSES): A multifactor scale that measures eight categories of life satisfaction: pleasure in daily activities, meaningfulness of life, goodness of fit between desired and achieved goals, mood tone, self-concept, perceived health, financial security, and social contact. See Salamon, M.J., & Conte, V.A. (1981). *The SCLSES and the eight categories of life satisfaction.* Contact Psychological Assessment Resources, Inc., P.O. Box 98, Odessa, FL 33556.

Self-Directed Search (SDS): A self-administered, self-scored instrument based on Holland's occupational types. This relatively inexpensive survey assesses respondent experiences, abilities, and interests in the world of work. Although the SDS can be self-interpreted, a counselor may be utilized to interpret the instrument. Contact Consulting Psychologists Press, Inc., 577 College Avenue, Palo Alto, CA 94306.

Social Readjustment Rating Scale (SRRS): This instrument evaluates the effects of life changes preceding the onset of illness in individuals. A total life-stress score is obtained as a measure of cumulative effects of life changes. See Holmes, T.H., & Rahe, R.H. (1967). The Social Readjustment Rating Scale. *Journal of Psychosomatic Research, 11,* 213–218.

Stroop Color and Word Test (SCWT): 300 stimulus items help direct and diagnose brain dysfunction. Subjects are asked to name colors printed on the three-page instrument. The data yield information about cognitive flexibility, selective attention, creativity, and strength of automatic verbal processing response. Contact Stoelting Company, 1350 S. Kostner Avenue, Chicago, IL 60623.

Thematic Apperception Test (TAT): A projective personality technique consisting of 19 cards of vague black and white pictures. Subjects are asked to describe the depicted event, what led up to that event, and the outcome of the event. Intensive training is required to administer and interpret the TAT. Contact Harvard University Press, 79 Garden Street, Cambridge, MA 02138.

Wechsler Memory Scale (WMS): This easily administered instrument assesses mnemonic functioning in seven subtests: personal and current information, orientation, mental control, logical memory, memory span, visual reproduction, and associate learning. Scores are considered equivalent to the intelligence quotient. Contact The Psychological Corporation, 7500 Old Oak Boulevard, Cleveland, OH 44130.

Zung Self-Rating Depression Scale (SDS): 20 items administered orally or by self tap four subscale indices—well-being, depressed-mood, optimism, and somatic symptoms. The items, developed through clinical observations of depressed persons, are rated by the subject as applicable to themselves "a little," "some," "a good part," or "most of the time." See Zung, W. (1965). A self-rating depression scale. *Archives of General Psychiatry, 1*, 63–70.

REFERENCES

Adams, D. (1969). Correlates of life satisfaction among the elderly. *The Gerontologist, 11*, 64–69.

Agee, J. (1967). *A death in the family.* New York: Grosset & Dunlap.

Aiken, L.R. (1980). Problems in testing the elderly. *Educational Gerontology, 5*, 119–124.

Aldous, J. (1987). New views on the family life of the elderly and near elderly. *Journal of Marriage and the Family, 49*, 227–234.

American Association of Retired Persons. (1986a). *A profile of older Americans.* Washington, DC: Author.

American Association of Retired Persons. (1986b). *Work and retirement: Employees over 40 and their views.* Washington, DC: Author.

American Association of Retired Persons. (1988). *Working Age, 3*(4), p.2.

American Association of Retired Persons. (undated). *A portrait of older minorities.* Washington, DC: Author.

American Health Care Association. (undated, a). *Myths and realities of living in a nursing home.* Washington, DC: Author.

American Health Care Association. (undated, b). *Reactions to nursing home admission.* Washington, DC: Author.

American Health Care Association. (undated, c). *Thinking about a nursing home? A consumer's guide to choosing a long term care facility.* Washington, DC: Author.

American Psychiatric Association. (1980). *Diagnostic and statistical manual of mental disorders, Third edition.* Washington, DC: Author.

Atchley, R.C. (1977). *The social forces in later life* (2nd ed.). Belmont, CA: Wadsworth.

Bach, R. (1977). *Illusions: The adventures of a reluctant messiah.* New York: Dell.

Barbado, C.A., & Feezel, J.D. (1987). The language of aging in different groups. *The Gerontologist, 27*(4), 527–531.

Barnes, G.M. (1982). *Alcohol and youth: A comprehensive bibliography.* Westport, CT: Greenwood Press.

Barnes, R., & Raskind, M. (1984). Long-term clinical management of the dementia patient. In J.P. Abrahams & V.J. Crooks (Eds.), *Geriatric mental health* (pp. 75–96). New York: Grune & Stratton.

Barnhill, L.R., & Longo, D. (1980). Fixation and regression in the family life cycle. In J.G. Howells (Ed.), *Advances in family psychiatry* (Volume II, pp. 51–64). New York: International Universities Press.

193

Baruth, L.G., & Huber, C.H. (1984). *An introduction to marital theory and therapy.* Monterey, CA: Brooks/Cole.

Baum, S.K. (1983–84). Age identification in the elderly: Some theoretical considerations. *International Journal of Aging and Human Development, 18*(1), 25–30.

Baum, S.K., & Boxley, R.L. (1983). Depression and old age identification. *Journal of Clinical Psychology, 39*(4), 584–590.

Bearden, L.J., & Head, D.W. (1985). Attitudes of rehabilitation professionals toward aging and older persons. *Journal of Applied Rehabilitation Counseling, 17*(1), 17–19.

Beck, W. (1984). *A structured addictions assessment interview for selecting treatment.* Toronto, Canada: Addiction Research Foundation.

Berger, H. (1983). Alcoholism in the elderly. *Postgraduate Medicine, 73*(1), 329–330.

Bergman, J.A. (1981). Prepared statement. In U.S. Congress, House Select Committee on Aging, *Abuse of older persons* (Comm. Pub. No. 97–289). Washington, DC: U.S. Government Printing Office.

Berkowitz, S. (1978). Informed consent, research, and the elderly. *The Gerontologist, 18*(3), 237–243.

Blai, B. (1987). *Accidents and alcohol abuse among older Americans.* Ann Arbor, MI: ERIC/CAPS.

Blake, R. (1982). Assessing the counseling needs of older persons. *Measurement and Evaluation in Counseling and Development, 15*(3), 188–193.

Blau, P.M. (1961). *Exchange and power in social life.* New York: Wiley.

Blazer, D. (1982). *Depression in later life.* St. Louis: Mosby.

Blazer, D., Hughes, D.C., & George, L.K. (1987). The epidemiology of depression in an elderly community population. *The Gerontologist, 27*(3), 281–287.

Blieszner, R. (1986). Trends in family gerontology research. *Family Relations, 35*(4), 555–562.

Block, M.R., & Sinnott, J.D. (1979). *The battered elder syndrome: An exploratory study.* College Park: University of Maryland Center on Aging.

Boszoromenyi-Nagy, P. (1980). Invisible loyalties—intergenerational therapy. In A.S. Gurman & D.P. Knisern (Eds.), *Handbook of family therapy.* New York: Brunner/Mazel.

Bowen, M. (1978). *Family therapy in clinical practice.* New York: Aronson.

Bowers, M.K., Jackson, E.N., Knight, J.A., & LeShan, L. (1975). *Counseling the dying.* New York: Aronson.

Bradburn, N., & Caplovitz, D. (1965). *Reports on happiness: A pilot study of behavior related to mental health.* Chicago: Aldine.

Brammer, L.M., & Abrego, P.J. (1981). Intervention strategies for coping with transitions. *The Counseling Psychologist, 9*(2), 19–36.

Braun, K.L., & Rose, C.L. (1987). Family perceptions of geriatric foster family and nursing home care. *Family Relations, 36*, 321–327.

Bray, J.H., Williamson, D.S., & Malone, P.E. (1984). *Personal authority in the family system questionnaire manual.* Houston: Texas Women's University.

Bridges, W. (1983). *Transitions: Making sense of life's changes.* Menlo Park, CA: Addison-Wesley.

Brody, E. (1985). Parent care as a normative family stress. *The Gerontologist, 25*(1), 19–29.

Brody, E., & Schoonover, C.B. (1986). Patterns of parent-care when adult daughters work and when they do not. *The Gerontologist, 26*(4), 372–381.

Brody, E.M., Johnsen, P.T., Fulcomer, M.C., & Lang, A.M. (1983). Women's changing roles and help to elderly parents: Attitudes of three generations of women. *Journal of Gerontology 38*(5), 597–607.

Brody, J.A. (1981). *Alcohol and alcohol abuse. White House Conference on Aging, background paper.* Bethesda, MD: National Institute on Aging.

Brotman, H. (1982). *Every ninth American.* (Committee Pub. No. 97–332). Washington, DC: U.S. House of Representatives.

Brown, B., & Chiang, C. (1984). Drug and alcohol abuse among the elderly: Is being alone the key? *International Journal of Aging and Human Development, 18*(1), 1–12.

Brubaker, T.H. (1985). *Later life families.* Beverly Hills, CA: Sage.

Buehler, C. (1967). Human life as a central subject of humanistic psychology. In J. Bugental (Ed.), *Challenges in humanistic psychology* (pp. 83–91). New York: McGraw-Hill.

Bulcroft, K., & O'Connor, M. (1986). The importance of dating relationships on quality of life for older persons. *Family Relations, 35,* 397–401.

Buscaglia, L. (1982). *Freddie the leaf.* Thorofare, NJ: Charles B. Slack.

Busse, E.W., & Blazer, D.G. (Eds.). (1980). *Handbook of geriatric psychiatry.* New York: Van Nostrand Reinhold.

Butler, R. (1975). *Why survive? Growing old in America.* New York: Harper & Row.

Butler, R.N. (1963). The life review: An interpretation of reminiscence in the elderly. *Psychiatry, 26,* 65–75.

Butler, R.N. (1980). A humanistic approach to our last days. *Death Education, 3,* 359–361.

Butler, R.N. (1982). Senile dementia: Reversible and irreversible. *The Counseling Psychologist, 12*(2), 74–96.

Butler, R.N., & Lewis, M.I. (1982). *Aging and mental health: Positive psychosocial and biomedical approaches.* St. Louis: Mosby.

Cantor, M. (1983). Strain among caregivers: A study of experience in the United States. *The Gerontologist, 23*(6), 597–604.

Caregivers in the workplace. (1988). *Working Age, 3*(5), 4–5.

Carnegie, D. (1936). *How to win friends and influence people.* New York: Pocket Books.

Chandler, J.T., Rachal, J.R., & Kazelskis, R. (1986). Attitudes of long-term care personnel toward the elderly. *The Gerontologist, 26*(5), 551–555.

Chenowith, B., & Spencer, B. (1986). Dementia: The experience of family caregivers. *The Gerontologist, 26*(3), 267–272.

Cherlin, A. (1983). A sense of history: Recent research on aging and the family. In M. Riley, B. Hess, & K. Bond (Eds.), *Aging in society: Selected reviews of recent research.* Hillsdale, NJ: Erlbaum.

Cherlin, A.F., & Furstenberg, F.F. (1986). *The new American grandparent: A place in the family, a life apart.* New York: Basic Books.

Cicirelli, V.G. (1983a). Adult children and their elderly parents. In T.H. Brubaker (Ed.), *Family relationships in later life* (pp. 31–46). Beverly Hills, CA: Sage.

Cicirelli, V.G. (1983b). Adult children's attachment and helping behavior to elderly parents: A path model. *Journal of Marriage and the Family, 45*(4), 815–825.

Cicirelli, V.G. (1983c). Personal strains and negative feelings in adult children's relationships with elderly parents. *Academic Psychology Bulletin, 5*(1), 31–36.

Cook, P., & Stewart, E. (1985). *Meeting guidance needs of older adults.* Columbus, OH: The National Center for Research in Vocational Education.

Coser, L.A., & Rosenberg, B. (1976). *Sociological theory: A book of readings.* (4th ed.). New York: Macmillan.

Cox, H. (1988). *Later life: The realities of aging* (2nd ed.). Englewood Cliffs, NJ: Prentice-Hall.

Crook, T., & Cohen, G. (1984). Future directions for alcohol research in the elderly. In J.T. Hanford & T. Samorajski (Eds.), *Alcoholism in the elderly* (pp. 277–282). New York: Raven Press.

Crumbaugh, J.C., & Maholick, L.T. (1969). *Manual of instructions for the Purpose in Life Test.* Munster, IN: Psychometric Affiliates.

Cumming, E., & Henry, W.E. (1961). *Growing old.* New York: Basic Books.

Cunningham, W.R., & Brookbank, J.W. (1983). *Gerontology: The psychology, biology, and sociology of aging.* New York: Harper & Row.

Davidson, P.O. (1976). *The behavioral management of anxiety, depression, and pain.* Larchmont, NY: Brunner/Mazel.

Davidson, W.B., & Cotter, P.R. (1982). Adjustment to aging and relationships with offspring. *Psychological Reports, 50,* 731–738.

de Saint-Exupéry, A. (1943). *The little prince.* New York: Harcourt, Brace & World.

Decker, D.L. (1980). *Social gerontology: An introduction to the dynamics of aging.* Boston: Little, Brown.

Dickstein, L.S. (1972). Death concern: Measurement and correlates. *Psychological Reports, 30,* 563–571.

Dobson, J.E., & Dobson, R.L. (1985). The sandwich generation: Dealing with aging parents. *Journal of Counseling and Development, 63,* 572–574.

Dohrenwend, B.S., Krasnoff, L., Askenasy, A.R., & Dohrenwend, B.P. (1978). Exemplification of a method for scaling life events: The PERI Life Events Scale. *Journal of Health and Social Behavior, 19,* 205–229.

Dowd, J.J. (1981). Aging as exchange: A preface to theory. In C.S. Kart & B.B. Manard, *Aging in America: Readings in social gerontology* (2nd ed.) (pp. 58–78). Sherman Oaks, CA: Alfred.

Dupree, L., & Schonfeld, L. (1985, August 23–25). *High risk situations for elderly alcohol abusers.* Paper presented at the annual convention of the American Psychological Association, Los Angeles.

Duvall, E.M. (1971). *Family development* (4th ed.). Philadelphia: Lippincott.

Dye, C.J., & Richards, C.C. (1980). Facilitating the transition to nursing homes. In S.S. Sargent (Ed.), *Nontraditional counseling and therapy with older adults* (pp. 100–118). New York: Springer.

Edwards, D.W. (1985). An investigation of the use and abuse of alcohol and other drugs among 50 aged male alcoholics and 50 aged female alcoholics. *Journal of Alcohol and Drug Education, 30*(2), 24–30.

Epstein, L.J. (1976). Depression in the elderly. *Journal of Gerontology, 31*(3), 278–282.

Erikson, E.H. (1963). *Childhood and society.* New York: Norton.

Essex, M.J., Klein, M.J., & Benjamin, L.S. (1985). Intimacy and depression in older women. *Psychiatry, 48,* 159–178.

Eyde, D.R., & Rich, J.A. (1983). *Psychological distress in aging: A family management model.* Rockville, MD: Aspen Systems.

Fabry, J., Haley, T., & Cahill, K. (1982). Assessment of organic dysfunctions in older persons. *Measurement and Evaluation in Counseling and Development, 15*(3), 240–248.

Falck, H.S., & Kane, M.K. (1978). *It can't be home: Social and emotional aspects of residential care* (DHEW Pub. No. (ADM) 78–313). Washington, DC: U.S. Department of Health, Education, and Welfare.

Feinauer, L.L. (1983, November). *Multigenerational households: Problems and solutions from three points of view.* Paper presented at the Annual Scientific Meeting of the Gerontological Society, San Francisco, CA.

Feinauer, L.L., Lund, D.A., & Miller, J.R. (1987). Family issues in multigenerational households. *The American Journal of Family Therapy, 15*(1), 52–61.

Finnerty-Fried, P. (1982). Instruments for the assessment of attitudes toward older persons. *Measurement and Evaluation in Counseling and Development, 15*(3), 201–210.

Flanagan, J.C. (1982). *New insights to improve the quality of life at age 70.* Palo Alto, CA: American Institutes for Research in the Behavioral Sciences.

Frankl, V.E. (1956). *Man's search for meaning.* New York: Pocket Books.

Franklin Research Center. (1980). *Elder Abuse.* Washington, DC: U.S. Department of Health and Human Services.

Fry, P.S. (1984). Development of a geriatric scale of hopelessness: Implications for counseling and intervention with the depressed elderly. *Journal of Counseling Psychology, 31*(3), 322–331.

Fry, P.S. (1986). *Depression, stress, and adaptations in the elderly.* Rockville, MD: Aspen Systems.

Gallagher, D., Thompson, L.W., & Levy, S.M. (1980). Clinical psychological assessment of older adults. In L.W. Poon (Ed.), *Aging in the 1980s: Psychological issues.* Washington, DC: American Psychological Association.

Gallagher, D.E., & Thompson, L.W. (1982). Psychosocial factors affecting adaptation to bereavement in the elderly. *International Journal of Aging and Human Development, 14*(2), 79–95.

Ganikos, M.L. (1977). The expressed counseling needs and perceptions of counseling of older adult students in selected Florida community colleges. *Dissertation Abstracts International, 38*, 6533A (University of Florida).

George, L.K. (1980). *Role transitions in later life.* Monterey, CA: Brooks/Cole.

Gerfo, M.L. (1980). Three ways of reminiscence in theory and practice. *International Journal of Aging and Human Development, 12*(10), 39–47.

Giordano, N.H., & Girodano, J.A. (1984). Elder abuse: A review of the literature. *Social Work, 29*, 232–236.

Glick, I.O., Weiss, R.S., & Parkes, C.M. (1974). *The first year of bereavement.* New York: Wiley

Goebel, B.L., & Boeck, B.E. (1987). Ego integrity and fear of death: A comparison of institutionalized and independently living older adults. *Death Studies, 11*, 193–204.

Gomberg, E.S. (1982). Alcohol use and alcohol problems in the elderly. *Alcohol and Health Monograph No. 4: Special Population Issues.* Rockville, MD: NIAAA.

Graham, K. (1986). Identifying and measuring alcohol abuse among the elderly: Serious problems with existing information. *Journal of Studies on Alcohol, 47*(4), 322–326.

Gross, D., & Capuzzi, D. (1981). The elderly alcoholic: The counselor's dilemma. *Counselor Education and Supervision, 20*(3), 185–192.

Gwynther, L.P., & George, L.K. (1986). Caregivers for dementia patients: Complex determinants of well-being and burden. *The Gerontologist, 26*(3), 245–266.

Hagestad, G. (1979). Problems and promises in the social psychology of intergenerational relations. In R. Fogel, E. Hatfield, S. Kiesler, & T. March (Eds.), *Stability and change in the family.* Annapolis, MD: National Research Council.

Hagestad, G.O., & Lang, M.E. (1986). The transition to grandparenthood. *Journal of Family Issues, 7*(2), 115–130.

Haley, J. (1973). Strategic therapy when a child is presented as the problem. *Journal of the American Academy of Child Psychiatry, 12*, 641–659.

Haley, W.E., Brown, S.L., & Levine, E.G. (1987). Experimental evaluation of the effectiveness of group intervention for dementia caregivers. *The Gerontologist, 27*, 376–382.

Hansson, R.O., Jones, W.H., Carpenter, B.N., & Remondet, J.H. (1986). Loneliness and adjustment to old age. *International Journal of Aging and Human Development, 24*(1), 41–53.

Harris, D.K., & Cole, W.E. (1980). *Sociology of aging.* Boston: Houghton Mifflin.

Harris, L., & Associates. (1974). *The myth and reality of aging in America.* Washington, DC: National Council on the Aging.

Harris, L., & Associates. (1981). *Aging in the eighties: America in transition.* Washington, DC: National Council on the Aging.

Hartwigsen, G. (1987). Older widows and the transference of home. *International Journal of Aging and Human Development, 25*(3), 195–207.

Hatch, R.C., & Franken, M.L. (1984). Concerns of children with parents in nursing homes. *Journal of Gerontological Social Work, 7*(3), 19–30.

Havighurst, R.J. (1972). *Developmental tasks and education.* (3rd ed.). New York: Longman.

Havighurst, R.J., Neugarten, B.L., & Tobin, S.S. (1968). Disengagement and patterns of aging. In B.L. Neugarten, (Ed.), *Middle age and aging.* Chicago: University of Chicago Press.

Hayes, J., & Nutman, P. (1981). *Understanding the unemployed.* New York: Tavistock.

Hayflick, L. (1977). The cellular basis for biological aging. In C.E. Finch & L. Hayflick (Eds.), *Handbook of the biology of aging* (pp. 159–186). New York: Van Nostrand Reinhold.

Henton, J., Cate, R., & Emory, B. (1984). The dependent elderly: Targets for abuse. In W.H. Quinn & G.A. Hughston, *Independent aging* (pp. 149–162). Rockville, MD: Aspen.

Herr, J.J., & Weakland, J.W. (1979). *Counseling elders and their families.* New York: Springer.

Herr, J.J., & Weakland, J.W. (1984). Conducting family therapy with elder clients. In J.P. Abrahams & V.J. Crooks (Eds.), *Geriatric mental health* (pp. 123–134). New York: Grune & Stratton.

Hess, B.B., & Waring, J.M. (1978). Changing patterns of aging and family bonds in later life. *The Family Coordinator, 27,* 303–314.

Hill, R. (1971). Modern science theory and the family. In M.B. Sussman (Ed.), *Sourcebook in marriage and the family* (4th ed.) (pp. 302–313). Boston: Houghton-Mifflin.

Hine, V.A. (1979–80). Dying at home: Can families cope? *Omega, 10,* 175–180.

Hitchcock, A.A. (1984). Work, aging, and counseling: Current trends. *Journal of Counseling and Development, 63*(4), 258–259.

Hoelter, J. (1979). Multidimensional measurement of fear of death. *Journal of Consulting and Clinical Psychology, 47,* 996–999.

Hoffman, L.W., McManus, K.A., & Brackbill, Y. (1987). The value of children to young and elderly parents. *International Journal of Aging and Human Development, 25*(4), 309–322.

Holmes, T.H., & Rahe, R.H. (1967). The social readjustment rating scale. *Journal of Psychosomatic Research, 11,* 213–218.

Homans, G.C. (1961). *Social behavior: Its elementary forms.* New York: Harcourt, Brace & World.

Honore, F.M. (1984). Responding to loneliness: Counseling the elderly. *Canadian Counsellor, 18*(3), 123–129.

Hooyman, N.R., & Lustbader, W. (1986). *Taking care: Supporting older people and their families.* New York: Free Press.

Horn, J.L., Skinner, H.A., Wanberg, K.W., & Foster, F.M. (1984). *Alcohol Dependence Scale.* Toronto, Canada: Addiction Research Foundation.

Horne, J. (1985). *Caregiving: Helping an aging loved one.* Glenview, IL: Scott, Foresman.

Horowitz, A. (1985). Sons and daughters as caregivers to older persons: Differences in role performance and consequences. *The Gerontologist, 25*(6), 612–617.

Horowitz, A., & Shindelman, L.W. (1981). *Reciprocity and affection: Past influences on current caregiving.* Paper presented at the annual meeting of the Gerontological Society of America, Toronto, Canada.

Horowitz, M.J., Weiss, D.S., Kaltreider, N., Krupnick, M.S., Marmar, C., Wilner, N., & DeWitt, K. (1984). Reactions to the death of a parent. *Journal of Nervous and Mental Disease, 172*(7), 383–391.

Hovestadt, A.J., Anderson, W.T., Piercy, F.P., Cochran, W.S., & Fine, M. (1985). A-family-of-origin scale. *Journal of Marital and Family Therapy, 11*, 287–297.

Howells, J.G. (1975). *Principles of family psychiatry.* New York: Brunner/Mazel.

Hwalek, M.A., & Sengstock, M.C. (1986). *A screening instrument for identifying elderly at risk of abuse and neglect.* Paper presented at the annual scientific meeting of the Gerontological Society of America, New Orleans, LA.

Hynes, A.M., & Hynes-Berry, M. (1986). *Bibliotherapy, the interactive process: A handbook.* Boulder, CO: Westview Press.

Jackson, D.D. (1965). The study of the family. *Family Process, 4*, 1–20.

Jacobi, J. (1962). *The psychology of C.G. Jung.* New Haven, CT: Yale University Press.

Jacobs, S., & Douglas, L. (1979). Grief: A mediating process between a loss and illness. *Comprehensive Psychiatry, 20*, 165–176.

Jacobsen, J.J. (1988). *Help! I'm parenting my parents.* New York: Benchmark Press.

Jarvis, G.K., & Boldt, M. (1980). Suicide in the later years. *Essence: Issues in the Study of Aging, Dying, and Death, 4*(3), 145–158.

Johnson, C.L. (1985). Grandparenting options in divorcing families: *An anthropological perspective.* In V.L. Bengtson & J.F. Robertson (Eds.), *Grandparenthood.* Beverly Hills, CA: Sage.

Johnson, E.S., & Bursk, B.J. (1977). Relationships between the elderly and their adult children. *The Gerontologist, 17*, 90–96.

Johnson, E.S., & Spence, D.L. (1982). Adult children and aging parents: An intervention program. *Family Relations, 31*, 115–121.

Johnson, R. (1982). Assessing retirement maturity. *Measurement and Evaluation in Counseling and Development, 15*(3), 221–227.

Johnson, R. (1986). *Generations . . . the game.* St. Louis, MO: St. John's Mercy Medical Center.

Johnson, R. (1987). *Aging parents: How to understand and help them.* Liguori, MO: Liguori Publications.

Johnson, R.P. (1988). How to stay young in a fast aging world: Part II. *Co-Op Networker: Caregivers of Older Persons, 4*(1), 1–4.

Johnson, S. (1984). *The precious present.* New York: Doubleday.

Jones, C.T. (1981). *Life is tremendous.* Wheaton, IL: Living Books.

Kaminsky, M. (Ed.). (1984). *The uses of reminiscence: New ways of working with older adults.* New York: Haworth Press.

Kane, R.A., & Kane, R.L. (1983). *Assessing the elderly.* Lexington, MA: Lexington Books.

Kart, C.S. (1981). *The realities of aging: An introduction to gerontology.* Boston: Allyn & Bacon.

Kart, C.S., & Palmer, N.M. (1987). How do we explain differences in the level of care received by the institutionalized elderly? *Journal of Applied Gerontology, 6*(1), 53–66.

Kastenbaum, R. (1969). Death and bereavement in later life. In A.H. Kutscher (Ed.), *Death and bereavement.* Springfield, IL: Charles C Thomas.

Kastenbaum, R. (1971). Age: Getting there on time. *Psychology Today, 5*(7), 52–54, 82–84.

Kastenbaum, R. (1977). *Death, society, and human experience.* St. Louis: Mosby.

Kastenbaum, R., & Costa, P.T. (1977). Psychological perspectives on death. *Annual Review of Psychology, 28,* 225–249.

Keith, P.M. (1986). The social context and resources of the unmarried in old age. International Journal of Aging and Human Development, *23*(2), 81–96.

Kelly, S., & Remley, T.P. (1987). Understanding and counseling elderly alcohol abusers. *American Mental Health Counselors Association Journal, 9*(2), 105–113.

Kenny, J., & Spicer, S. (1984). *Caring for your aging parent: A practical guide to the challenges, the choices.* Cincinnati, OH: St. Anthony Messenger Press.

Kermis, M.D. (1984). *The psychology of human aging: Theory, research, and practice.* Boston: Allyn & Bacon.

Kieffer, J. (1980). Kicking the premature retirement habit. *Journal of Career Development, 13*(2), 39–51.

Kiernat, J.M. (1984). The use of life review activity. In I. Burnside (Ed.), *Working with the elderly: Group processes and techniques* (pp. 298–307). Monterey, CA: Wadsworth.

Kivett, V.R. (1985). Grandfathers and grandchildren: Patterns of association, helping, and psychological closeness. *Family Relations, 34*(4), 565–571.

Kivnick, H. (1981). Grandparenthood and the mental health of grandparents. *Aging and Society, 1,* 365–391.

Kleemeier, R.W. (Ed.). (1961). *Aging and leisure: A research perspective into the meaningful use of time.* New York: Oxford University Press.

Kramer, J. (1984). *Treating families of demented patients: Two group models.* Paper presented at the annual meeting of the Western Psychological Association, Los Angeles.

Kramer, M., Taube, C.A., & Redick, R.W. (1975). Patterns of use of psychiatric facilities: Past, present, and future. In C. Eisdorfer & M.P. Lawton (Eds.), *The psychology of adult development and aging* (pp. 428–528). Washington, DC: American Psychological Association.

Krause, N. (1987). Satisfaction with social support and self-rated health in older adults. *The Gerontologist, 27*(3), 301–308.

Krieger, S.R., Epting, F.R., & Leitner, L.M. (1974). Personal constructs, threat, and attitudes toward death. *Omega, 5*, 299–310.

Kübler-Ross, E. (1969). *On death and dying.* New York: Macmillan.

Kübler-Ross, E. (1975). *Death: The final stage of growth.* Englewood Cliffs, NJ: Prentice-Hall.

Kushner, H.S. (1981). *When bad things happen to good people.* New York: Avon Books.

Kuypers, J.A., & Bengston, V.L. (1973). Competence and social breakdown: A social-psychological view of aging. *Human Development, 16*, 37–49.

LaBarge, E. (1981). Counseling patients with Senile Dementia of the Alzheimer Type and their families. *Personnel and Guidance Journal, 60*(3), 139–143.

Lawrence, P. (1981). Applying helping skills with special populations. In. J.E. Myers & M.L. Ganikos (Eds.)., *Counseling older persons, Volume II, Basic helping skills for service providers* (pp. 187–232). Alexandria, VA: American Association for Counseling and Development.

Lawson, D.M., & Gaushell, H. (1988). Family autobiography: A useful method for enhancing counselors' personal development. *Counselor Education and Supervision, 28*(2), 162–168.

Lawton, M.P. (1975). The Philadelphia Geriatric Center Morale Scale: A revision. *Journal of Gerontology, 30*, 85–89.

Lee, G.R., & Ishi-Kuntz, M. (1987). Social interaction, loneliness, and emotional well-being among the elderly. *Research on Aging, 9*(4), 459–482.

Lemon, B.W., Bengtson, V.L., & Peterson, J.A. (1972). An exploration of the activity theory of aging: Activity types and life satisfaction among in-movers to a retirement community. *Journal of Gerontology. 27*, 511–523.

Lester, D.A. (1966). *A scale measuring the fear of death: Its construction and consistency.* Unpublished manual. Richard Stockton State College.

Lindemann, E. (1944). Symptomatology and management of acute grief. *American Journal of Psychiatry, 10*, 141–148.

Lowenthal, M.F. (1964). *Lives in distress.* New York: Basic Books.

Lowry, J.H. (1985). Predictors of successful aging in retirement. In E.B. Palmore (Ed.), *Normal aging III* (pp. 394–404). Durham, NC: Duke University Press.

Lynch, J.J. (1977). *The broken heart: The medical consequences of loneliness.* New York: Basic Books.

Mace, N.L., & Rabins, P.V. (1981). *The 36-hour day; A family guide to caring for persons with Alzheimer's disease, related dementing illnesses, and memory loss in later life.* Baltimore: Johns Hopkins University Press.

Macione, A.R. (1979). Macione Physical and Mental Competence for Independent Living in the Aged scale. *Research for clinical nursing: Its strategies and findings.* Proceedings of the seventh annual nursing research conference. Tucson, AZ: University of Arizona.

Maddox, G.L. (1970). Themes and issues in sociological theories of human aging. *Human Development, 13*, 17–27.

Maiden, R.J. (1985, March 21–24). *Caregiving for dementia in family members: Caregiving burden and prospects for effective intervention.* Paper presented at the annual meeting of the Eastern Psychological Association, Boston, MA.

Markides, S.K. (1986). Minority status, aging, and mental health. *International Journal of Aging and Human Development, 23*(4), 285–300.

Markides, S.K., Levin, J.S., & Ray, L.A. (1987). Religion, aging, and life satisfaction: An eight-year, three-wave longitudinal study. *The Gerontologist, 27*(5), 660–665.

Masciocchi, C. (1985). The challenge of caregiving: Families of older rehabilitation patients. *Rehabilitation Research and Training Center in Aging Newsletter, 2*(2), 1–4.

Maslow, A.H. (1954). *Motivation and personality.* New York: Harper & Row.

Matthews, S.H. (1987). Provision of care to old parents: Division of responsibility among adult children. *Research on Aging, 9*(1), 45–60.

May, R. (1958). Contributions of existential psychotherapy. In R. May, E. Angel, & H.F. Ellenberg (Eds.), *Existence: A new dimension in psychiatry and psychology.* New York: Basic Books.

McDaniels, C. (1982). *Leisure: Integrating a neglected component in life planning.* Columbus, OH: The National Center for Research in Vocational Education.

McDowell, C.F., & Clark, P. (1982). Assessing the leisure needs of older persons. *Measurement and Evaluation in Counseling and Development, 15*(3), 228–239.

McGinnis, A.L. (1979). *The friendship factor.* Minneapolis, MN: Augsburg.

McGoldrick, M., & Gerson, R. (1985). *Genograms in family assessment.* New York: Norton.

McIntosh, J.L., & Santos, J.F. (1981). Suicide among minority elderly: A preliminary investigation. *Suicide and Life-Threatening Behavior, 11*(3), 155–166.

McKenzie, B., & Campbell, J. (1987). Race, socioeconomic status, and the subjective well-being of older Americans. *International Journal of Aging and Human Development, 25*(1), 43–61.

Menninger, K. (1961). Reading as therapy. *ALA Bulletin, 55,* 316–319.

Miller, S.J. (1982). Aging parents and their middle-aged children. *Educational Horizons, 50,* 179–183.

Mines, R.A., Rockwell, L., & Hull, S.B. (1980). Plans and attitudes of family members for caring for aged parents: Implications for counseling. *Counseling and Values, 24*(3), 175–183.

Minuchin, S. (1974). *Families and family therapy.* Cambridge, MA: Harvard University Press.

Mishara, B.L., & Kastenbaum, R. (1980). *Alcoholism and old age.* New York: Grune & Stratton.

Molinari, V., & Reichlin, R.E. (1985). Life review reminiscence in the elderly: A review of the literature. *International Journal of Aging and Human Development, 20*(2), 81–92.

204   ADULT CHILDREN AND AGING PARENTS

Montgomery, D.R., & Still, J.A. (1984). Adult day care: A bibliography. *Catholic Library World, 56*(3), 135–137.

Morgan, L.A. (1981). Aging in a family context. In R.H. Davis (Ed.), *Aging: Prospects and issues* (pp. 98–112). Los Angeles: University of Southern California.

Moss, M., & Moss, S.Z. (1983). The impact of parental death on middle aged children. *Omega, 14*(1), 65–75.

Moss, M., Moss, S.Z., & Moles, E.L. (1985). The quality of relationships between elderly parents and their out-of-town children. *The Gerontologist, 25*(2), 134–140.

Motto, J.A. (1980). Suicide risk factors in alcohol abuse. *Suicide and Life-Threatening Behavior, 10*(4), 230–238.

Mutran, E., & Reitzes, D.C. (1984). Intergenerational support activities and well-being among the elderly: A convergence of exchange and symbolic interaction perspectives. *American Sociological Review, 49*, 117–130.

Myers, E. (1986). *When parents die: A guide for adults.* New York: Viking.

Myers, J.E. (1978). The development of a scale to assess counseling needs of older persons. *Dissertation Abstracts International, 39*, 7165A (University of Florida).

Myers, J.E. (1983). A national survey of geriatric mental health services. *American Mental Health Counselors Association Journal, 5*(2), 69–74.

Myers, J.E. (1988a). *Infusing gerontological counseling into counselor preparation: Curriculum Guide.* Alexandria, VA: AACD.

Myers, J.E. (1988b). The mid/late life generation gap: Adult children and aging parents. *Journal of Counseling and Development, 66*, 331–335.

Myers, J.E., & Loesch, L.C. (1981). The counseling needs of older persons. *The Humanist Educator, 20*, 21–35.

Myers, J.E., & Rimmer, S. (1982). Assessment of older persons [special issue]. *Measurement and Evaluation in Counseling and Development, 15*(3).

Myers, J.E., & Shelton, B. (1987). Abuse and older persons: Issues and implications for counselors. *Journal of Counseling and Development, 65*, 376–380.

National Alliance for Business. (1985). *New directions for an aging workforce: An analysis of issues and options for business.* Washington, DC: Author.

National Conference on Social Welfare. (1981). *Long term care: In search of solutions.* Washington, DC: Author.

National Council on Alcoholism. (1972). Criteria for the diagnosis of alcoholism. *American Journal of Psychiatry, 129*, 127–135.

National Institute on Aging. (1986). *Age page: When you need a nursing home.* Washington, DC: U.S. Government Printing Office.

Neugarten, B.L. (1968). *Middle age and aging.* Chicago: University of Chicago Press.

Neugarten, B.L., Havighurst, R.J., & Tobin, S. (1961). The measurement of life satisfaction. *Journal of Gerontology, 16*, 134–143.

Neugarten, B.L., Havighurst, R.J., & Tobin, S.S. (1968). Personality and patterns of aging. In B.L. Neugarten (Ed.), *Middle age and aging*. Chicago: University of Chicago Press.

Neugarten, B.L., & Weinstein, K.K. (1964). The changing American grandparent. *Journal of Marriage and the Family, 26*, 199–204.

Nichols, W., & Everett, C.A. (1986). *Systemic family therapy: An integrative approach*. New York: Guilford Press.

Okun, B.F. (1984). *Working with adults: Individual, family, and career development*. Monterey, CA: Brooks/Cole.

Osgood, N. (1985). *Suicide in the elderly: A practitioner's guide to diagnosis and mental health intervention*. Rockville, MD: Aspen Systems.

Owen, G., Fulton, R., & Markusen, E. (1982). Death at a distance: A study of family survivors. *Omega, 13*(3), 191–225.

Palmore, E. (1977). Change in life satisfaction: A longitudinal study of persons aged 46–70. *Journal of Gerontology, 32*(3), 311–316.

Pastorello, T. (1986). *Contributions to successful aging by familial caretakers as differentiated by sex of caretakers: Social policy implications*. Paper presented at the annual meeting of the Gerontological Society of America, Chicago.

Patrick, L.F., & Moore, J.S. (1985). *Life event types and attributional styles as predictors of depression in the elderly*. Paper presented at the annual meeting of the Eastern Psychological Association, Boston, MA.

Patterson, R. (1978). Community mental health centers: A survey of services for the elderly. In *Issues in mental health and aging, Volume Three: Services* (pp. 26–30). DHEW Publication No. (ADM) 79–65. Washington, DC: U.S. Government Printing Office.

Paulus, T. (1972). *Hope for the flowers*. New York: Paulist Press.

Peck, R.C. (1968). Psychology developments in the second half of life. In B.L. Neugarten (Ed.), *Middle age and aging*. Chicago: University of Chicago Press.

Peppers, L.G., & Stover, R.G. (1977). The elderly abuser: A challenge for the future. *Journal of Drug Issues, 9*, 73–83.

Perlick, D., & Atkins, A. (1984). Variations in the reported age of a patient: A source of bias in the diagnosis of depression and dementia. *Journal of Consulting and Clinical Psychology, 52*(5), 812–820.

Pierce, R.L., & Trotta, R. (1986). Abused parents: A hidden family problem. *Journal of Family Violence, 1*, 99–110.

Pillemer, K., Wolf, R.S., & Gwynther, L.P. (1987). Elder abuse: Conflict in the family. *Journal of Gerontology, 42*, 234–235.

Powell, J. (1976). *Fully human, fully alive*. Niles, IL: Argus.

Powell, J. (1978). *Unconditional love*. Niles, IL: Argus.

Power, P.W., & Dell Orto, A.E. (1980). *Role of the family in rehabilitation of the disabled*. Baltimore: University Park Press.

Quinn, W.H. (1983). Personal and family adjustment in later life. *Journal of Marriage and the Family, 45*(1), 57–73.

Quinn, W.H., & Keller, J.F. (1983). Older generations of the family: Relational dimensions and quality. *American Journal of Family Therapy, 11*, 23–30.

Rabins, P., Mace, N., & Lucas, M.J. (1982). The impact of dementia on the family. *Journal of the American Medical Association, 248*, 333–335.

Raffoul, P.R., Cooper, J.K., & Love, D.W. (1981). Drug misuse in older people. *The Gerontologist, 21*(2), 146–150.

Rakowski, W., & Clark, N.M. (1985). Future outlook, caregiving, and care-receiving in the family context. *The Gerontologist, 251*(6), 618–623.

Rando, T.A. (1986). *Loss and anticipatory grief.* Lexington, MA: Lexington Books.

Raphael, B. (1983). *The anatomy of bereavement.* New York: Basic Books.

Reedy, M., & Birren, J.E. (1980, September). *Life review through guided autobiography.* Poster presented at the annual meeting of the American Psychological Association, Montreal, Canada.

Reichard, S., Livson, F., & Peterson, P.G. (1962). *Aging and personality: A study of 87 older men.* New York: Wiley

Remnet, V.L. (1987). How adult children respond to role transitions in the lives of their aging parents. *Educational Gerontology, 13*, 341–355.

Riker, H.C., & Myers, J.E. (1989). *Retirement counseling: A handbook for action.* New York: Hemisphere.

Riley, M.W. (1971). Social gerontology and the age stratification of society. *The Gerontologist, 11*, 79–87.

Robertson, J.F. (1977). Interaction patterns in three-generation families: Towards a theoretical perspective. *International Journal of Aging and Human Development, 6*, 103–110.

Rose, A.M. (1965). The subculture of aging: A framework for research in social gerontology. In A.M. Rose & W.A. Peterson, (Eds.), *Older people and their social world* (pp. 3–16). Philadelphia: Davis.

Ryan, M.J. (1957). Bibliotherapy and psychiatry: Changing concepts. *Special Libraries, 48*, 197–199.

Salamon, M.J., & Conte, V.A. (1981). Salamon-Conte Life Satisfaction in the Elderly Scale. Odessa, FL: Psychological Assessment Resources.

Salmon, H. (1981). How can I make the best use of support networks? In J.E. Myers (Ed.), *Counseling older persons, Volume III, Trainer's manual for basic helping skills* (pp. 183–192). Alexandria, VA: American Association for Counseling and Development.

Satir, V. (1974). *Conjoint family therapy.* Palo Alto, CA: Science and Behavior Books.

Schaie, K.W., & Geiwitz, J. (1982). *Adult development and aging.* Boston, MA: Little, Brown.

Schlossberg, N. (1984). *Counseling adults in transition: Linking practice with theory.* New York: Springer.

Schonfeld, L., & Dupree, L.W. (1984, August). *Strategies for recognizing and treating elderly alcohol abusers.* Paper presented at the annual convention of the American Psychological Association, Toronto, Ontario, Canada.

Selan, B.H., & Schuenke, S. (1982). The late life care program: Helping families cope. *Health and Social Work, 7*(3), 192–197.

Select Committee on Aging, U.S. House of Representatives. (1981). *Abuse of older persons* (Comm. Pub. No. 97–289). Washington, DC: U.S. Government Printing Office.

Sengstock, M., Barrett, S., & Graham, R. (1984). *Abused elders: Victims or villains of circumstances?* Detroit, MI: Wayne State University Institute on Gerontology.

Shanas, E. (1980). Older people and their families: The new pioneers. *Journal of Marriage and the Family, 42*, 9–15.

Sheehan, N.W., & Nuttall, P. (1988). Conflict, emotion, and personal strain among family caregivers. *Family Relations, 37*(1), 92–98.

Shifflett, P.A., & Blieszner, R. (1988). Stigma and Alzheimer's disease: Behavioral consequences for support groups. *Journal of Applied Gerontology, 7*(2), 147–160.

Shoham, H., & Neuschatz, S. (1985). Group therapy with senile patients. *Social Work, 30*(1), 69–72.

Shomaker, D. (1987). Problematic behavior and the Alzheimer patient: Retrospection as a method of understanding and counseling. *The Gerontologist, 27*(3), 370–375.

Siegel, J.S. (1976). *Current population reports: Special studies: Demographic aspects of aging and the older population in the United States.* Series P–23, No. 59. Washington, DC: U.S. Bureau of the Census.

Silverstein, S. (1961). *The giving tree.* New York: Random House.

Simons, R.L., & West, G.E. (1984–85). Life changes, coping resources, and health among the elderly. *International Journal of Aging and Human Development, 20*(3), 173–179.

Simonton, L.J., & Haugland, S.M. (1986). *Assessing caregiver information needs: A brief questionnaire.* Paper presented at the annual scientific meeting of the Gerontological Society, Chicago, IL.

Skinner, B.F., & Vaughn, M.E. (1983). *Enjoy old age.* New York: Warner Books.

Smallegan, M. (1985). There was nothing else to do: Needs for care before nursing home admission. *The Gerontologist, 25*(4), 364–369.

Smyer, M.A., & Hofland, B.F. (1982). Divorce and family support in later life: Emerging concerns. *Journal of Family Issues, 3*(1), 61–77.

Sneegas, J.J. (1986). Components of life satisfaction in middle and later life adults: Perceived social competence, leisure participation, and leisure satisfaction. *Journal of Leisure Research, 18*(4), 248–258.

Solomon, B. (1984). Minority aging in mental health settings: Clinical issues. In J.P. Abrahams & V. Crook (Eds.), *Geriatric mental health* (pp. 183–197). Orlando, FL: Grune & Stratton.

Sommers, T., & Shields, L. (1987). *Women take care: The consequences of caregiving in today's society.* Gainesville, FL: Triad Pub. Co.

Sommerstein, J.C. (1986). Assessing the older worker: The career counselor's dilemma. *Journal of Career Development, 13*(2), 52–56.

Special Committee on Aging. (1980). *Aging and mental health: Overcoming barriers to service.* Washington, DC: U.S. Government Printing Office.

Special Committee on Aging. (1983). *Developments in aging: 1983, Vol. 1*. Washington, DC: U.S. Government Printing Office.

Sprey, J., & Matthews, S.H. (1982). Contemporary grandparent: A systemic transition. *Annals, AAPSS, 464*, 91–103.

Steinmetz, S.K. (1979). Battered parents. *Society, 15*, 54–55.

Steinmetz, S.K., & Amsden, D.J. (1983). Dependent elders, family stress, and abuse. In T.H. Brubaker (Ed.), *Family relationships in later life* (pp. 178–192). Beverly Hills, CA: Sage.

Stern, D.S., & Kastenbaum, R. (1984). Alcohol use and abuse in old age. In J.P. Abrahams & V.J. Crooks (Eds.), *Geriatric mental health* (pp. 153–168). New York: Grune & Stratton.

Sterns, H.L., Weis, D., & Perkins, S.E. (1984). A conceptual approach to counseling older adults and their families. *The Counseling Psychologist, 12*(2), 55–61.

Stinnett, J.L., & Schechter, J.O. (1983). A quantitative inventory of alcohol disorders (QIAD): A severity scale for alcohol abuse. *American Journal of Alcohol and Drug Abuse, 9*, 413–430.

Stockwell, T., Hodgson, R., Edwards, G., Taylor, C., & Rankin, H. (1979). The development of a questionnaire to measure severity of alcohol dependence. *British Journal of Addictions, 74*, 79–87.

Stoller, E.P. (1983). Parental cargiving by adult children. *Journal of Marriage and the Family, 45*(4), 851–865.

Stone, R., Cafferata, G.L., & Sangl, J. (1987). Caregivers of the frail elderly: A national profile. *The Gerontologist, 27*(5), 616–626.

Stricherz, M., & Cunnington, L. (1982). Death concerns of students, employed and retired persons. *Omega, 12*, 373–379.

Strom, R., & Strom, S. (1987). Preparing grandparents for a new role. *Journal of Applied Gerontology, 6*(4), 476–486.

Subak-Sharpe, G.J., & MacLean, H. (1988, September 1). Where there's a will there's a way: Practical checklists for you and your parents. *Family Circle*, 35–38.

Suicide, Part I. (1986). *Harvard Medical School Mental Health Newsletter, 2*(8), 1–4.

Suicide, Part II. (1986). *Harvard Medical School Mental Health Newsletter, 2*(9), 1–4.

Supiano, K.P. (1980). The counseling needs of elderly nursing home residents. In C.J. Pulvino & N. Colangelo (Eds.), *Counseling for the growing years: 65 and over* (pp. 233–246). Minneapolis, MN: Educational Media.

Sweeney, T.J. (1981). *Adlerian counseling: Proven concepts and strategies*. Muncie, IN: Accelerated Development.

Sweeney, T.J. (1989). *Adlerian counseling: A practical approach for a new decade*. Muncie, IN: Accelerated Development.

Sweeney, T.J., & Myers, J.E. (1986). Early Recollections: An Adlerian technique with older people. *Clinical Gerontologist, 4*(4), 3–12.

Sweeney, T.J., & Myers, J.E. (1988). *Video resources for infusion of gerontological counseling into counselor preparation*. Alexandria, VA: AACD.

Templer, D.I. (1970). The construction and validation of a death anxiety scale. *Journal of General Psychology, 82,* 165–177.

Terry, R. (1982). Brain disease in aging, especially senile dementia. In R. Terry, C. Bolis, & G. Toffano (Eds.), *Neurology, aging, and its implication in human neurological pathology, Volume 8* (pp. 43–52). New York: Raven Press.

Timberlake, E.M. (1980). The value of grandchildren to grandmothers. *Journal of Gerontological Social Work, 3*(1), 63–76.

Tolbert, E.L. (1980). *Counseling for career development* (2nd ed.). Boston: Houghton Mifflin.

Treas, J. (1983). Aging and the family. In D.S. Woodruff & J.E. Birren (Eds.), *Aging: Scientific perspectives and social issues* (pp. 92–108). Los Angeles: University of California.

Troll, L.E. (1980). Grandparenting. In L.W. Poon (Ed.), *Aging in the 1980s: Psychological issues.* Washington, DC: American Psychological Association.

Troll, L.E. (1982a). *Continuations: Adult development and aging.* Monterey, CA: Brooks/Cole.

Troll, L.E. (1982b). Family life in middle and old age: The generation gap. *Annals of the American Academy of Political and Social Science, 464,* 38–46.

Troll, L.E., Miller, B.J., & Atchley, R.C. (1979). *Families in later life.* Belmont, CA: Wadsworth.

U.S. Department of Education. (1988). *Profile of adult education participants: Final report.* Washington, DC: Author.

U.S. Department of Health, Education, and Welfare. (1973). *Nursing home care* (SRS 73–24902). Washington, DC: Author.

Wasow, M. (1986). Support groups for family caregivers of patients with Alzheimer's disease. *Social Work, 31*(2), 93–97.

Wass, H. (1977). Views and opinions of elderly persons concerning death. *Educational Gerontology, 2,* 15–26.

Wass, H., & Forfar, C.S. (1982). Assessment of attitudes toward death: Techniques and instruments for use with older persons. *Measurement and Evaluation in Counseling and Development, 15*(3), 210–220.

Wass, H., & Myers, J.E. (1982). Psychosocial aspects of death among the elderly: A review of the literature. *Personnel and Guidance Journal, 61*(3), 131–137.

Wass, H., & Myers, J.E. (1984). Death and dying: Issues for educational gerontologists. *Educational Gerontology, 10,* 65–81.

Waters, E. (1984). Building on what you know: Individual and group counseling with older persons. *The Counseling Psychologist, 12*(2), 52–64.

Waters, E., & Weaver, A. (1981). Specialized techniques to help older people. In J.E. Myers, (Ed.), *Counseling older persons, Volume III, A trainer's manual for basic helping skills* (pp. 147–170). Alexandria, VA: AACD.

Waters, E., Weaver, A., & White, B. (1980). *Gerontological counseling skills: A training manual.* Rochester, MI: Oakland University.

Wedl, L. (1982). *Bibliotherapy: A counseling tool to promote creative aging in older persons.* Unpublished manuscript.

West, J.D. (1988). Marriage and family therapy assessment. *Counselor Education and Supervision, 28*(2), 169–180.

Westcott, N. (1983). Application of the structured life-review technique in counseling elders. *Personnel and Guidance Journal, 62,* (3), 180–181.

Whanger, A.D., & Myers, A.C. (1984). *Mental health intervention and therapeutic assessment with older persons.* Rockville, MD: Aspen.

Wilhite, B., & Teaff, J.D. (1986). Nursing home recreation: An unchanging diet of bingo, birthdays and Bible? *Parks and Recreation, 21*(8), 38–42, 63.

Williams, M. (1983). *The velveteen rabbit.* New York: Simon & Schuster.

Williams, W.V., & Polak, P.R. (1979). Follow-up research in primary prevention: A model of adjustment to acute grief. *Journal of Clinical Psychology, 35,* 35–45.

Winoground, I.R., Fisk, A., Kirsling, R., & Keyes, B. (1987). The relationship of caregiver burden and morale to Alzheimer's disease patient function in a therapeutic setting. *The Gerontologist, 27*(3), 336–339.

Wisniewski, W., & Cohen, D. (1984). *Older women: A population at risk for mental health problems.* Paper presented at the annual scientific meeting of the Gerontological Society of America, San Antonio, TX.

Wolberg, L.R. (1977). *The technique of psychotherapy.* New York: Grune & Stratton.

Wolfe, S.M., Fugate, L., Hulstrand, E.P., & Kamimoto, L.E. (1988). *Worst pills, best pills: The older adult's guide to avoiding drug-induced death or illness.* Washington, DC: Public Citizen Health Research Group.

Worden, J.W. (1982). *Grief counseling and grief therapy—A handbook for the mental health practitioner.* New York: Springer.

Wrenn, C.G. (1979). Caring for others when they need you the most. *The Humanist Educator, 3,* 98–105.

Yesavage, J.A., Brink, T.L., Rose, T.L., Lum, O., Huang, V., Aday, M., & Leirer, V. (1983). Development and validation of a geriatric depression screening scale: A preliminary report. *Journal of Psychiatric Research, 17,* 37–49.

Zarit, J.M. (1981). *Family relationships and burden in long-term care.* Paper presented at the annual meeting of the Gerontological Society of America, Toronto, Canada.

Zarit, S., Orr, N., & Zarit, J. (1985). *The hidden victims of Alzheimer's disease.* New York: New York University Press.

Zarit, S., & Zarit, J. (1984). Depression in later life: Theory and assessment. In J.P. Abrahams & V.J. Crooks (Eds.), *Geriatric mental health* (pp. 21–40). New York: Grune & Stratton.

Zarit, S.H. (1980). Relatives of the impaired elderly: Correlates of feelings of burden. *The Gerontologist, 20*(6), 649–655.

Zarit, S.H. (1983). *Interventions with families of impaired elderly.* Paper presented at the annual scientific meeting of the Gerontological Society of America, San Francisco.

Zung, W.K. (1980). *Handbook of geriatric psychiatry.* New York: Van Nostrand Reinhold.

Zweibel, N.R. (1984). *Analysis of family decision-making in selection of alternatives to institutionalization: A tool for service planners and providers.* Paper presented at the annual scientific meeting of the Gerontological Society, San Antonio, TX.

INDEX